Margaret Fuller

❖

WHETSTONE OF GENIUS

BY

MASON WADE

AUGUSTUS M. KELLEY • PUBLISHERS

CLIFTON 1973

First Published 1940
(New York: The Viking Press, Inc.)
Copyright 1940 by Hugh Mason Wade

RE-ISSUED 1973 BY
AUGUSTUS M. KELLEY · PUBLISHERS
Clifton New Jersey 07012
By Arrangement with THE VIKING PRESS

Library of Congress Cataloging in Publication Data

Wade, Mason, 1913-
   Margaret Fuller, whetstone of genius.

   (Viking reprint editions)
   Bibliography: p.
   1. Ossoli, Sarah Margaret (Fuller)
marchessa d', 1810-1850.
PS2506.W3 1973   818'.3'09 [B]   72-122077
ISBN 0-678-03178-9

PRINTED IN THE UNITED STATES OF AMERICA
by SENTRY PRESS, NEW YORK, N. Y. 10013

TO

MY MOTHER AND FATHER
AND COPI

Acknowledgments

I AM under a great obligation to a host of students of the period, and to many others who aided my work in one way or another. No words can do more than acknowledge my debt to Mr. Van Wyck Brooks, whose *Flowering of New England* first set me thinking on Margaret Fuller, who guided my approach to the subject, and who was kind enough to read the completed manuscript; to Mrs. Arthur Nicholls, Margaret's niece, for her permission to make free use of family papers; to Professor Odell Shepard, for advice and for supplying me with copies of all the entries relating to Margaret in Alcott's *Journals*; to Mr. Frederic Wolsey Pratt, for permission to print these extracts; to Dr. Norman Holmes Pearson, for making the manuscript of the forthcoming collected edition of Hawthorne's letters available to me, and for emendations in the text of the *Italian Notebooks*; to the Estate of W. T. H. Howe, for permission to quote from the Hawthorne-Fuller correspondence; to Professor Newton Arvin, for enlightenment on the vexed subject of Hawthorne's relations with Margaret; to Mrs. Gamaliel Bradford, for permitting me to use her husband's notes on Margaret; to Miss Evelyn Winslow Orr, for making available to me her unpublished studies on Margaret; to Dr. Merrill Moore and Miss Barbara Rogers, for clarifying the psychological problems involved; to Mr. Zoltán Haraszti, for his courtesy and assistance at the Boston Public Library; to Miss Robin Williams, for aid in research at the Harvard College Library; to Miss Harriet Colby, for her invaluable editorial advice and encouragement; to Mr. Curtice Hitchcock, for his friendly interest; to those many who freely offered to me their recollections of Margaret.

Cornish, New Hampshire   M. W.
January 1940

VIKING REPRINT EDITIONS

Contents

INTRODUCTION   xi

Part I. FORMATION, 1810–1839

I. A CAMBRIDGE CHILDHOOD   3
II. EXILE IN GROTON   20
III. A TEACHER IN BOSTON AND PROVIDENCE   34

Part II. FIRST FLOWERING, 1839–1844

IV. TRANSCENDENTALISM   53
V. THE CONVERSATIONS   68
VI. THE "DIAL" AND EMERSON   82
VII. BROOK FARM AND HAWTHORNE   102
VIII. THE WEST AND FEMINISM   119

Part III. FEMINISM AND FRUSTRATION, 1844–1847

IX. HORACE GREELEY'S "TRIBUNE"   139
X. MR. JAMES NATHAN   160
XI. ENGLAND AND SCOTLAND   172
XII. FRANCE AND ITALY   180

Part IV. FULFILLMENT, 1847–1850

XIII. "MY ITALY"   215
XIV. REVOLUTION AND SIEGE   234
XV. THE LAST YEAR   254
XVI. AFTERGLOW   273

APPENDIX   287
BIBLIOGRAPHICAL NOTE   295
INDEX   298

Illustrations

Facing page

WILLIAM ELLERY CHANNING   38

HARRIET MARTINEAU   44

MARGARET FULLER   68

RALPH WALDO EMERSON   82

NATHANIEL HAWTHORNE   102

HENRY DAVID THOREAU   110

TITLE-PAGE OF *WOMAN IN THE NINETEENTH CENTURY*   132

HORACE GREELEY   140

JAMES RUSSELL LOWELL   146

MARGARET'S REVIEW OF *THE RAVEN*   154

MARGARET FULLER IN ROME   234

THE MEMORIAL, AT CAMBRIDGE   274

Introduction

THE flowering of New England culture in the thirties, forties, and fifties of the last century is now commonly regarded as the greatest era of American literature, and one which has set a sharp stamp on our national life. This renaissance or golden age has been much discussed from many points of view in recent years, and it has now been made clear that it was more of an Indian summer, as Santayana has called it, than a renaissance, for Boston enjoyed supremacy as the Athens of America during but a few brief decades, and then its glory passed to New York, the modern Rome.

In our day there has been much reweighing of the roles played by the leading figures of those years, and new estimates of their relative importance have been made. George Bancroft, the Channings, Edward Everett, Oliver Wendell Holmes, James Russell Lowell, Longfellow, Prescott, George Ticknor, Julia Ward Howe, and John Greenleaf Whittier have been left largely undisturbed in the niches of the hall of fame to which they attained in their own time; and while they gather dust in obscurity, Emerson, Thoreau, Hawthorne, Theodore Parker, Bronson Alcott, Orestes Brownson, and Emily Dickinson have been given more prominence. It is curious that Margaret Fuller, who in her own time and for some years thereafter was regarded as one of the most brilliant members of the New England constellation and the peer of Emerson, Thoreau, and Parker, has been neglected, so that her reputation has waned while the fame of the others has increased. She is still mentioned in all discussions of the period; but she is not read or taken seriously, and consequently has become a strange, misty figure, living chiefly in apocryphal anecdotes. She is a myth and a legend.

Yet so acute a critic of American thought as V. L. Parrington has judged that "no other woman of her generation in America is so well worth recalling." To him, "a sensitive emotional nature offers the best of social barometers, and Margaret Fuller's tragic life, despite its lack of solid accomplishment, was an epitome of the great revolt of the New England mind against Puritan asceticism and Yankee materialism. She was the emotional expression of a rebellious generation that had done with the past and was questioning the future. Not a scholar like Theodore Parker, not a thinker like Thoreau, not an artist like Emerson, she was a ferment of troubled aspirations, an enthusiasm for a more generous culture than New England had known." He considers her a far richer nature than her books reveal, and blames her failure on the narrow world that bred her: "Perhaps no sharper criticism could be leveled at New England than that it could do no better with such material, lent it by the gods." To Van Wyck Brooks, "Margaret Fuller sums up the whole story of Transcendentalism—its cause and its cure. She was eminently caused by Transcendentalism and her unique distinction lies in having been cured of it." He observes that it has been the tradition in America to laugh at the first half of Margaret's story, but that it is wiser to pay attention to the second half, which is a moral to every American idealist.

The forgotten or neglected facts of her dramatic life bear out these high opinions, which are largely unshared by other contemporary critics. As she emerged from a puritanically rigorous childhood, which made her bookish for life, she displayed such a precociousness that she impressed her contemporaries as an almost intolerably intellectual young woman. The romanticism, the idealism, the liberalism, the humanitarianism of the new Europe which was rising from the old found fertile soil in her mind, and she did much to make their force felt in America. She was the intimate friend of Dr. Channing, Emerson, Alcott, Hawthorne, and of a host among the younger generation. She was a Feminist as well as a Transcendental radical and critic, and gave a lasting impetus to that cause by her actions and writings. She was the first editor of the *Dial,* the most representative publication of the golden era in New England. When the ferment of Transcendentalism subsided, she left Boston and became the first woman to act as literary critic for one of America's great newspapers, Horace Greeley's *New York Tribune.* In this post she rivaled Edgar Allan Poe as the only American critic of note before 1850. In addition she lent her aid to numerous reform movements. She went to Europe as the *Tribune's* special correspondent, and was received as an honored guest by Carlyle, George Sand, the Brownings, and other notables with whom she had already won some regard by her writings. She spent the closing years of her brief life in Italy, whither she had felt drawn since childhood, and was caught up in the revolutionary fervor of the closing years of the forties, which seemed to promise to build a new Europe, devoid of tyranny, injustice, and oppression. She was an intimate friend of Mazzini, the leading spirit of the Roman revolution, and she knew as no other foreigner did how that movement rose and fell. She found a husband among its supporters, and, when the cause collapsed, was obliged to flee from Italy with him and their child and her chronicle of the revolt. They perished by shipwreck when their flight had brought them to American shores.

Margaret died at forty, just when the full fruition of her talents was at hand, for with marriage she seemed to attain the psychological balance which had evaded her in early life. She came back fired with the spirit of the new age that was dawning in Europe, but the messenger and the message both were lost. It was a tragic waste, yet perhaps the most fitting end for a life of ceaseless struggle against all manner of handicaps, with the prizes always vanishing just as the goal was reached.

Her contemporaries felt the tragedy of her loss most keenly, and she was not forgotten while those who had known her were still alive. As time went by, her many friends tended to idealize her in their minds, and by opposition those who had disliked her tended to make her name the watchword for all that was pretentious, eccentric, and ridiculous. She was a haunting ghost who, for more than forty years after her death, troubled the memories of the singularly long-lived generation to which she had belonged. A whole literature of reminiscences by all who had had any contact with her came into being, and many of the writers who concerned themselves with her were, as Andrew MacPhail put it, "little less hysterical and quite as absurd" as some of them made her out. The legend swelled as the reality faded from men's minds. There are good reasons why the real Margaret Fuller has been lost sight of, despite all the attention that has been paid to her memory. Her brother made an attempt to collect her writings in five volumes, but the collection is poorly edited, incomplete, and by no means representative. She was a great talker, and only secondarily a writer. Her life was cut off just as her most creative period might have been expected. Her conversation is almost completely lost; her letters and journals, which give a far more adequate idea of her capabilities than her formal writings, are scattered and in many cases unpublished. Her history of the Roman revolution, which she considered her best work, is thought to have been lost in the shipwreck, for no trace of it has been found.

After her death she suffered from the biographical attentions of her friends, who in their sentimentalism suppressed many of the facts of her life and made of this passionate woman a wooden and unreal figure, from whom it was natural that later generations should turn in disgust. The *Memoirs of Margaret Fuller Ossoli,* which Emerson, William Henry Channing, and James Freeman Clarke produced in collaboration two years after her death, is shockingly inadequate and unreliable. As Carlyle observed in his comment on it to Emerson, if you seek a fact in it, "you are answered (so to speak) not in words, but by a symbolic tune on the bagpipe, symbolic burst of wind-music from the brass-band." These friends of Margaret, in their regard for her memory, inked out, scissored, or pasted over a third of the never-to-be-duplicated mass of material they had before them, and thus blocked the path for all who might follow them. Mazzini and Robert Browning wrote their recol-lections of Margaret for inclusion in the *Memoirs*, but their important contributions were lost and never rediscovered. The majority of those who have subsequently concerned themselves with her career have either followed the precedent set by her first biographers or have lost the main outlines of the real woman in the complex maze of her character. For, as Gamaliel Bradford pointed out, "Margaret had so many selves that you can peel her like an onion." The process of discovering the true Margaret has become no easier through the activities of the myth-makers.

The recent revival of interest in the great era of New Eng-land letters has brought to light, however, much source ma-terial which is of great value in an attempt to do fuller justice to the woman whose life epitomizes that era. New light on Brook Farm, on Emerson, Hawthorne, Alcott, Parker, Emily Dickinson, and Brownson also illuminates Margaret Fuller. New methods of studying documents make it possible to re-cover some of the material that her first biographers suppressed. The rapid advances of the new science of psychology permit a sounder and more critical use of a technique which did much to explain the inexplicable in such characters as hers when it was enthusiastically applied in the first wave of literary Freud-ianism. And since the critical revaluing of our cultural heritage is under way, it seems essential to trace out once more, but in these new lights, the life of one who was, as Van Wyck Brooks has it, "not so much a great writer, but a great woman writing."

For Margaret Fuller was too vivid a person to be allowed to remain a shade, and had too much importance as an influence to be neglected in any reweighing of her contemporaries. She

was a whetstone of genius; she possessed the gift of bringing
out the brilliance in her friends, and where they lacked talent
she made them rise far above their natural limitations. Her
crudities and absurdities are those of the pioneer, and are in
large measure due to the enthusiasm with which she blazed the
trail for those who won greater recognition as they followed in
her path. Longfellow, who was no friend of hers and had felt her
critical sting, remarked long after her death: "It is easy enough
now to say and see what she then saw and said, but it demanded
insight to see and courage to say what was entirely missed by
that generation." She was a potent force in the Feminist movement; she did much to make the masterpieces of German literature familiar in a country where the language was hardly
known when she began the work; she fostered the growth of
interest in art; and she proclaimed the dawn of a new day in
America, when our literature and art would no longer be de-
rivative and imitative, but rather the unique flowering of our
own traditions and culture. She was ahead of her time, yet
very much of it. New England's greatest era becomes more
understandable in the light of Margaret Fuller's life. Emerson
can be read without reference to his historical background, as
Shakespeare often is, but Margaret Fuller brings that background to life for us, so that greater figures than she become
more clearly defined and better understood.

FORMATION

1810–1839

❧ CHAPTER I ❧

A Cambridge Childhood

The child fed with meat instead of milk becomes too soon mature.

—M. F.

SARAH MARGARET FULLER was born on May 23, 1810, in Cambridgeport, Massachusetts. She was the first child of Timothy and Margaret Crane Fuller, whose marriage was less than a year old at her birth. In honor of his first-born, Timothy planted two elms in front of his house on Cherry Street. These two trees, growing side by side and gradually interlacing their branches, typified the way in which the lives of father and daughter were linked throughout Margaret's childhood and youth.

Timothy Fuller was a lawyer and a budding politician, a man of some consequence in the community but of no popularity, partly because of his eccentricities of opinion—he was a Unitarian and a Jeffersonian—and partly because of the self-assertiveness and arrogance which were reputed to be the heritage of the Fullers. He was the son of a poor country minister and had worked his way through Harvard. Because of the role he had taken in a student rebellion against certain regulations, he was denied the right of being first honor man in his class and was graduated with second honors, as his father had been before him. Timothy doubtless inherited his independence of mind from his father, who had stoutly maintained Tory opinions from the pulpit during the Revolutionary War until the Minute Men, who made up the bulk of the congregation,

3

brought about his discharge. The Reverend Mr. Fuller promptly brought suit against the town for his salary, but was unsuccessful in the courts and even had to bear the costs of the affair. Despite these reverses, the indomitable clergyman refused to leave the town which had thus rejected him, and settled down to raise his family on a near-by farm.

When Timothy entered Harvard he had already determined to follow the law rather than the ministry. Twelve years after his graduation in 1801, he decided to combine politics with his profession and became a member of the Massachusetts Senate. In 1817 he was elected to Congress as a Representative, and eight years later became speaker of the Massachusetts House. In 1828 he was chosen a member of the Executive Council. His caustic tongue served him well in election contests, but was a handicap in his law practice, which never proved of much profit to him. Shrewd, energetic, and capable as he was, his almost total lack of endearing personal qualities left him dependent upon his family for friendship. And even in the family circle his domineering nature caused much friction.

At thirty-one he had married a girl ten years his junior, who had no money and many poor relations. Mrs. Fuller, though hardly more than a girl, had been a school teacher before her marriage. Timothy dominated his wife so thoroughly that her influence on their daughter seems to have been confined largely to the physical act of motherhood and to have ended with Margaret's emergence from infancy. Although Timothy paid lip-service to a firm belief in the equality of the sexes, it was not in his character to treat his wife as a partner with rights equal to his own. Nor was it in Mrs. Fuller's to protest: she was a gentle soul. Margaret described her as "one of those fair and flower-like natures, which sometimes spring up even beside the most dusty highways of life—a creature not to be shaped into a merely useful instrument, but bound by one law with the blue sky, the dew, and the frolic birds. Of all persons whom I have known, she had in her most of the angelic—of that spontaneous love for every living thing, for man and beast and tree, which restores the golden age." She bore her husband nine children in sixteen years, and was described on her tombstone as a "true woman." For the rest, she effaced herself, or was effaced by the domineering Timothy, and after his death it was Margaret, whom he had trained to be his instrument, who managed the family and reared the younger children. Mrs. Fuller's only indulgence was the hours she devoted to tending the flowers in her garden. One of her sons wrote of her: "Duty was her daily food. Self-sacrifice was as natural to her as self-gratification is to others." There have been many such women in New England since the Puritans made it their home.

Margaret's earliest recollection was of the death of a sister two years younger than herself. In later life she found it significant that her first experience of life was one of death. At thirty she still remembered vividly the sense of loss, wonder, and mystery that she felt:

I remember coming home and meeting our nursery-maid, her face streaming with tears. That strange sight of tears made an indelible impression. I realize how little I was of stature, in that I looked up to this streaming face; and it has often seemed since that, full grown for the life of this earth, I have looked up just so, at times of threatening, of doubt, of distress, and just so has some being of the next higher order of existence looked down, aware of a law unknown to me, and tenderly commiserating the pain I must endure in emerging from my ignorance.

She took me by the hand and led me into a still and dark chamber—then drew aside the curtain and showed me my sister. I see yet that beauty of death! The highest achievements of sculpture are only the reminder of its severe sweetness. Then I remember the house all still and dark—the people in their black clothes and dreary faces—the scent of the newly made coffin—my being set up in a chair and detained by a gentle hand to hear the clergyman—the carriages slowly going, the procession slowly doling out their steps to the grave. But I have no remembrance of what I have since been told I did—insisting with loud cries that they should not put the body in the ground. . . . She who would have been the companion of my life was severed from me, and I was left alone. This has made a vast difference in my lot.

Thus, at the outset of life, death deprived Margaret of a natural companion and fixed melancholy memories in her mind. The strange course of her childhood brought no other companions to replace the lost sister, and nothing to banish these memories.

As soon as Margaret could talk and toddle about alone, Timothy Fuller took complete charge of his daughter's life. He taught her her first lessons; he supervised her dress, manners, behavior, and what little recreation she was allowed. She came to him at a time when he felt the need of companionship, and he treated her as a living mind, not as a plaything. When the first locks were cut from her hair, he wrote verses hymning her head as the temple of immortal intellect. But he was not an indulgent parent. He demanded from little Margaret the same strict adherence to the virtues of clear judgment, courage, honor, and fidelity that he exacted from himself. He had high expectations for his daughter, and he did not intend that she should fail to realize them through idleness.

Timothy Fuller had hoped that his first child would be a son who could be reared in his pattern as his heir. After the birth of his second daughter, he decided to give Margaret the rigorous classical education which was conventional for a boy in an era when Harvard freshmen were fourteen years of age— but in Margaret's case he started instruction even earlier than was usual for a boy. He was not a man to be balked in his purposes; he had the Puritan's rigidity of mind and will. A brilliant son—one who could fittingly follow in his steps—he would have; and since the Lord had seen fit to give him a daughter instead, he would rear her as he would have reared the much-desired son. In later life, when he had several sons, his feelings had already become centered on Margaret. Perhaps it was just as well, for none of the Fuller boys showed much intellectual promise.

It was serious instruction that Margaret received from her father when she was hardly more than a baby. She was taught Latin and English grammar simultaneously, and began reading Latin at six. For some years afterward she read it daily and was expected to translate to her father without breaks or hesitation. He set rigorous standards for the little girl, demanding accuracy and clearness in everything. Margaret was not allowed to speak unless she could make her meaning perfectly intelligible, to express a thought unless she could give a reason for it, to make a statement unless she was sure of all particulars. Since Timothy found the Romans the best exemplars of the virtues he was trying to inculcate, Margaret was given Virgil, Horace, and Ovid to read when she was six and seven. At first this was a mere burden of study to her; soon it became a habit and a passion. She idolized Caesar and her thoughts were filled with the stern Romans of the books she read.

Timothy Fuller was a man of business, even in the education of his daughter. He hoped to make his daughter the heir of all he knew, and as much more as he could give her the means of acquiring. He thought to gain time by developing her intellect as early as possible, so Margaret's hours were filled with many tasks, often on subjects beyond her age. When he returned home from his office in the evening, he heard her recitations. She was often kept up very late, because he was subject to many interruptions and because his own mental habits and his ambition for her made him a severe and conscientious teacher. Then, with over-strained and over-stimulated nerves, she was packed off to bed. The effects of this forcing process soon made themselves felt: Margaret became the victim by

night of spectral illusions, nightmares, and somnambulism. She
dreaded going to bed:

> No one knew why this child, already kept up so late, was
> still unwilling to retire. My aunts cried out upon the "spoiled
> child, the most unreasonable child that ever was—if brother
> could but open his eyes to see it—who was never willing to go
> to bed." They did not know that, so soon the light was taken
> away, she seemed to see colossal faces advancing slowly
> toward her, the eyes dilating and each feature swelling loath-
> somely as they came, till at last, when they were about to
> close upon her, she started up with a shriek which drove them
> away, but only to return when she laid down again. They did
> not know that, when at last she went to sleep, it was to dream
> of horses trampling over her, and to awake once more in
> fright; or, as she had just read in her Virgil, of being among
> trees that dripped with blood, where she walked and walked
> and could not get out, while the blood became a pool and
> plashed over her feet, and rose higher and higher, till soon
> she dreamed it would reach her lips. No wonder the child
> arose, and walked in her sleep, moaning all over the house,
> till once, when they heard her, and came and waked her,
> and she told them of what she had dreamed, her father
> sharply bid her "leave off thinking of such nonsense, or she
> would be crazy"—never knowing that he was himself the
> cause of all these horrors of the night. Often she dreamed of
> following to the grave the body of her mother, as she had
> done that of her sister, and woke to find the pillow drenched
> with tears. These dreams softened her heart too much, and
> cast a deep shadow over her young days; for then, and later,
> the life of dreams—probably because there was in it less to
> distract the mind from its own earnestness—has often seemed
> to her more real, and been remembered with more interest,
> than that of waking hours.

The psychological connections between these dreams and the

realities of Margaret's childhood are clear. The Latin she began to read at six was too strong an intellectual diet for an immature mind, and it is not surprising that the horrendous images of Virgil haunted her dreams. The trampling horses, which commonly figure in the dreams of adolescent girls and hysterical women, suggest that Margaret was sexually precocious on the unconscious level. And the frequent recurrence of the dream about attending her mother's funeral was a natural result of Timothy Fuller's exclusion of his wife from the child's life, and of Margaret's vivid impressions of her sister's death.

Denied the companionship of other children, Margaret found refuge from the stern masculine world of her lessons and the strictly ordered life of the Fuller household in the garden behind the Cherry Street house. Here her mother had planted flowers and fruit trees, and the child found the place full of delight. She loved to study the roses, violets, lilies, and pinks from every side; she picked the most beautiful blossoms, kissed them and pressed them to her bosom with a passion that she could not explain. She determined to be as perfect and as beautiful as they. At sunset Margaret liked to watch the golden sky through the black frame of the garden gate, but she never ventured through it to the fields beyond. These placid hours in the garden were the happiest of her childhood.

Once her lessons were done, the child was encouraged to make use of the large closet of books which served Timothy Fuller as a library. Here she found and read the French Jacobins, the Queen Anne authors who were her father's favorites, and Smollett, Fielding, and other English novelists. At eight she discovered Shakespeare and read him avidly, although she was sternly reproved when discovered lost in *Romeo and Juliet* on a Sunday that should have been devoted to more godly pursuits. Then she came upon Cervantes and Molière, though these authors were not quite so much to her taste as the English poet who made the great Romans come to life again. Her thoughts came to dwell more and more in the new worlds which these books opened to her. And the more she read and daydreamed about the proud beings of these worlds, the tamer her own existence became. She looked about her for Roman or Shakespearean figures, and found only "the shrewd, honest eye, the homely decency, or the smartness of a New England village on Sunday." She despaired of her own powers, so faint and meager in comparison with those of her idols. Later she was to realize that too much of life had been devoured in the bud through books.

When Margaret was thirteen her bookish and solitary life was interrupted by a passionate attachment to an English-woman whom she first saw at church. This stranger, with her foreign ways and manners, satisfied the child's need for some-thing more glamorous than was offered by prosaic Cambridge. The Englishwoman was a typical product of European culture. When Margaret came to know that culture at first hand, she was able to speak contemptuously of "how wearisome now ap-pears that thorough-bred *millefleur* beauty, the distilled result of ages of European culture!" But to the little girl craving the exotic, even such things as the stranger's dress, arrangement of her hair, and self-possession and reserve were fascinating. When she forced herself upon the visitor—this was always Margaret's way in later life with anyone who attracted her—she found her both elegant and captivating, accomplished as a painter in oils and as a harpist, and a great reader of the ro-mances of Sir Walter Scott. Margaret worshiped this paragon among women, and the stranger was touched by the odd little girl's devotion. She gave her admirer a bunch of golden amaranths, which Margaret kept for seventeen years.

But the Englishwoman's visit to Boston came to an end in a few months and she returned home. Margaret was desolated, although her friend promised to write regularly—as a matter of fact, the correspondence was kept up for many years. For her "the light of life was set and every leaf was withered"—at thirteen! She ate nothing, grew thin, abandoned herself to melancholy, and suffered all the torments of the lovelorn. At first her father could make nothing of this, and then he began to wonder if his cherished scheme of upbringing was, after all, a sound one for a young girl. He suddenly became aware for the first time of the child's need for companionship and play. He decided that a change of scene would end this melancholy, and proposed to send her off to school. Margaret had no relish for the prospect. On the rare occasions when she had associated with other girls, she had not been a social success. She was not their schoolmate, she seemed to scorn their games, and her bookish life had bred a repelling aloofness and a manner which appeared haughty.

The school chosen by Timothy Fuller for his daughter was that of the Misses Prescott at Groton, some forty miles from Cambridge. Margaret attended this school during her fourteenth and fifteenth years, and her experiences there are revealed in an autobiographical story called "Mariana." At first she got along well enough with her schoolmates, who found her different, surprising, and captivating with her strange ways. But she gradually displayed other characteristics which turned her companions from her. She had the impulse for leadership and demanded a strict faithfulness from her followers, while she herself would follow no one. She was prone to infatuations and expected from those thus favored a devotion equal to her own. She was given to capricious withdrawals into solitude, yet expected to be made welcome by the others when her need for solitude was satisfied. The teachers could not understand this strange child who would be quiet all day and then in the evening would spin about like a whirling dervish, declaiming verses and acting parts that fitted into her fantasies. Such excitement rendered her sleepless and she would try to continue her performance after the others had gone to bed. Discouraged in that, she would lie down only to begin walking in her sleep. This habit was regarded as most alarming and various measures were taken to cure it—among them, putting her on a milk diet.

But none of the cures worked. She rebelled against the restraints and routine of the school, and asserted her individuality by dressing oddly. Finally she found an outlet from the drab everyday life of the school in the theatricals which she dominated, playing the principal parts and directing the whole enterprise.

During these entertainments the girls were allowed the use of rouge. Margaret would not leave off painting her cheeks after the play was over, as the others did, and answered the jeers of her companions by saying that she did it because it made her look pretty. One day when she came late to dinner, as she often did under the plea of suffering from headaches, she found that all the other girls had painted heavy circles on their cheeks. Even the teachers and the servants joined in the laugh which followed her startled glance around the room. It was a hard joke to take, but she had been trained in the Roman virtues and tried to reveal no trace of discomfort. It was only after dinner that she went to her room, locked the door, and threw herself upon the floor in convulsions. As soon as this was discovered, everyone was kindness itself. But Margaret did not forgive the slight which had been put upon her by her schoolmates.

She brooded upon her wrongs and decided upon a revenge. She took advantage of the confidences which came her way to fan up the flames of envy and jealousy among her companions. It was only too easy, she found, to set friends at odds by a word here and a glance there. Soon the school was a hotbed of dissension and Margaret could enjoy her success as a "genius of discord." Her role was soon discovered, however, and she was summoned before the principal to answer charges of slander and falsehood. At first Margaret confronted with poise the eight older girls who were her accusers, and defended herself eloquently. But when she could no longer hold out against the truth, she suddenly threw herself down, dashing her head with all her force against the iron hearth, before which she had been standing, and lay there senseless. For several days she refused to talk or eat. She was stricken with repentance for her course of action during the preceding months, and thought: "Too late sin is revealed to me in all its deformity, and sin-defiled, I will not, cannot live. The main-spring of life is broken." The same Puritan conscience which had made her implacable in revenge now reduced her to inhuman despair.

Finally Margaret was brought back to health through the efforts of one of the teachers, who confessed to a similar experience in her own life. But it was a different Margaret who took her place in the school for the short time that she remained there. She put aside her pride and begged the forgiveness of her schoolmates; she did her best to be warm-hearted and so earned some affection from them. Her fiery will seemed to have gone from flame to coal, and she found no capacity for resentment or trickery left in her nature. The incident had seared Margaret's soul deeply and indelibly.

The sympathetic teacher who had rallied Margaret from despair was not forgotten after her pupil had returned home. For five years Margaret wrote to her and gave detailed accounts of her intellectual development. Upon her return home she began a course of self-culture which she administered to herself in staggering doses:

I rise a little before five, walk an hour, and then practice on the piano until seven, when we breakfast. Next I read French—Sismondi's Literature of the South of Europe—till eight, then two or three lectures in Brown's Philosophy. About half-past nine I go to Mr. Perkins' school and study Greek until twelve, when, the school being dismissed, I recite, go home, and practice again until dinner, at two. Sometimes, if the conversation is very agreeable, I lounge for half an hour over the dessert, though rarely so lavish of time. Then, when I can, I read two hours in Italian, but I am often interrupted. At six I walk or take a drive. Before going to bed I play or sing for half an hour or so, to make all sleepy, and about eleven, retire to write a while in my journal, exercises on what I have read, or a series of characteristics which I am filling up according to advice. Thus, you see, I am learning Greek, and making acquaintance with metaphysics, and French and Italian literature.

In these letters Margaret confessed herself frankly. Ambition was the all-powerful motive behind this industry. She was determined to win at least distinction, though she saw that long years of labor were necessary to achieve the *succès de société* which seemed so poor beside the ideal of perfection that she cherished. She hoped to combine grace and pleasing qualities with mental genius. Undismayed by her lack of natural tact and polish, she set herself to cultivate these virtues and to discipline her intellectual powers, which she found "sufficient, I suppose." To her mind, an ardent spirit could overcome all hindrances. Certainly it carried her well along her chosen road, for even in the erudite Cambridge of that day it was a rare sixteen-year-old girl who devoted her letters to serious discussions of such topics as the Holy Alliance, the romance of Anastius, the Castilian ballads, Epictetus, Milton, and Racine. She worked out a parallel between Byron and Rousseau for her correspondent. After much debating of the relative merits of the brilliant de Staël and the useful Edgeworth, she determined to model herself on the former.

In the following year she mentioned that she was reading the older Italian poets, beginning with Berni, and studying the philosophy of John Locke as an introduction to English metaphysics. Remarking solemnly: "I read very critically," she plans to follow up this last with Madame de Staël's work on Locke's system. At last she had found a companion who shared the love of knowledge which she felt to be prodigiously kindled in her soul of late—one Miss Francis, who as Lydia Maria Child was to become celebrated both in England and in America as a

novelist and anti-slavery writer. Margaret valued her freedom
from cant and pretense, her charming conversation and spirited
thinking. As they studied Locke together, Margaret observed a
peculiar purity of mind in her friend, who was soon to under-
take the editorship of a magazine for children. But Margaret
did not let the charms of her new idol eclipse her feeling for
her old friend. Five years after the painful episode at the Prescott School, it is pleasant to find her writing: "Can I ever forget
that to your treatment in that crisis of youth I owe the true life
—the love of Truth and Honor?"

Margaret's life in Cambridge after her return from school
was not so wholly devoted to study as her letters to her former
teacher would indicate. She began to take the place in society
that was hers as the daughter of a man of rising consequence in
the community. Timothy Fuller had been active in John Quincy
Adams's first campaign for the Presidency, and in the summer
of 1826 he gave a party for the great man at his home in
Cambridge. The President had not been entertained in Boston
since Washington's time, and this reception established Timothy
Fuller as a social rival to the Federalist aristocrats, though it
doubtless taxed his resources. Margaret wore a pink silk dress
on this occasion, and impressed the company as a buxom young
woman of eighteen or twenty, though actually she was barely
sixteen. She was as precocious physically as mentally. She was
beginning to find friends among the more serious-minded
young men of the class of 1829 at Harvard, who esteemed her
conversation, although many young people were frightened
away by her tendency to sarcasm.

One of her circle at this time, Frederick Henry Hedge, found
that she had no pretensions to beauty, but a face that aroused
interest and made one desirous of nearer acquaintance. There
was evidence of a mighty force in it, without indication of the
direction that force might take. As one studied that face, never
seen in repose, great possibilities and talent seemed to vie with
indifference and caprice. She escaped plainness on the strength

of her abundant blond hair, excellent teeth, and particularly her brilliant eyes, which shot piercing glances at those with whom she conversed—glances all the more disconcerting because the busy eyes were usually half closed from near-sightedness. And she had an odd way of carrying her head on her long swaying neck, which reminded her friends of a swan and her enemies of a snake.

Good conversation was highly esteemed in the Cambridge of that day. Margaret soon discovered that she had a talent for it, which brought her the intellectual companionship that she so much desired. In James Freeman Clarke, who was related to her by a remote family connection and whom she called cousin, she found a confidant with whom she could discuss her studies and her intellectual aspirations. He was impressed by her ability to magnetize others, when she wished, so that they opened their natures to her. This was not the result of a vulgar curiosity on her part, but rather of her conviction that every human being was an individual and hence worth knowing. In this way she could discover whether an acquaintance possessed the one thing she demanded of her friends—that aspiration to a higher life than the common which her favorite Goethe called "extraordinary generous seeking."

Where this aspiration existed, Margaret asked for no notable originality of intellect or greatness of soul. Wherever she found it, she cultivated the friendship of the person who possessed it. Her circle of intimates offered the greatest variety of character, but they all had this aspiration and they all were drawn to Margaret by the compelling magnetism which she could exert at will. Some were young beauties, some elderly students. Some were worldly, some were creatures of the spirit. Some were witty, and some were dull. Margaret held the motley group together by her wit and fancy, her insight and imagination, her resources of learning and rhetoric. Clarke thus described her fascination for her friends:

Margaret was, to persons younger than herself, a Makaria
and Natalia. She was wisdom and intellectual beauty, filling
life with charm and glory "known to neither sea nor land."
To those of her own age she was sibyl and seer—a prophetess
revealing the future, pointing the path, opening their eyes to
the great aims only worthy of pursuit in life. To those older
than herself she was like the Euphorion in Goethe's drama,
child of Faust and Helen—a wonderful union of exuberance
and judgment, born of romantic fullness and classic limita-
tion. They saw with surprise her clear good sense balancing
her flow of sentiment and ardent courage. They saw her
comprehension of both sides of every question, and gave
her their confidence, as to one of equal age, because of so
ripe a judgment.

Of course, there were those who were not dazzled at first
sight by Margaret's intellectual attainments and many who felt
an active dislike and distaste for her upon a first meeting, because of her rough manners and highhanded ways. In some
people she aroused a feeling of physical revulsion. Emerson,
who became one of her closest friends, at first felt uncomfort-
able when in the same room with her. Others could not tolerate
her egotism and the domineering manner that she had inherited
from Timothy Fuller. Horace Mann went so far as to say that
she possessed the unpleasantness of forty Fullers. But if Margaret thought a person's company valuable or interesting, she
sought it without regard to that person's opinion of her. She paid
no attention to repulses, and the curious power of her personality usually won over in the end anyone upon whom it was
directed. James Clarke dubbed her "sagacious of her quarry,"
and tells of one woman who repelled Margaret's advances for
several years, but at last became dearly attached to her.
Throughout Margaret's life many became her friends in just
this way. She seldom lost a friend once made. She had the talent

of inviting confidences from people not given to crying on the nearest shoulder, and she knew how to keep each intimacy separate and inviolate. Her friendship was constant and inspiring, and those who enjoyed it found the ordinary things of life made more lustrous.

As Margaret began to figure in the intellectual life of Cambridge, she attracted the attention of Mrs. Farrar, a Harvard professor's wife and the author of a *Manual for Young Ladies*. Mrs. Farrar soon came to take a kindly interest in the girl and attempted to mold her character in more feminine lines than those of the masculine upbringing which Timothy Fuller had given it. Here was a brilliant ugly duckling to metamorphose, and one who repaid her for her efforts by idolizing her. For Margaret was becoming acutely conscious of her lack of the feminine charms which attracted her in other girls and drew young men to them. She enjoyed the intellectual admiration which was paid her, but it was cold comfort when her thoughts began to turn to love and marriage. Under Mrs. Farrar's guidance she came to know her faults, but it was no easy matter to overcome them. The pattern that Timothy Fuller had imposed upon her character was too deeply embedded to be altered at will. Mrs. Farrar was able to give some polish to Margaret's bearcub manners, but the feminization of her character was not to be completed until late in life.

Since beauty and the social graces seemed to be denied her by nature, Margaret determined to be "bright and ugly," and cultivated her mental powers. While her contemporaries chose their partners for life, she remained unsought and went her way alone. She formed a romantically melancholy idea of what the future held for her, which she revealed in a letter to James Clarke:

From a very early age I have felt that I was not born to the common womanly lot. I knew that I should never find a being who could keep the key to my character; that there would be none on whom I could always lean, from whom I could always learn; that I should be a pilgrim and sojourner on the earth, and that the birds and foxes would be surer of a place to lay the head than I. . . .

I mourned that I should never have a thorough experience of life, never know the full riches of my being; I was proud that I was to test myself in the sternest way, that I was always to return to myself, to be my own priest, pupil, parent, child, husband, and wife. All this I did not understand as I do now; but this destiny of the thinker, and (shall I dare to say it?) of the poetic priestess, sibylline dwelling in the cave or amid the Libyan sands, lay yet enfolded in my mind. . . .

Yet, as my character is, after all, more feminine than masculine, it would sometimes happen that I put more emotion into a state than I myself knew. I really was capable of attachment, though it never seemed so until the hour of separation. And if a connexion was torn up by the roots, the soil of my existence showed an unsightly wound, which long refused to clothe itself in verdure. . . .

I think I may say I have never loved. I but see my possible life reflected on the clouds. As in a glass darkly, I have seen what I might feel as child, wife, mother, but I never have really approached the close relations of life. A sister I have truly been to many—a brother to more—a fostering nurse to, oh, how many! The bridal hour of many a spirit, when first it was wed, I have shared, but said adieu before the wine was poured out at the banquet. And there is one I always love in my poetic hour, as the lily looks up at the star from amid the waters; and another whom I visit as the bee visits the flower, when I crave sympathy. Yet those who live would scarcely consider that I am among the living—and I am isolated, as you say.

❧ CHAPTER II ❧

Exile in Groton

Heaven's discipline has been invariable to me. The seemingly most pure and noble hopes have been blighted; the seemingly most promising connexions broken. The lesson has been endlessly repeated: "Be humble, patient, self-sustaining; hope only for occasional aids; love others, but not engrossingly, for by being so much alone your appointed task can best be done." What a weary work is before me, ere that lesson shall be fully learned. . . . Yet I will try to keep the heart with diligence, nor even fear that the sun is gone out, because I shiver in the cold and dark!—M. F.

IN THE spring of 1833 Timothy Fuller moved his family from Cambridge to a farm which he had acquired in Groton. The re-election of Andrew Jackson to the Presidency the previous fall had completed the ruin of his political ambitions. He had lost his zest for politics with the collapse of his hope of being rewarded with an ambassadorship for his services in behalf of John Quincy Adams. His law practice, never highly remunerative, was beginning to dwindle away, perhaps because his clients had no confidence in a man so obviously embittered by disappointment. So, at fifty-five, Timothy Fuller retired to the country to bring up his family, as his father had before him. He found that he enjoyed life on the farm and only wished that he had taken the step earlier. Here he was undisputed master of a little world of his own, and he began to forget his disappointment in the work of the farm. But none of the considerations which combined to make Timothy certain that his decision was a wise one had any weight with Margaret. She made no attempt to conceal her displeasure at the change in the

Fullers' way of life. At twenty-three, it was desperately hard to exchange the stimulating intellectual and social atmosphere of Cambridge for the lifeless calm of a little country village. The forty miles between the two places raised a barrier in all her intimacies, and she saw herself condemned for life to the sad lot of the unmarried elder daughter of a country family. The boys would be free to go out into the world as they grew up, but she would have to stay on at home, for such was the custom of the age.

Margaret soon found herself too busy to have time for brooding. She was charged with the education of the younger children, for Timothy devoted such leisure as the farm allowed him to study, since he was planning to write on American history. Margaret gave five to eight hours a day to her four pupils, instructing them in three languages, geography, and history. Since her mother was often ill, she had a heavy burden of domestic duties. The family could afford only one servant now, and that meant more work for the grown-up daughter. Timothy sought her companionship in his studies, and they read Jefferson's letters and discussed the outlines of American history together. And with her unquenchable zeal for self-improvement, Margaret somehow found time during the first winter in Groton to complete a course of study which included European history, the elements of architecture, and the works of Alfieri, Goethe, and Schiller. She also began to try her hand at writing, but was unable to complete anything that satisfied her. Somehow it was easier to sketch out plans for future execution, "in a season of more joyful energy when my mind has been renovated and refreshed by change of scene or circumstance." She did write, however, an essay in defense of Brutus, which delighted her father so much that he brought about its anonymous publication in a Boston paper. No less a person than George Bancroft replied to it, only to be worsted by his unknown opponent's rejoinder. Timothy Fuller swelled with pride at this proof of the superior education he had given his daughter, and informed her that he was "mightily gladdened" by the way in which she was instructing her brothers and sister. He even held out to her the prospect of a trip abroad as a reward for her efforts. Margaret set her heart upon this goal, and labored all the harder to attain it.

Timothy Fuller's idyllic picture of the life that his family could lead in Groton was never realized. The Fullers found that the habits of town life had ill prepared them for the rigors of dwelling on a farm. They paid a heavy toll of hardship and misfortune for the change. Mrs. Fuller's health broke down under the strain, and she was often ill. The baby fell sick and died. One of the older children met with a serious accident and had to be nursed for months. Antagonism broke out between father and sons. Eugene, the eldest, left home and took a post as tutor to a family in Virginia. William, the second son, also rebelled against his father's domineering ways and quit the farm, so that only Arthur and Richard, the two youngest boys, were left with the womenfolk at home.

Margaret never succeeded in reconciling herself to Groton and pained her father by her lack of interest in the place. Soon after he acquired the farm, he built a retreat for her in a little clump of woods near the house, but she never used it. She accepted the heavy burden of work that fell upon her shoulders with a seeming cheerfulness that scarcely masked a fundamental discontent. If the country must be their home, why could not her father have chosen Concord, where she had friends who shared her interests and where the railroad offered easy access to Boston and Cambridge? Here in Groton she was buried from the world, and she saw no possibility of realizing any of her cherished plans. But she had too much strength to be crushed, and kept her world of dreams intact, deep within herself, while the surface of her life was devoted to uncongenial duties. After two years of such repressed conflict and too heavy a burden of toil, she fell ill with brain fever. For nine days and nights she was in agony, nursed constantly by her mother.

Timothy Fuller, fearing for the life of his favorite child, for once allowed himself to express his feelings and told her one morning: "My dear, I have been thinking of you in the night, and I cannot remember that you have any faults. You have defects, of course, as all mortals have, but I do not know that you have a single fault." These words from a father who conscientiously refrained from praise as hurtful reduced Margaret to tears. When she grew better and her recovery was assured, he astonished the family by the fervency of his prayers of thanksgiving. To his wife he said: "I have no room for a painful thought now that our daughter is restored."

During this illness Margaret had felt that she was going to die. She had met the prospect calmly and without fear. Indeed, as she thought of the struggle that awaited her if she recovered and how improbable it was that the future would bring her what she wished, she had felt willing to go. But she was to discover that it was harder to face the death of another than of oneself. For she was hardly restored to health before Timothy Fuller was suddenly taken sick and died within twenty hours. His disease was diagnosed as Asiatic cholera, of which there had been an epidemic during the previous year. Shortly before his death, he had been busy with the ditching of some low-lying meadows on the farm, and it was thought that this might have contributed to his sudden illness. In any case, the change from professional work to farm labor had worn down a constitution which was naturally weak, although he had attempted to fortify it by temperance, diet, exercise, and bathing in cold water. To his family, however, he had seemed a pillar of strength and they were utterly unprepared for his untimely death. Mrs. Fuller was prostrated by the loss of her husband, and the children feared that they would lose her too. So it was his daughter, not his wife, who closed the eyes of Timothy Fuller as he lay on his deathbed.

Margaret was never able to speak of the grief she felt at her father's death. She kept seeing his image wherever she went.

She was tormented by conscientious scruples about matters in which she had failed him in love or duty. The sylvan grove that he had reserved for her use, indeed every corner of the farm, was a painful reminder of unfulfilled affection. There was nothing to sustain her but the thought that God, who had seen fit to restore her to life when she was so willing to leave it, must have some good work for her to do. It soon became clear what this work was. Mrs. Fuller was by nature unfitted to deal with a world from which her husband had always sheltered her. Margaret had to take the place of the head of the family. Timothy had never confided anything about his business affairs to his wife or children, and they were utterly unable to cope with the disordered condition in which his sudden death left the family fortunes. Margaret's uncle, Abraham Fuller, set about disentangling these business matters, but the rest of the responsibility fell upon her. Soon after her father's death she wrote to a friend:

> I have often had reason to regret being of the softer sex and never more than now. If I were an eldest son, I could be guardian to my brothers and sister, administer the estate, and really become the head of the family. As it is, I am very ignorant of the management and value of property, and of practical details. I always hated the din of such affairs, and hoped to find a lifelong refuge from them in the serene world of literature and the arts. But I am now full of desire to learn them, that I may be able to advise and act where it is necessary. The same mind which has made other attainments can in time compass these, however uncongenial to its nature and habits.

In such a spirit she set about filling her father's place, making use of the mental traits that he had developed in her. Her mother, who had only patience and faith to carry through this difficult time, and the children depended upon her strength as they had on Timothy's. His desire to re-create his personality in his oldest child was thus fulfilled.

Abraham Fuller's investigation of his brother's affairs soon revealed that the family was in straitened circumstances. Timothy had left an estate of some twenty thousand dollars, but this was so tied up that little money would be available for months. Margaret's dream of a trip to Europe seemed doomed to be unrealized. During the summer of 1835, before her father's death in September, she had paid a visit to the Farrars in Cambridge and at their home had become friendly with Harriet Martineau, the English Feminist. This encounter had served to whet her appetite to study European civilization at first hand, and she had made tentative plans to travel to England with the Farrars the following summer. But now Uncle Abraham dismissed the scheme as impossible when she broached it to him, and it was becoming obvious to Margaret herself that she could not be spared from home, even if the money were available. But she could not bring herself to abandon her cherished dream, which offered such relief from the struggles and privations of the present. She was too strong-minded to despair, and noted in her journal for New Year's Day, 1836: "My difficulties are not to be compared with those over which many strong souls have triumphed." All that spring there are indications that she was still debating the question with herself, and there are frequent prayers for divine guidance. As late as April, she was writing to Mrs. Farrar:

If I am not to go with you, I shall be obliged to tear my heart by a violent effort from its present objects and natural desires. But I shall feel the necessity and will do it, if the life blood follows through the rent.

By May she had finally made up her mind, with the aid of certain passages in her little New Testament which she found authoritative in deciding the matter. In her journal for the twenty-third of this month she wrote:

Circumstances have decided that I must not go to Europe and shut upon me the door, as I think, forever, to the scenes I could have loved. Let me now try to forget myself and act for others' sakes. What I can do with my pen, I know not. At present I feel no confidence or hope. The expectations that so many have been led to cherish by my conversational powers, I am disposed to deem ill-founded. I do not think that I can produce a valuable work. I do not feel in my bosom the confidence necessary to sustain me in such undertakings —the confidence of genius. But I am now just recovered from bodily illness and still heart-broken by sorrow and disappointment. I may be renewed again and feel differently. If I do not soon, I will make up my mind to teach. I can thus get money, which I will use for the benefit of my dear, gentle, suffering mother, my brothers, and sister. This will be the greatest consolation to me, at all events.

So she put aside her thoughts of Europe and dealt with the practicalities of family life in Groton. While her mother occupied herself with the dairy and the running of the house, Margaret took charge of the children. She also conducted the frequent family conferences, which her brother Richard recalled as so fearful and gloomy that "for years I saw starvation or the poorhouse in the dim perspective of distance—inevitable and the only question as to their approach being one of time." In the schoolroom Arthur was bright and Ellen diligent, but Richard was slow to learn. Margaret tried to arouse ambition in them by urging them to emulate the excellence of distinguished characters in history. She herself was so quick of mind and rapid in learning that dullness on the part of her pupils hurt her more than deliberate unkindness might have done. Through her struggles with the children she learned the patience without which a teacher is doomed to failure, although she found the progress of her young scholars "unpromising and unsatisfactory" by her high standards. She developed a sense of humor which saved her from despair when Richard, being asked where Turkey in Asia was, would reply that it was in Europe. The children found her an exacting mistress and worked hard to earn the praise of which she was as chary as her father.

So scholarly was the atmosphere at the Fuller farm that even the hired man felt its influence. This young man, who had been nicknamed "The Elephant" by the boys because of his bulk and heavy tread, was dazzled by Margaret's intellectual attainments and sought to emulate them. He ransacked books to seek out long words, which he collected and scattered through his own compositions. He constantly plagued Margaret with these singular productions, which he wanted her to show to her friends for criticism. She passed on one to Mrs. Farrar, who promptly included it in her *Manual* as a striking example of the dangers to be avoided in letter-writing. It read:

Dear Mother: My pen, which has long lain in idleness, has at length resumed its original important task. This will arrive in time to inform you that I have been and am still at work upon Mrs. Fuller's farm. Were I called upon to demonstrate in behalf of my eyes, I should say they were poor. . . .

"The Elephant" also took it upon himself to rub in the Fullers' poverty on the little boys, and made dire references to the washtub as the future occupation of their brilliant sister. He quailed, however, before Margaret's rebukes and soon left the farm "to fly about," as he put it, "from bush to bush seeking better food." His weakness for a ponderous vocabulary led him into a career as a phrenologist.

One of the causes of "The Elephant's" flight may well have been Margaret's supercilious attitude toward the young man and his pitiful pretensions to erudition. Preoccupied as she was with the idea of self-culture, she had only contempt for the vulgar herd who lacked her high aspirations. She was thinking of her humble neighbors in Groton when she wondered why God suffered "these grub-like lives, undignified even by pas-

sion—these lifelong quenchings of the spark divine." Very early
in life, she had come to the conclusion that the only object
in being was growth. She had had a period when she sought
knowledge as a means of gaining admiration, and when talent
had seemed to her the key to fame and position. As she
matured, she was less swayed by vanity as a motive and experienced a profound desire to develop her whole nature by a full
experience of life. Her reading of Goethe clarified this aim of
life which she evolved out of her own mind. It was this doctrine
of self-culture which supplied the energy that she devoted to
study and intellectual labor. Her friend James Clarke saw this
great idea of hers as the root and spring of her life; to him, it
was a "high, noble one, wholly religious, almost Christian."
But he was distressed by its fundamental selfishness, and noted
that it resulted in superciliousness toward the common run of
humanity and an idolatrous worship of genius and power. He
also blamed on it the sharp conflicts with circumstances and
duties which gave Margaret so much unhappiness.

Her illness and her father's death led Margaret into a consideration of religious problems, and a revaluation of her personal philosophy. She was no longer content, as she had been at
nineteen, to dismiss religion as a youthful need of sentimental or
feeble natures, but not of such as hers. At that time she had
written to a friend that she held no opinion about religion and
was determined not to form one. She drew her rules of life
from just two articles of faith: a belief in what she called
Eternal Progression, and in a God, "a Beauty and Perfection to
which I am to strive all my life for assimilation." Two years
later she had had a first religious experience. On Thanksgiving
Day, 1831, she had gone to church to please her father, though
she "almost always suffered much in church from a feeling
of disunion with the hearers and dissent from the preacher."
She was melancholy, and the grateful and joyful tone of the
services had only jarred upon her mood. She could hardly wait
until the end, and as soon as the services were over, she walked

through the fields as fast as she could, which was her custom when emotionally disturbed. The drab November landscape offered nothing to rouse her spirit from the gloom which had descended upon it. She walked on for hours, and then suddenly, as the sun shone out for a moment, a strange insight came to her. She seemed to see the plight of the human soul under the limitations of time and space and human nature, and how it must overcome these obstacles:

> I saw that there was no self; that selfishness was all folly, and the result of circumstance; that it was only because I thought self real that I suffered; that I had only to live in the idea of the ALL, and all was mine. This truth came to me, and I received it unhesitatingly; so that for that hour I was taken up into God.

From that day on, she was never completely engaged in self, though the guiding aim of her life gave her a strong tendency toward preoccupation with it. In her journal she prayed: "May God enable me to see the way clear, and not to let down the intellectual, in raising the moral tone of my mind." The removal of her family to Groton went counter to all her inclinations, and she found it difficult to subdue them. But finally she felt "the Holy Ghost descend upon her," and there came to her meekness and love and patience to obey in order to know. After that, she still knew suffering, but never felt "in discord with the grand harmony." The shock of her father's death made difficulties and duties very distinct in her mind, and she had much recourse to prayer that she might combine what was due to others with what was due to herself.

In the following March Margaret recorded in her journal: "I am having one of my intense times, devouring book after book. I have been examining myself with severity, and am shocked to find how vague and superficial is all my knowledge." She felt the need of a religious basis for thought, and she set about a serious examination of the evidence for Christianity.

It seemed high time that she stopped contenting herself with superficial and unthinking notions. Too long had she put off the reasoning out of her religious ideas, perhaps in the unconscious fear that they, once revealed, might put her outside the wide embrace of the Unitarian faith in which she had been reared by her father. Her nature demanded complete freedom to think its own thoughts and to use its critical judgment. It was fortunate that the Unitarian Church of that day was so broad in its views that she felt no necessity to leave its fold, and thus was spared any addition to her burden of emotional conflict.

This concern with religious matters did not keep Margaret from carrying out an ambitious scheme of general studies. In her letters and journals of this period she comments on and quotes from Goethe, Shelley, Wordsworth, Sir James Mackintosh, Herschel, Harriet Martineau, Southey, Carlyle, Coleridge, Heine, Novalis, Körner, and a host of others. In her reading she found escape from the prison of life at Groton. During the summer of 1836 she paid a visit of three weeks to Emerson at Concord, having made his acquaintance the previous year through Miss Martineau. He was somewhat exhausted by her insatiable appetite for serious discussion, but was much impressed by her intelligence and accomplishments. He compared her rate of reading with Gibbon's, and the comparison was unjust only in that Margaret had many demands upon her time and energy, while the great historian enjoyed the leisure that wealth affords. Perhaps it was a belated recognition of this difference that led him to remark to Harriet Martineau, when she expressed her regret that Margaret would be unable to go to Europe with her and the Farrars that fall: "Does Margaret Fuller, supposing her to be what you say, believe her progress to be dependent on whether she is here or there?" Seemingly her visit to Concord had strongly impressed him with her determination to make the best of her lot, and her ability to do so.

About this time Margaret also began to think seriously of eking out the Fullers' slender income by the product of her pen. She dismissed from her mind her earlier extravagant notion of writing six historical tragedies, with which she had got no further than the planning of three. Until she had re-educated herself to her satisfaction, she did not dare to think of beginning her dearest project, a life of Goethe. Her earlier attempts at composition had made her distrustful of her ability to write and sure that her true talent was for conversation, where contact with other minds brought out the best that was in her. Writing seemed "mighty dead" compared with good talk, but in her isolation at Groton it was only by writing that she could turn her talents to account. Her reading had given her a familiarity with German literature such as few Americans possessed at this time, and in a letter to a friend about her literary plans she speaks of writing on this subject:

> With regard to what you say about the American Monthly, my answer is I would gladly sell some part of my mind for lucre, to get the command of time; but I will not sell my soul; that is, I am not willing to have what I write mutilated or what I say dictated to suit the public taste. . . . It is my earnest wish to interpret the German authors of whom I am most fond to such Americans as are ready to receive. Perhaps some might sneer at the notion of my becoming a teacher; but where I love so much, surely I might inspire others to love a little; and I think this kind of culture would be precisely the counterpoise required by the utilitarian tendencies of our day and place. . . . I hope a periodical may arise, by and by, which may think me worthy to furnish a series of articles on German literature, giving room enough and perfect freedom to say what I please.

But it was to be some years yet before Boston shared her enthusiasm for German literature and such a magazine as she described appeared.

In the meantime the need for money became more acute, and the struggle to maintain the Fuller family on the farm more difficult. A casual incident in Margaret's life at Groton at this time influenced her strongly. She paid a visit to some poor neighbors, an aged mother and her daughter, and was so much struck by the meanness and misery of their life that she wrote an account of it. As she wrote, the thought came to her that such might be the fate of her mother and herself if they kept up the hopeless battle to make ends meet on the farm. Shortly afterwards she sought a position in Boston, and found one as a teacher of languages at Amos Bronson Alcott's Temple School. Alcott was impressed by her attainments and the boldly speculative trend of mind, and recorded his first judgment of her in his endless journals in these flattering terms: "Not wanting in imaginative power, she has the rarest good sense and discretion."

Margaret looked forward with delight to the prospect of her new career. She felt no lack of confidence in her power to teach, and the life in Boston promised to give all the intellectual stimulus, through contact with other minds, that had been lacking in Groton. At the same time she would be able to contribute to the welfare of her family more substantially than she had by her presence. Before she went off to take up her new post, in August 1836, she wrote a farewell to Groton:

> The place is beautiful in its way, but its scenery is too tamely smiling and sleeping. My associations with it are most painful. There darkened around us the results of my father's ill-judged exchange—ill-judged so far at least as regarded himself, mother, and me—all violently rent from the habits of our former life and cast upon toils for which we were unprepared: there my mother's health was impaired and mine destroyed; there my father died; there were undergone the miserable perplexities of a family that had lost its head; there I passed through the conflicts needed to give up

all which my heart had for years desired, and to tread a path for which I had no skill and no call, except that it must be trodden by someone and I was ready. Wachuset and the Peterboro hills are blended in my memory with hours of anguish as great as I am capable of suffering. I used to look at them towering to the sky and feel that I, too, from birth had longed to rise, and though for a moment crushed, was not subdued.

But if those beautiful hills and wide, rich fields saw this sad lore well learned, they also saw some precious lessons given in faith, fortitude, self-command, and unselfish love. There, too, in solitude the mind acquired more power of concentration and discerned the beauty of strict method; there, too, the heart was awakened to sympathize with the ignorant, to pity the vulgar, to hope for the seemingly worthless, and to commune with the divine spirit of Creation, which cannot err, which never sleeps, which will not permit evil to be permanent, or its aim of beauty in the smallest particular eventually to fail.

The pattern of her character was set; the statue was emerging from the block. The years that lay ahead were to modify this pattern but not to change it for another until the tragic close of her life.

CHAPTER III

A Teacher in Boston and Providence

Perhaps some might sneer at the notion of my becoming a teacher; but where I love so much, surely I might inspire others to love a little.

—M. F.

BRONSON ALCOTT had realized many of his theories of educational reform in his Temple School, so called because the classes were held in the Masonic Temple. He had had a hard struggle to educate himself as a poor farmer's son, and his study of Plato and Coleridge had convinced him that conventional education was misdirected. He conducted his school on the principle that the function of the teacher was to develop genius, not to impart knowledge. By the use of the Socratic method, he hoped to draw out the natural gifts of the children. His schoolroom was a pleasant place, with pictures on the walls. Busts of Plato, Socrates, and Milton stood upon pedestals, and a portrait of Dr. Channing had a place of honor as tribute to the modern immortal. The children were encouraged to win self-knowledge through the keeping of journals; recreations and amusements formed part of the school life. There was no wielding of the birch in punishment, and a system of self-government was fostered. These were radical innovations for the day, and attracted the attention of tradition-governed Boston. The year that Margaret taught at the Temple School was the third of its short-lived existence. The success that it enjoyed that year was

34

interrupted by the publication of Alcott's *Conversations with Children on the Gospels,* and a decline set in. Its eventual collapse two years later was brought about by Alcott's insistence on accepting a Negro pupil on the same basis as the other children, who were hastily withdrawn by their horrified parents, till only his own daughters Anna and Louisa were left. Though the very mention of its name awakened scandal in Boston, the Temple School served as the prototype of a number of flourishing establishments in England, where Alcott's disciples came to regard him as the greatest leader in education since Pestalozzi.

The book which contributed to the school's failure was an innocent enough record of Alcott's attempt to develop clear ideas of Biblical personages and events through questioning his pupils. But it was greeted in the press with a storm of vituperation. Charges of obscenity and blasphemy were leveled at the book, and Mr. Alcott was admonished by the *Boston Courier* to hide his head in shame. He was branded as an ignorant and presuming charlatan, and as a corrupter of youth. Alcott himself took the incident quietly—all through his life his philosophic calm was rarely disturbed—and pasted the article from the *Courier* into his journal, noting: "All this stir will do good—serving to bring better views into notice." But his assistants at the school, Margaret Fuller and Elizabeth Peabody, were roused to defend him among their friends. Margaret wrote to Harriet Martineau that Alcott was:

a true and noble man . . . whose disinterested and resolute efforts for the redemption of poor humanity all independent and faithful minds should sustain, since the "broadcloth" vulgar will be sure to assail them. A philosopher worthy of the palmy times of ancient Greece; a man whom Carlyle and Berkeley . . . would delight to honor; a man whom the worldlings of Boston hold in as much honor as the worldlings of ancient Athens did Socrates.

The Boston Socrates regarded Margaret as the fortunate possessor of "more of that unspoiled integrity of being so essential to the apprehension of truth in its unity than any person of her sex whom I meet," and enjoyed the freedom, elegance, and skill of her conversation. He judged that leisure and encouragement would do much to foster the growth of her already great intellectual powers.

Margaret found some encouragement, but not much leisure during her stay in Boston. In addition to teaching Latin and French at the Temple School, she gave private instruction in German and Italian. One evening a week she read German— chiefly the works of De Wette and Herder—aloud to Dr. Channing, who already employed her fellow teacher, Elizabeth Peabody, as his literary assistant. With this stimulus to her interest in German literature, she resumed the planning of her life of Goethe, and devoted considerable time to studying the subject and thinking about it. And despite all these preoccupations, she continued her omnivorous reading on a wide range of subjects. It is no wonder that at the end of the winter she complained of ill health:

> I am still quite unwell, and all my pursuits and propensities have a tendency to make my head worse. It is but a bad head—as bad as if I were a great man! I am not entitled to so bad a head by anything I have done; but I flatter myself it is very interesting to suffer so much, and a fair excuse for not writing pretty letters, and saying to my friends the good things I think about them.
>
> I was so desirous of doing all that I could that I took a great deal more upon myself than I was able to bear. Yet now that twenty-five weeks of incessant toil are over, I rejoice in it all, and would not have done an iota less. I have fulfilled all my engagements faithfully; have acquired more power of attention, self-command, and fortitude; have acted

in life as I thought I would in my lonely meditations; and have gained some knowledge of means. Above all—blessed be the Father of our spirits!—my aims are the same as they were in the happiest flight of my youthful fancy. I have learned, too, at last, to rejoice in all past pain, and to see that my spirit has been judiciously tempered for its work. In the future I may sorrow, but can I ever despair?

When she began her teaching in the fall, she had felt her enthusiasm for her favorite studies waning when she seemed to be buying and selling them. It had been hard to achieve a proper point of view in the matter. She felt vulgarized, profaned, and divided from her intimate friends. She was alone for the first time in many years, and loneliness brought on melancholy. Illness plagued her, and she thought that she might die when her work was but just begun. But in her new role she could not abandon herself to melancholy, as she often had before; it was necessary to smile brightly and talk wisely, no matter how gloomy her mood. Finally this dark mood passed from her as she achieved a friendly intimacy with Alcott, Elizabeth Peabody, and Dr. Channing.

She seems to have been a good teacher. One class that she introduced to German could read twenty pages at a lesson by the end of three months. Another read through during the year Schiller's *Don Carlos, Die Künstler,* and *Das Lied von der Glocke;* Goethe's *Hermann und Dorothea, Götz von Berlichingen, Iphigenie, Clavigo,* and the first part of *Faust;* Lessing's *Minna, Nathan,* and *Emilia Galotti;* parts of Tieck's *Phantasus* and nearly the whole first volume of Richter's *Titan.* Her Italian class read parts of Tasso, Petrarch, Ariosto, Alfieri, and the whole of the *Divina Commedia.* One of her private pupils was a little blind boy, to whom she taught Latin orally and read the history of England and Shakespeare's historical plays in the space of ten weeks. The tremendous amount of work

done during this one winter by her pupils and herself is ample
indication of the swiftness of her mind and the pitch to which
she keyed up her students.

Margaret found it difficult to slow down to suit the pace of
minds less rapid than her own. She complained that Dr. Channing took in subjects "more deliberately than is conceivable to
us feminine people, with our habits of ducking, diving, or flying
after the truth." She was willing to admit, however, that he
made better use of what he got, and was able to view it in a
steadier light. There was more talking than reading during her
evenings with him, but she enjoyed the talk, from which she
got much food for thought. The Doctor had a way of treating
even one so young and obscure as Margaret upon equal terms,
and this pleased her. She felt no constraint in talking with him,
and could value his thought properly without being bound to
tiresome formalities of respect on account of his age and rank
in the intellectual world. In the pulpit he could make her feel
"purged as if by fire."

Her quickness of spirit enabled her to search out the essence
of an idea while another was fumbling to express it. A passage
in her journal, which records a conversation between Alcott and
herself, shows how quickly she could seize upon the weak
points of his rather misty idealism:

Mr. A. O for the safe and natural way of Intuition! I cannot
grope like a mole in the gloomy passages of experience. To
the attentive spirit, the revelation contained in books is only
so far valuable as it comments upon, and corresponds with
the universal revelation. Yet to me, a being social and sympathetic by natural impulse, though recluse and contemplative
by training and philosophy, the character and life of Jesus
have spoken more forcibly than any fact recorded in human
history. This story of incarnate love has given me the key to
all mysteries and showed me what path should be taken in
returning to the Fountain of the Spirit. Seeing that other

WILLIAM ELLERY CHANNING

redeemers have imperfectly fulfilled their tasks, I have sought a new way. They all, it seemed to me, had tried to influence the human being at too late a day and had laid their plans too wide. They began with men; I will begin with babes. They began with the world; I will begin with the family. So I preach the Gospel of the Nineteenth Century.

M. But, preacher, you make *three* mistakes.

You do not understand the nature of Genius or creative power.

You do not understand the reaction of matter on spirit.

You are too impatient of the complex; and not enjoying variety in unity, you become lost in abstractions, and cannot illustrate your principles.

Alcott took no offense at such a shattering attack upon the philosophical theory which was the basis of his educational principles; it served merely to raise his high opinion of Margaret's capabilities. He understood that Margaret brought the same disposition to conversation as a gladiator to the arena, but there were many who did not understand that it was a passion for truth which gave her such brusque manners in conversation. Her quickness and sharpness of mind repelled less sturdy intellects, and made them echo the remark of Emerson's friend: "Miss Fuller *remembers;* it is ill-bred to remember."

She lived at too fast a pace during this first winter away from home. She was so eager to satisfy as a teacher and make use of all her new opportunities that she nearly ruined her health; she did damage it severely. Her constitution was never after this able to meet the demands she imposed upon it, and she suffered much from physical lassitude and periodic headaches of great intensity. Since her vigorous mind knew no limits to its endurance when it was set upon a goal, she made no concessions to illness. She came to believe that pain gave tension to her powers, that illness brought better understanding, and continued to read and write even when forced to her

bed. But by April she had decided that illness was no longer
"interesting" and that she must somehow lighten her burden
of petty and distracting tasks. She wrote to her old friend
Henry Hedge:

> I have learned much and thought little, an operation
> which seems paradoxical and *is* true. I faint with desire to
> think and surely shall, the first opportunity, but some out-
> ward requisition is ever knocking at the door of my mind
> and I am as ill placed as regards a chance to think as a
> haberdasher's prentice or the President of Harvard Univer-
> sity.
>
> I intend to get perfectly well, if possible, for Mr. Carlyle
> says, "It is wicked to be sick."

She told Emerson that she regarded Concord as her Lethe
after her present purgatory. From his first acquaintance with
her he had been alarmed by the rate at which she lived, so
much more rapid and violent than his own. As he followed
out his chosen and carefully guarded way of life in Concord,
he had a foreboding that her destiny was threatened with
shocks and reverses beyond the power of friendship to avert or
relieve. For her part, she found his equilibrium provoking, and
tried to disturb it by taunting him with shunning life.

Just as she was casting about for some way to free herself
of the burden that had been too much for her strength, a
tempting proposal was made to her. She was offered a teaching
post at the Greene Street School in Providence, Rhode Island,
and the salary set was a thousand dollars a year for four hours'
daily instruction. This meant that she would have leisure to
follow out her own interests, and yet be able to give far more
substantial assistance to her family. The salary was a very high
one for the times, unprecedently so for a woman teacher.
Alcott was cheered by the offer that had come to his assistant,
and noted in his journal that "it promises somewhat more
honorable than has been awarded heretofore to genius and

acquirement given to interests of human culture." Margaret was somewhat reluctant to leave Boston, for Providence was more noted for its flourishing business than its intellectual life, and she felt that in time she could derive sufficient income from her private classes to continue where she was. But she finally decided to accept the offer and its assurance of immediate financial independence. In bidding farewell to Alcott and his ill-fated school, she assured him that she sympathized with his educational creed, although she had found it imperfect in details. The roundness of his world had given her much intellectual pleasure.

This Greene Street School, at which she was to teach for two years, was a newly established private institution, for which a beautiful building had been provided. Margaret was permitted to become its guiding genius, and called herself its lady superior. As she set about classifying her new students in the fall of 1837, she experienced some of the real problems of the educator. She found a wide gulf between herself and her pupils, wider than seemed possible. The "deplorable ignorance and absolute burial of the best powers" that she found in some of the children gave her a better understanding of how such a man as Alcott could devote his life to reforming elementary education. She felt that great advances could be made in educational methods if she could devote five or six years to this new school. As an apostle of the new ideas which were beginning to radiate from Boston, she was given more or less free rein in her administration. Her enthusiastic advocacy of reformed methods found more support than she had expected from unenlightened Providence, and she told one lady who was numbered among the city's elect and had shown an intelligent understanding of her proposals: "Why, *you* deserved an education!" Her goal was the development of "general activity of mind, accuracy in processes, constant looking for principles, and search after the good and the beautiful." Alcott's influence is clearly evident in this program.

During her stay in Providence, Margaret began to interest herself for the first time in people and events outside her own life. She defied the disapproval of her employer and attended a Whig caucus, where she heard Tristram Burgess, who was known as the "old bald eagle." He was famed as a rhetorician, but a too-apparent trickery in his ornate and declamatory way of speaking displeased Margaret. She went to hear Joseph John Gurney, who was heralded in Providence as one of the most distinguished and influential English Quakers, and found him a "thick-set, beetle-browed man, with a well-to-do-in-the-world air of pious solidity." His manner seemed as wooden as his matter, and his only merit as a speaker was his distinct elocution. His thought seemed narrow, and his sincerity corrupted by spiritual pride.

> One could not but pity his notions of the Holy Ghost, and his bat-like fear of light. His Man-God seemed to be the keeper of a madhouse rather than the informing Spirit of all spirits. After finishing his discourse, Mr. G. sang a prayer, in a tone of mingled shout and whine, and then requested his audience to sit awhile in devout meditation. For one, I passed the interval in praying for him, that the thick film of self-complacency might be removed from his spirit, so that he might no more degrade religion.

More to her taste were the visitors who came to lecture at the school. There was Richard Henry Dana, the poet, cousin to Dr. Channing and an old Newport boy. He had been banished from his post as assistant editor of the *North American Review* for upholding the English Romantic poets against the slurs of his professorial colleagues, who still dwelt in the eighteenth century. A somewhat disappointed and embittered man, he now found children his favorite audience. He had read Wordsworth and Coleridge to Alcott's charges at the Temple School, and now in Providence he was giving a course of readings in the English dramatists, beginning with Shakespeare. Margaret sympathized with his aim: never to pander to the popular love of excitement, but to tell quietly, without regard to brilliancy or effect, what struck him in these poets. But she feared that his genuine refinement led him to undervalue the "cannon-blasts and rockets which are needed to rouse the attention of the vulgar." She did not feel that the novelist John Neal, who spoke to her girls on the destiny and vocation of woman in America, was in danger of making this mistake. Neal was a Yankee intellectual soldier of fortune. He had been a shop-keeper, clerk, teacher of drawing and fencing, auctioneer, merchant, editor, lawyer, a journalist in England, and had lived for three years with Jeremy Bentham. Margaret liked his lecture: "He gave truly a manly view, though not the view of common men," yet she felt that she might quarrel with his definitions in almost every subject and thought that his method of argument was not quite fair, for he used reason only as an accessory to wit, sentiment, and assertion. She was conscious of the brilliancy and endless resource which had enabled him to write a three-volume novel in the space of twenty-seven days, and regretted her lack of opportunity to form a closer acquaintance with him. His talk started her thinking along Feminist lines, though she felt: "I should not like to have my motives scrutinized as he would scrutinize them, for I prefer rather to disclose them myself than to be found out." The seed he planted in her mind found nourishment from the natural bent of her character, and was to bear fruit in later years.

The sharpening of Margaret's critical powers, evident in her strongly etched portraits of distinguished visitors to Providence, did some damage to her friendship with Harriet Martineau, when those powers were loosed upon the latter's work. For in 1837 Miss Martineau published her *Society in America*, which embodied her observations of this country during her extended tour, and Margaret undertook to give her friend an account of its reception by the American press and to offer her own judgment on it. The critics of the day anticipated their modern

colleagues by displaying a tendency to abuse the patronizing
English visitor. Margaret divided them into two classes:

> The one, consisting of those who knew you but slightly,
> either personally or in your writings. These have now read
> your book; and seeing in it your high ideal standard, genuine
> independence, noble tone of sentiment, vigor of mind and
> powers of picturesque description, they value your book very
> much and rate you higher for it.
>
> The other comprises those who were previously aware of
> these high qualities, and who, seeing in a book to which
> they had looked for a lasting monument to your fame, a
> degree of presumptuousness, irreverence, inaccuracy, hasty
> generalization, and ultraism on many points, which they did
> not expect, lament the haste in which you have written and
> the injustice which you have consequently done to so impor-
> tant a task and to your own powers of doing and being. To
> this class I belong.

Margaret particularly disliked the emphasis on Abolitionism,
which seemed to haunt almost every page. She was willing to
admit that the subject was a great one, but felt that the book
had other purposes to fulfill, which had been neglected in Miss
Martineau's enthusiasm for the anti-slavery cause. And perhaps
she took offense at her friend's observation that "in my progress
through the country I met with a greater variety and extent of
female pedantry than the experience of a lifetime in Europe
would afford." This struck close to home, and revived the differences that had arisen between them during their discussions at
the Farrars' hospitable home. Miss Martineau had appreciated
Margaret's "admirable candor, the philosophical way in which
she took herself in hand, her genuine heart, her practical insight," and her evident natural powers and the confidence she
had in them had led the Englishwoman to expect great things
of her. For her part, Margaret idolized this older woman who

HARRIET MARTINEAU

Engraving by J. C. Armytage

had refused to submit to convention in an age when it was not thought proper for young ladies to try to excel in studies and with the pen. She found renewed strength amid the difficulties which beset her when the visitor encouraged her literary ambitions, and told her how Jane Austen had been compelled to cover up her manuscripts with a piece of muslin-work, kept on the table for that purpose, whenever "genteel" people called. Margaret had felt a passionate attachment to Harriet Martineau, similar to her feeling for the visiting Englishwoman of her lonely childhood and the kind teacher at the Misses Prescott's school; she had prayed: "May her noble mind be kept firmly poised in its native truth, unsullied by prejudice and error, and strong to resist whatever outwardly or inwardly shall war against its high vocation." But Harriet Martineau had felt that Margaret was living and moving in a too-ideal world, and could not make her respect the Abolitionists, "who acted instead of talking finely, and devoted their fortunes, their peace, their repose, and their very lives to the preservation of the principles of the republic." To one with her passion for liberty, such efforts were vastly more important than fanciful and shallow philosophizing. The tone of Margaret's sharply critical analysis of her book served only to confirm her fears that her young friend was being caught up by the destructive pedantry of Boston, though the sting of some of the criticism was relieved by Margaret's closing remarks:

I have thought it right to say all this to you, since I felt it. I have shrunk from the effort, for I fear that I must lose you. Not that I think that all authors are like Gil Blas' archbishop. No; if your heart turns from me, I shall still love you, still think you noble. I know it must be so trying to fail of sympathy at such a time where you expect it. And besides, I felt from the book that the sympathy between us is less general than I had supposed, it was so strong on several points. It is strong enough for me to love you forever, and I could no more have been happy in your friendship, if I had not spoken out now.

After this, one begins to understand how Margaret's habit of castigating her friends for their faults and weaknesses was noted by all her contemporaries, though always with the comment that she could take the greatest personal liberties without irreparably damaging a friendship. Harriet Martineau was somewhat stung by the patronizing airs of one eight years her junior and as yet unknown to the fame which she herself enjoyed, but continued to take a friendly interest in Margaret's career.

During her teaching years in Providence, Margaret paid as many visits to Boston as she could. She thought of herself only as a temporary exile from that citadel of the intellect, and returned to it as eagerly as a homing pigeon to its loft. On these visits she would spend hours in conversation with her friends, a morning with Emerson, an afternoon with Alcott, a day with Dr. Channing, "that valuable reproving angel." The worlds of music and art opened to her at this time, and she took to frequenting the concert halls and theaters, though the Athenaeum's art collection captured more of her interest. Her journals of this period are full of discussions of various musical compositions, plays, and pictures. Of music she wrote: "The Ton-Kunst, the Ton-Welt, gives me now more stimulus than the written Word; for music seems to contain everything in nature, unfolded in perfect harmony." Her taste was classical: she preferred Haydn, Mozart, and particularly Beethoven. She was much impressed by the talent of Fanny Kemble, whom she saw in *Much Ado about Nothing* and did not like, but whose performance in *The Stranger* moved her to tears and to observe: "This is genius. . . . I should like to recall her every tone and look." In Emerson's company she saw Fanny Elssler, the famous ballet dancer, and at the conclusion of the performance, the two deeply moved friends turned to each other and remarked:

"Margaret, this is poetry."

"Waldo, this is religion."

But it was painting and sculpture that captured more of her attention than these other new interests. Art was a subject very much in the Boston air at this period. In 1823 the Athenaeum had acquired a collection of plaster casts of classical sculpture, chosen by Canova, and now in 1838, through the Brimmer donation, a series of engravings of the chief masterpieces of European painting was added. Margaret spent hours poring over these reproductions, and reading Condivi, Vasari, Cellini, Duppa, Fuseli, and Von Wagen on art. She came to regard the artist as the only fortunate man, for he could satisfy his spirit by the power of creation. She delighted in Flaxman and Retzsch and their sense of form. "He who expresses his thought in form is secure as man can be against the ravages of time." The Athenaeum became a refuge from her periodic agonies of mind; she went to it when she felt the need of some high influence to rouse her from the sickly sensitiveness which she despised but could not conquer. There she seemed to breathe her native atmosphere, and calm could be regained. She drew comfort from Michelangelo's Sibyl. "Such is female Genius; it alone understands the God." But she mourned that her creative genius did not equal her apprehensiveness. Nevertheless, she devoted many pages of notes to the works of art she knew only through reproductions. To Emerson, who shared her enthusiasm for art but, as always, was less passionate about it, her taste was "more idiosyncratic than universal; she mistook the emotions that were aroused in her by art for those the artist intended." And since she was an abnormally sensitive person, with strong imaginative powers, it is not surprising that her art criticism often has very little to do with the actual subject. She has been mocked for making solemn judgments of great paintings which she knew only through colorless prints and engravings, but almost all American art knowledge of this period had a similarly inadequate foundation. As yet there were few Maecenases who valued art collections as a symbol of success, and their taste was uncertain. By her passionate interest in European art, Margaret helped to remedy this condition and to start the flood of masterpieces flowing across the Atlantic.

In the summer of 1839 Washington Allston, Boston's own painter, who had his studio in Margaret's native Cambridgeport, gave an exhibition of his work. She wrote a "Record of Impressions" of this event which is far from lacking in critical penetration, although she felt obliged to defend her qualifications by stating that true appreciation was not to be attained "by unthinking repetition of the technics of foreign connoisseurs, or by a servile reliance on the judgment of those who assume to have been formed by a few hasty visits to the galleries of Europe." She saw how Allston lapsed into the sentimental and picturesque when he aimed at the spiritual and noble. She caught some glimpse of the forces which had prevented Allston, like his brother-in-law and particular friend, Richard Henry Dana, from successfully making use of his brilliant talents. He was both painter and man of letters, but there was too much of the literary in the Boston and Cambridge world for a painter to flourish there. Margaret noted a "certain bland delicacy" in his work; it came to cancel out more and more the Titian-like qualities of his early canvases done in Europe. On his studio wall he had written: "The only competition worthy of a wise man is with himself." Perhaps he had reflected too much on this text, for the lack of competition with fellow craftsmen seems to have been the reason why his talent went to seed, and the great "Belshazzar's Feast," begun in his youth, was still unfinished at his death. He became a great legend in Boston, but not a great painter. It was the younger men who stayed abroad to work who reaped the rewards: Greenough, Crawford, Powers.

The Allston exhibition created a stir in Boston, but the commissions went to the studios of the artistic exiles in Italy, who were following the lead of Canova in exploiting the Greco-

Roman tradition. Mr. Allston was all very well, but to the Boston mind art was something Italian and it was the Italian genius that colored the life of Boston in 1839 and 1840. As Emerson remarked: "Our walls were hung with prints of the Sistine frescoes; we were all petty collectors; and prints of Correggio and Guercino took the place, for the time, of epics and philosophy." Margaret's artistic enthusiasms were thus a natural outgrowth of her early love for classical and modern Italian literature, and served to increase her desire to know Italy at first hand.

But Margaret's new interests did not divert her from old ones. During her second year in Providence she translated Eckermann's *Conversations with Goethe*, for publication in George Ripley's new library of standard foreign works in English. The effort that this required, in addition to the energy devoted to her teaching and her other activities, brought on ill health again. Her sufferings were such during this winter that when she later showed her journal for this period to Emerson, she removed some leaves which showed "too sickly a tone." She felt weary and in need of rest; her mind longed for freedom from outward demands, for concentration and tranquil thought. She became convinced that the teaching of children was not her appointed work in the world, and decided to give up her post in Providence. It was something of a wrench to part from her pupils. During the last week of school she gave the classes in philosophy, rhetoric, poetry, and moral science short lectures on the true objects of study and advice on their future course. On the last day she expressed her pleasure that "the minds of so many had been opened to love of good and beauty." Then she bade farewell to the boys who had been under her care and whom she had governed in a "resolute yet gentle manner." The girls felt her departure more keenly and wept as she bade each one a tender good-by. Margaret was aware of the danger to a teacher of taking too great pleasure in being beloved, but the adoration of her pupils had been welcome to her and this final evidence of it was deeply moving. She wept with them.

II

FIRST FLOWERING

1839–1844

✤CHAPTER IV✤

Transcendentalism

The grandsire of Transcendentalism was the French Revolution; its mother was a mystical philosophy; its father was the Puritan spirit— rapture and revolution were in its veins.—N. C. GODDARD

THROUGH conversation and correspondence with her Boston friends, Margaret had kept in touch with the intellectual ferment that had begun to swell during her year with Bronson Alcott at the Temple School. During her absence in Providence the stir had become a spiritual and philosophical movement of some proportion, and since its leaders were her friends, she was caught up in it when she returned to Boston. With Transcendentalism, as the movement came to be called, she rose to fame, for an important role in it was soon thrust upon her and out of necessity her powers developed a precocious maturity. But she had no thought of this when in the summer of 1839 she rented a house in Jamaica Plain, just outside Boston, which she and her family occupied for the next two years. For the farm in Groton had finally been sold and the struggle to keep it going abandoned. Her brother Arthur was to go to college this fall, and fifteen-year-old Richard was thinking of finding commercial employment, since scholarship was not his strong point. Mrs. Fuller was quite ready to lay down the burden of running the family, which she had assumed during Margaret's absence, and so her eldest daughter again became the head of the house. It was her efforts as a tutor, conductor of conversation classes, editor, and writer, that supported the Fullers for

the next few years. The immediate needs of the family had
been met in some measure through her two remunerative years
of teaching in Providence. Margaret felt free to launch her
cherished scheme of private classes and to devote herself to
the intellectual life of Boston.

It was a stirring time for the Boston intellectuals. The new
movement was primarily religious in character, though it
branched out into many other fields as it developed, and since
Boston had long been a hotbed of theological argument, there
was much vigorous discussion. From the turn of the century
the rigorous Calvinism of the Puritans had been crumbling
under the onslaughts of the Unitarian movement, whose prophet
was Dr. Channing. Before men knew it, the iron orthodoxy of
two hundred years' standing was replaced, at least in Boston,
by the more liberal Unitarianism. By 1830 the latter was the
accepted church of the prosperous folk of both Boston and
Cambridge. Its liberalism did not lap over into the rest of the
accepted set of opinions; Boston remained Federalist and conservative in all else. Hardly was it established before the
younger generation began the movement which was at once a
revolt against what Emerson called the "pale negations of
Boston Unitarianism" and the logical culmination of Channing's
thought. There was a new spirit abroad in New England; anything which smacked of the old order was suspect. Revolt and
reform were in the air. A host of new influences came to bear
on the people of a rapidly developing country. The political
triumph of the democratic idea brought about a reweighing of
the traditional ideas of morality and religion. The outward
reformation had been accomplished with the founding of the
Republic, and now it was time to turn inward.

In this new era of individualism in all things, the "young
men were born with knives in their brains," as Emerson put it,
"a tendency to introversion, self-dissection, anatomizing of
motives." Out of their reading of the Greek and Roman philosophers, of the Oriental writers, who first became known in

America at this time, and of the new theology, philosophy, and sociology of De Wette, Hegel, Kant, Schelling, Fichte, Schleiermacher, Rousseau, Coleridge, Cousin, Fourier, they evolved new ideas of human nature, new personal creeds, even new systems of society. Their idealism was largely derived from modern German sources, which most of them knew only through French and English paraphrases, but it also stemmed ✓ from the antinomianism of John Cotton, Anne Hutchinson, Roger Williams, and Jonathan Edwards. They carried further the redemption of the human spirit by the earlier Unitarianism from its degraded state under Calvinism; they exalted it by attributing to it a godlike nature. They carried Channing's toleration and liberalism so much further that many of them abandoned all dogma and religious system, and were content to be pantheists rather than Christians. Emerson, George Ripley, John Sullivan Dwight left the pulpit behind them to read and write about the new ideas, and to have freedom to practice them in their own lives. There were others, notably Theodore Parker, Frederick Henry Hedge, William Henry Channing, and James Freeman Clarke, who found no difficulty in promulgating the gospel of the "Newness" from the pulpit, though they gravely disturbed their congregations by their radicalism. Some of the group, among them Alcott and Thoreau, found no place for any church in their personal creeds. The diversity of religious opinion which followed the breaking-up of the Puritan orthodoxy was made evident to all observers in the sabbatarian Chardon Street Convention of 1840. For all his fondness for the "Newness," Emerson was appalled by this gathering.

Madmen, madwomen, men with beards, Dunkers, Muggletonians, Come-outers, Groaners, Agrarians, Seventh-Day Baptists, Quakers, Abolitionists, Calvinists, Unitarians, and Philosophers—all came successively to the top, and seized their moment, if not their hour, wherein to chide, or pray, or preach, or protest.

The exaltation of the human spirit by the new creeds brought with it a perfectionism whose manifestations were often curious and alarming to the possessors of staid and unenthusiastic minds.

The movements of protest were not confined to the religious field. Emerson and his circle were troubled by the rise of materialism to dominance in American life. The rapid growth of the country made more bitter the struggle in New England to maintain economic supremacy over the West and South. The swelling prosperity of the early years of the century vanished in the financial crash of 1837, and intensified the widespread interest in social experiment. Between 1825 and 1845 over fifty new communities based upon various radical social and economic programs came into being. Some of the men who became known as Transcendentalists were interested in such schemes, notably Alcott and George Ripley; others, like Emerson and Thoreau, were not. The movement included both individualists and socialists, and never had a social program of its own, apart from a tendency toward withdrawal from conventional social life and religious worship. Brook Farm was associated with the Transcendentalists in the public mind, but many of the leaders of the movement quarreled with the scheme and thought that the ideal of plain living and high thinking could be best realized by them as individuals.

Aside from their common idealism and insistence on freedom of discussion, the Transcendentalists were not united in their ideas. Emerson speaks of a general belief prevailing in Boston at that time that "there was some concert of doctrinaires to establish certain opinions and inaugurate some movement in literature, philosophy, and religion," and protests that the supposed conspirators were wholly innocent of any such design. What happened was that a group of men and women who read, wrote, and thought with unusual vigor were drawn together by their common interests for purposes of discussion of their solitary studies. They came together by many different paths, and their

grand-daughter of a president of Harvard College and of a chief justice. Elizabeth Peabody was already widely known as a progressive educator, and just about this time she opened a bookshop in her father's house in West Street, which served as headquarters and intellectual arsenal for the Transcendentalists. Here the English, German, and French reviews could be obtained, as well as the foreign books which were just coming into demand. George Ripley drew many of the translators for his *Specimens of Standard Foreign Literature* from those who frequented Miss Peabody's shop. The West Street house sometimes sheltered the meetings of the Transcendentalists, although Emerson's house in Concord, Dr. Francis's in Watertown, and Dr. Bartol's in Boston were the usual meeting places.

It was a rare group which gathered on these occasions. A good indication of its quality is furnished by the five individuals whom O. B. Frothingham, the historian of Transcendentalism, singled out to illustrate the various tendencies of the movement. There was Emerson the seer, who approached philosophy with the religious attitude natural in the descendant of eight generations of ministers. His *Nature*, published in 1836, is often considered the philosophical constitution of Transcendentalism. He was a Platonic Yankee, a practical idealist, with an absolute and perpetual faith in thought. He lived in a region of serene ideas. His idealism was derived from Jonathan Edwards and the Neo-Platonists, as well as from the sacred books of the East. He was little affected by the German idealists, with whom he was just becoming familiar at this time. His correspondence with Carlyle, which began in 1834, brought him into contact with the English Romantics, who owed a great debt to the Germans. By nature he was a solitary and not a social being, and thus recorded his reaction to an 1838 meeting of Hedge's Club:

I was unlucky in going after several nights of vigils, and heard as though I heard not, and among gifted men I had not one thought or aspiration. . . . I nevertheless read today with a wicked pleasure the saying ascribed to Kant, that "detestable was the society of mere literary men." It must be tasted sparingly to keep its gusto. . . . So all this summer I shall talk of Chenagoes and my new garden spout; have you heard of my pigs? I have planted forty-four pine-trees; what will my tax be this year?—and never a word more of Goethe or Tennyson.

This was no rare mood with him, for in the following year there is another mention in the *Journals* of his dissatisfaction with literary meetings and the muddiness of all conversation among literary men. It was otherwise with Alcott, the mystic of the movement, who drew his inspiration from the Greek and Roman philosophers. He lived for discussion. He had formed his beliefs on ideal laws and based his conduct upon them. He was an active mystic of the type of St. Bernard, conscious of his mission as a regenerator and as a teacher of wisdom. His Temple School was but the first of his attempts to translate his ideas into reality. His enthusiasm and passionate seriousness brought down upon him the derision of those who frowned upon the "Newness" to which he was ardently devoted.

Margaret, the critic, lacked the metaphysical background of the other leading Transcendentalists. The temper of her mind was enthusiastic rather than philosophical. But she had a confident faith in her own spiritual capacity, and, by extension, in that of others. To her, liberty was a condition of enlightenment, and enlightenment a condition of progress. She made up for her philosophical shortcomings by the extensiveness of her literary knowledge, for she had a better acquaintance with the foreign literatures than any of the other Transcendentalists. She introduced Emerson to Goethe, Channing to the German theologians. She said of herself: "I am merely 'Germanico,' and not 'transcendental.'" But the German literature that she loved so dearly was saturated with the idealism of the philosophers, and had given form and direction to her own natural idealism. Her critical and aspiring intellect made her seek out principles independent of time and place. She was a worshiper of beauty, which she derived from good and truth. And, finally, her great conversational talents made her valued in this circle of individualists, for she was better able than any of them to draw out the best in each and reconcile the differences which arose. Her old friend William Henry Channing, the Doctor's nephew, was surprised to see her "acknowledged as a peer of the realm in this new world of thought," where she soon became the umpire of discussion.

Theodore Parker, by nature a realist, was the preacher of this idealistic gospel, for Transcendentalism was far more of a gospel than a philosophy. Its chief disciples were drawn from the ministry; it had its oracles proceeding from a sacred shrine; there was an air of indefiniteness and mystery about it and its exclusive privileged truths; its method was introspection. It was fortunate in having as its preacher a man like Parker, who was at home among sensible things, yet possessed a vast interior devotional power. He was a man of tremendous energies, both mental and physical, had mastered some twenty languages, and was informed on the most abstruse subjects. He lived in a house jammed with books and was popularly supposed to have read everything of a serious nature ever written, but he was as much a man of action as a scholar. As befitted a Lexington farmer's son, he held to the gospel of manual labor. His sermon *On the Transient and the Permanent in Christianity*, given in May 1841, launched Unitarianism's second era and within ten years he was recognized as New England's greatest preacher. He completed the religious revolution which Dr. Channing had begun with his Baltimore sermon in 1819.

Transcendentalism's man of letters was George Ripley, who introduced the new trends of European thought into New England through his series of translations. He began as a minister, left the Church to establish Brook Farm, and ended as a journalist and encyclopedist in New York. His career was typical of the varied course which the lives of many of the lesser Transcendentalists took. His dream of the heaven on earth which Brook Farm was to be, attracted many to the movement. Among the lesser prophets were William Henry Channing, a young minister already known as a Christian socialist; Margaret's early friend James Freeman Clarke, who was both minister and man of letters; C. E. Bartol, later the founder of the Radical Club; John Sullivan Dwight, who left a pulpit in Northampton for Brook Farm and in after years established the first journal devoted to music in this country; Orestes Brownson, who passed through many sects in his search for light and was the editor of the *Boston Quarterly;* Dr. Francis, Samuel Longfellow, Thomas Wentworth Higginson, Samuel Johnson, David Wasson, and John Weiss.

Few of these men and women had the same notion of the movement in which they took part, and their confusion about the essential nature of Transcendentalism is reproduced by its historians. Some consider it purely local in activity and limited in scope; others hold it to be part of the spiritual stir which followed the French Revolution, or purely German in origin. One critic blames Transcendentalism for its lack of concern with practical matters and its tendency to abstract thought without contact with reality. Another views it as a movement which radically affected the institutions and practical interests of society in New England. Some consider it a philosophical system; others a religious one; still others a social and economic, or a literary and artistic movement.

Whatever it was, and there seems to be but little hope of ever finding a satisfactory label which will cover all its many facets, something of its nature and its effects can be recorded. For it supplied a spiritual dynamic which infused new vigor into New England and during the ten years of its most intense influence it brought the intellectual life of Boston into prominence both at home and abroad. It was a natural development of intellectual Protestantism in that it claimed for all men what Calvin had claimed for the elect. It differed from Unitarianism in its reliance on inner inspiration. It was idealistic and individualistic. It shared its belief in the inalienable worth of man, in the immanence of divinity in human instinct, with the reformers who launched the French Revolution. It was itself reformative in tendency; it encouraged self-culture in the individual and social reform in the community. As a religion it had pantheistic tendencies, and encouraged belief in marvels, wonders, and the symbolism which stems therefrom. Though it had no aesthetics, it was a literary and artistic movement, as well as a philosophical and religious one. Whatever the movement's intellectual content may be said to be, notice cannot fail to be taken of the concrete results of its spiritual ferment. It was the spirit of a new age in a new country, though the influence of many ancient traditions was evident in it, and during the golden age which it so confidently ushered in the intellectual dominated New England life for a short span of years.

At first the journal and the letter were the mediums of the new movement, as these men and women speculated and conjectured in the light of the "Newness." It was too early to look for systematic results, formulated on the printed page, and besides they were trying to escape from the dogmatic letter of the old order. Then as the group drew closer together, they turned to conversation as their chosen medium. It was far more a vocal than a literary era. The great men of the day were Dr. Channing, Edward Everett, Daniel Webster, and George Ticknor; sermons, orations, speeches, and lectures had more weight than books. It was natural that the younger generation should seek expression in discussions. The year 1839, which saw Margaret's return to Boston, seems to have been devoted to conversation by the Boston intellectuals. In one week that spring Bronson Alcott, the most insatiable talker of them all, made these entries in his *Journals:*

Monday, 29th April. This morning I rode to Concord. Dwight stepped into the stage at Lexington. We had miscellanious talk during the forenoon at Emerson's. . . . We had some conversation, after dinner, on high themes—the genesis of Nature—the dependence of the elements of the corporeal and physical world on the Soul, &c. . . . Dwight left towards evening. After tea we conversed on style—my Conversations —the future. . . .

Tuesday, 30th April. The day was rainy. Morning was given to talk on high matters. In the afternoon we rode to Waltham and supped with Mrs. Ripley. Eclecticism—Culture—were the topics discussed.

In the evening we had a general consideration of the age, men, means, &c. Channing, Brownson, Ripley, Furness, Hedge, Francis, Clarke, W. Channing, Dwight, Parker, Miss Fuller, Miss Peabody, Mrs. Ripley were severally spoken of. Also the relative fitness of preaching, lecturing, conversation, writing, to the quickness of the Soul.

Wednesday, 1st May. We conversed awhile, this morning, on Space and Time. . . . Afternoon; a walk, with miscellanious colloquy. Evening—Emerson read his lecture on Comedy before the Lyceum: after which, we had agreeable conversation at his house, with some of the villagers, on Conversation.

Thursday, 2nd May. More conversation. Walking. Evening, a concert of vocal and instrumental music. Conversation on music.

Friday, 3rd May. Walking, conversing, during the day. Evening—met a circle of persons at Mrs. Thorow's [Thoreau's mother] for conversation. Topic, *Futurity*. Various points of sight were taken. Knowledge—memory—hope—preexistance —Faith—Elements of the Soul—Incarnation—Miracles—were spoken of in illustration of the future life.

The pursuits of this week in Concord were not unusual in

Alcott's life. His *Journals* show that many hours that summer were devoted to serious discussions with Margaret or Theodore Parker or another. In the fall there were many meetings of a larger group for formal conversation, thus recorded by Alcott:

> Monday, 16th Sept. We rode to Watertown, dining on our way with E. Quincy, at whose house we found H. G. Wright. We discussed the doctrine of Non-Resistance.
>
> The following persons comprised our circle for Conversation, at the house of Dr. Francis: Emerson, Alcott, Channing, Hedge, Ripley, Dwight, Parker, Bartlett, Bartol, May, Stetson, Morrison, Mrs. Ripley, Miss Fuller.
>
> I proposed the Esoteric and Exoteric doctrine for discussion. The conversation was general, lively, continuous. Emerson, Channing, Ripley, Bartlett, had good words to say. I tried to show the roots of this doctrine in the functions of the Soul; descrimination the functions of Prophet, Scribe, Priest; the order of Revelation; Inspiration of all Scriptures, &c.
>
> This was one of our best interviews. It was marked by candour, independence, charity. Our best materials were gathered in this circle. But we are yet too feeble to execute works worthy of the position in which the good Soul has placed us. Yet we must watch and labor as becomes faithful disciples of hers, and she shall make us strong betimes.

Much the same group met only two days later at the Bartol house in Boston, and discussed the establishment of a magazine "designed as the organ of views more in accordance with the Soul." A great deal was said and nothing decided, though the general sentiment favored the setting up of a rival to the *Christian Examiner* and the *North American Review*. As the group's breach with orthodoxy grew wider and the opposition from these organs of tradition became sharper, the need of a journal of their own was felt more acutely and was often discussed in the frequent gatherings for conversation. John Heraud's *London Monthly Review* set an example which they hoped to follow. And meanwhile the interminable talk went on.

Was there ever such insatiable lust for conversation and self-culture? To be sure Alcott was one of the most visionary and impractical of the circle, and gave more of his time to it than most of the others. Late in this year of talk he was hardpressed by poverty and somewhat disgusted with idealistic conversation:

> Thursday, 19th Dec. I was invited to dine with Emerson, N. Frothingham, and Miss Fuller at George Bancroft's, but declined. Is it meet place for me at the tables of the fashionable, the voluptuous, the opulent? Am I not rather a present and living rebuke to all such? Above the temptations, what have I to do among the Sadducees? Do I not too deeply feel the injustice of my townsmen, to sit in their midst as a guest fed by their charity, and receiving my standing in society therefrom? No: I do not thus degrade myself: I hold my prerogatives from God: my integrity is my honor: magnanimously will I hold my course wide of fashion, usage. Want stares me and mine too fiercely in the face to suffer waste of time at the tables of the opulent. I seek the dwellings of the publicans, the workshops of the artisan rather, and make my appeal to them with more of hope.

Alcott accepted the will of Providence with a resignation worthy of a philosopher, though materially unhonored as such by his fellow citizens, and found employment working at a lathe for a dollar or two a day. It was enough to give the bare necessities of existence to a family that had come to accept penury as their lot, and Margaret at least honored him as the Anaxagoras of the joiner's shop. The other members of the circle were much more fortunate, and could afford to pass the time in talk. It was by no means mere idle talk, and its fruits soon began to appear. But the more material-minded and solid citizens shared the opinions of the New Yorker who referred to the group as zanies and of the Boston magnate who

told Margaret: "You know, *we* consider *those men* insane."
Boston was more amused than alarmed by the first manifestations of the movement, and it was not until 1841, when "those
men" launched Brook Farm, that public opinion shifted and
Emerson recorded: "The view taken of Transcendentalism in
State Street is that it threatens to invalidate contracts." It was
all very well. if somewhat scandalous, for a small group of
eccentrics to indulge in rash speculations but when they began
to practice their theories and endanger the sacred *status quo,*
Boston became seriously disturbed. These Transcendentalists
were no better than the Abolitionists, and should be dealt with
as severely.

CHAPTER V

The Conversations

You could hardly tell whether she were more like an unsexed version of Plato's Socrates or a Yankee Lyceum lecturer.—BARRETT WENDELL

IN THIS atmosphere, in which talk welled up as naturally as water from a spring, it is not surprising that Margaret was impelled to hold conversation classes. Her friend Elizabeth Peabody had supplied a precedent with her conferences for women in 1833 and 1836, which had consisted partly of lectures by her and the reading of essays by the class and partly of discussion. Margaret was conscious of the esteem in which her conversational talents were held by her contemporaries, and she had been convinced for some years now that conversation was her natural element. Madame de Staël had been her youthful model; what could be more logical than to set up as a "paid Corinne"? She discussed her plan with Alcott during the summer of 1839, and he was enthusiastic about the project. In his *Journals* he noted:

> She is purposing to hold Conversations with a circle of women in Boston, during the coming autumn and winter. This is a hopeful fact. She is the most commanding talker of the day, of her sex, and must sway society: such a position is worthy of her gifts. I trust those who shall hear her will reap a rich harvest of thought and become powers of like seed in the bosom of the Age.

MARGARET FULLER

From the painting by Chappel

A high tribute from perhaps the greatest talker of this age of talk!

But Margaret did not launch her scheme merely as a means of displaying publicly the conversational talents that had won recognition in private life. Like Alcott, she was under the constant necessity of earning money, and literary labor was as yet unremunerative and distasteful to her. John Neal's Providence lecture on the place of women in America had started a train of thought in her brain. In Sarah Ripley she found a deeply sympathetic audience for these ideas of hers. The classes would provide a center for all the educated and intelligent women of Boston, which for all its pretensions to intellectual refinement boasted nothing of the sort. Margaret knew that many of the older women felt the need of some such stimulus, and that the younger ones would welcome a place where they could discuss their doubts and difficulties in the light of others' experience. Even if her own role amounted to nothing more than guiding the conversation to higher topics than the usual exchange of personalities and commonplaces, the scheme might be worth while.

But she had a more ambitious purpose, whereby these classes could help aspiring women to free themselves from their traditional subserviency:

> It is to pass in review the departments of thought and knowledge, and to endeavor to place them in due relation to one another in our minds. To systematize thought and give a precision and clearness in which our sex are so deficient, chiefly, I think, because they have so few inducements to test and classify what they receive. To ascertain what pursuits are best suited to us in our time and state of society, and how we may make best use of our means for building up the life of thought upon the life of action.

She was going to emancipate her sex by sharing with them

the fruits of the masculine education she had received from Timothy Fuller. She felt that in her own life she had discovered the means by which the life of woman could be raised to a higher estate, if a serious circle could be assembled and would allow her to be its moving spring. She felt qualified to meet the needs of others, since she had felt her own profoundly and overcome them with some success. The difficulty would lie rather in "that sort of pride in them which wears the garb of modesty." Her pupils would have to be prepared to give up vague generalities, the art of coterie criticism, and the delicate disdains of good society. They must be willing to be called crude and tasteless by their less daring sisters as they pursued truth. It was only thus that they could attain "real health and vigor, which need no aid from rouge or candlelight to brave the light of the world." Her scheme was nothing less than a Feminist manifesto. Margaret wanted no passive partakers in her Conversations, no bashful if worshiping auditors. The discussion was to be general. She would open it with a general statement of the subject, and then call for the expression of opinions on one or another branch of the matter. If no one could deal successfully with it in conversation, one of the circle would prepare a written discussion to be read at the next meeting and considered critically. As topics she proposed the "endless profusion" offered by literature and the arts.

The scheme attracted considerable interest, and twenty-five women were present at the first meeting, which was held at the Peabody house in West Street on November 6, 1839. Emerson observed that "the circle comprised some of the most agreeable and intelligent women to be found in Boston and its neighborhood." The first course of Conversations was on Greek mythology, and thirteen meetings of two hours' duration were held. A letter from one of the circle to a friend in unenlightened New Haven shows how responsive Margaret's audience was:

As I sat there, my heart overflowed for joy at the sight of

the bright circle, and I longed to have you by my side, for I know not where to look for so much character, culture, and so much love of truth and beauty in any other circle of women and girls. The names and faces would not mean so much to you as to me, who have seen more of the lives of which they are the sign. Margaret, beautifully dressed (don't despise that, for it made a fine picture), presided with more dignity and grace than I had thought possible. The subject was beauty. Each had written her definition, and Margaret began with reading her own. This called forth questions, comments, and illustrations on all sides. The style and manner, of course, in this age are different, but the question, the high point from which it was considered, and the earnestness and simplicity of the discussion, as well as the gifts and graces of the speakers, gave it the charm of a Platonic dialogue. There was no pretension or pedantry in a word that was said. The tone of remark and question was as simple as that of children in a school class; and I believe everyone was gratified.

Since interest had increased during the first series of Conversations, a second followed, which was devoted to the fine arts. The support given to Margaret's enterprise during this first winter insured its success, and the Conversations became a Boston institution and were held each year until Margaret moved to New York in 1844.

The same talents that made her presence welcome at the gatherings of the Transcendentalists served her in good stead as the presiding genius of the Conversations. Her new role allowed her to indulge the strain of queenliness which seemed to be innate in her character. In the dreams of her lonely childhood she had sometimes thought she was not her parents' child, but a European princess confided to their care. She remembered how, when she was but a little girl, Timothy Fuller had noticed her walking among the apple trees with such an air and step that he remarked to her sister Ellen: *"Incedit regina."*

As she grew up, she had continued to idealize herself as a sovereign in the realm of the intellect. In a letter written the year before she began the Conversations, she spoke of herself as "without throne, sceptre, or guards, still a queen." She had displeased some by the way she brought her regal airs into company, and complacently assumed that her place was among the highest. As she became more generally known, her proud and haughty nature bred a host of extravagant anecdotes about her opinion of herself; of how she said quite coolly to her friends: "I now know all the people worth knowing in America, and I find no intellect comparable to my own," or in enumerating the merits of some person she stated: "He appreciates me." But it was the high aspiration and the absolute truthfulness of her character that impelled her to such excesses; she was conscious of her intellectual superiority, striving as she constantly did to increase it, and she said of herself what others often thought of themselves without expressing it. Among the women of her Conversation circle, she was under no necessity to defend her powers by the arrogant attitude which she sometimes felt obliged to assume among men who might not be willing to admit a woman's equality or superiority in intellectual matters. In the Feminist atmosphere of her classes, she was recognized as a credit to her sex, and a sort of adoration was cheerfully paid to one who labored to emancipate her sisters in the midst of her personal struggle to maintain her family. This adoration brought her powers to full flower; it made up for her periods of abject humility and self-condemnation. It supplied a need of her nature, which had been met in her youth by her passionate friendships with other girls and young women.

Though there is no question that Margaret had a special capacity for arousing the mood of adoration and discipleship, her conversational powers were really such as to justify the recognition they received in her classes. The evidence of all those who knew her is overwhelming on this point. Her nature seemed to be transformed by the atmosphere of good conversation. She possessed the gift of being in perfect tune with the company, and as she directed the flow of talk with masterly skill and grace, her face would take on a new and animated expression and she would seem beautiful to those who listened to her. She lived with such intensity at these moments that she made all those who were with her feel the miracle of existence more keenly. She seemed effulgent with thought and a penetrating wisdom, and could make common things shine with splendor. Her vision soared in these moments of all-conquering exaltation, and she carried her auditors with her. But she paid a price for these flights; the aftermath was always a mood of severe depression, in which she was tormented by racking headaches. While her great moments lasted she blended feminine receptiveness and masculine energy; she could take a germ of truth received from another and give it brilliant development of her own with incredible rapidity. Though she took the dominant role thus, she could make any other speaker feel glad the suggestion had been offered. For all her egotism, her wideranging sympathies and human insight brought her the confidence and admiration of her audience. Her personal influence was extraordinary, derived as it was solely from strength of mind and character and not dependent upon beauty, power, wealth, or fashion. To experience it at its most tender and cherishing, it was first necessary to submit to her; thereafter she was loving, faithful, and even humble. She seemed an embodiment of affection, conscience, courage, resource, and decision to those who thus became her intimates, and the path of each became clearer by association with her. She shaped the lives of others with more success than her own. She was a sibyl, giving forth wisdom with a wave of her lorgnette.

Her spell worked only in close contact, however, and as she had foreseen at the outset the Conversations excited a certain amount of ridicule from the conventional-minded. The spectacle of twenty or thirty of Boston's most consciously intellectual females sitting down, dressed in their best, in a parlor to discuss high questions had a certain absurdity about it to some of their contemporaries. Harriet Martineau christened them the "gorgeous pedants" and the name stuck. It was all too easy to poke fun at these earnest seekers after truth, with their self-conscious sense of intellectual superiority. To her their preoccupation with metaphysical idealism was "destructive of all genuine feeling and sound activity." But she had her Abolitionist ax to grind, and those who lacked her enthusiasm for that cause were likely to be labeled mere pedants if they nevertheless boasted intellectual pretensions. Though "fanciful and shallow conceits" were aired at the Conversations, some serious matters were dealt with soundly. From this circle came the moving force of the Feminist movement of the fifties, and a higher concept of woman. This development is clearly foreshadowed in Margaret's remarks at the opening of the first series:

> Women are now taught at school all that men are. They run over superficially even *more* studies, without being really taught anything. But with this difference: men are called on from a very early period to reproduce all that they learn. Their college exercises, their political duties, their professional studies, the first actions of life in any direction, call on them to put to use what they have learned. But women learn without any attempt to reproduce. Their only reproduction is for purposes of display. It is to supply this defect that these conversations have been planned.

This underlying theme was introduced again and again as the Conversations continued. Margaret was to develop it more fully in an article for the *Dial*, "The Great Lawsuit," which was in turn expanded into her book, *Woman in the Nineteenth Century*, a Bible to the early Feminists. The seed sown by John Neal and Margaret's natural inclinations was already germinating.

The membership of the Conversations was drawn from the best that Boston had to offer: representatives of the great merchant families, the wives and daughters of the Harvard faculty, the leading ministers, and other intellectuals. Some of the subscribers had long been Margaret's friends, and many more of them were to become her intimates through this contact with her. Among the "gorgeous pedants" were Mrs. George Bancroft, the historian's wife; Mrs. Barlow, who was shortly to disturb the young men at Brook Farm with her beauty; Lydia Maria Child, Margaret's childhood friend and now a well-known writer; Sarah Clarke, James Freeman Clarke's artist sister; Mrs. Emerson; Mrs. Farrar; Elizabeth Hoar, who was recognized in Concord as having many of Margaret's intellectual qualities; Mrs. Theodore Parker; Elizabeth Peabody and her sisters Mary and Sophia, who were engaged to Horace Mann and Nathaniel Hawthorne; Mrs. Josiah Quincy, wife of that model of a Boston man; Mrs. Ripley; Maria White, James Russell Lowell's talented fiancée. There were many others: Channings, Gardiners, Jacksons, Lees, Lorings, Putnams, Russells, Shaws, Sturgises, Tuckermans, Wards, and Whitings. Like the Transcendentalist meetings, the Conversations attracted occasional visitors as well as regular attendants. Margaret's influence in Boston society soon became considerable.

As the Conversations were continued winter after winter, new subjects were introduced, although mythology and the fine arts were not abandoned as topics. One series was devoted to ethics, and such influences on women as family, school, church, society, and literature were discussed. Another was concerned with such questions as: "Is the Ideal First or Last; Divination or Experience?" "Persons Who Never Awake to Life in This World," "Mistakes," "Faith," "Creeds," "Woman," "Demonology," "Influence," "Catholicism," "The Ideal." Still another was concerned with education; and culture, ignorance, vanity, prudence, patience, and health were the titles of the Conversations. In March 1841, Margaret opened an evening series for both men and women. She was much pressed for money at that time, and her need coincided with pressure from some of her masculine friends and some members of the day classes, who felt that joint sessions of men and women might be both valuable and interesting. Of this series of Conversations alone there is something like a verbatim account in the shorthand notes of Caroline Healey Dall. The only records of the others are Elizabeth Peabody's notes, which were used by Emerson in his memoir of Margaret. Mrs. Dall dismissed them with the comment: "Elizabeth wrote what she called an abstract every night; but an examination of her abstracts quoted by Mr. Emerson shows that what she wrote was not what anyone said, but the impression made upon her own mind by it." Mrs. Dall's record suffers from a similar subjectivity, however, for she states: "Of course, much was omitted as not worth recording, nor did I write down anything that I could not understand." By her own admission she was very young to take part in the Conversations, and there may well have been much said that was beyond her understanding. But her notes constitute the best record of these discussions, and a somewhat disappointing one. For in them is evident none of the charm of the Platonic dialogues to which the Conversations were likened by others who took part in them.

The subject of this series was Greek mythology as illustrated by art. A subscription for the ten Conversations cost twenty dollars, which was considered a very high price at a time when tickets for a series of Lyceum lectures sold for two dollars. About thirty persons usually attended, including Mr. and Mrs. George Ripley, Elizabeth Peabody, Frederick Henry Hedge, James Freeman Clarke, Emerson, Mrs. Farrar, Mr. and Mrs. Francis Shaw, Mrs. Ann Wilby Clarke, Mrs. Jonathan Russell and her daughter Ida, William White, William Story, Caroline Sturgis, Mrs. Samuel Ward, Jones Very, Elizabeth Hoar, Bronson Alcott, W. Mack, Sophia Peabody, Marianne Jackson, and Charles Stearns Wheeler. The group included a number of brilliant independent thinkers, and that proved to be the trouble with Margaret's new scheme. For the Conversations wan-

dered far afield from the set subject, and there was much
digression, quibbling over terms, and uttering of good things
which possessed little relevance. There was an unfortunate
disposition displayed by some of the celebrated men, which
shocked Margaret's adoring ladies: "Emerson pursued his own
train of thought. He seemed to forget that we had come
together to pursue Margaret's." Alcott was also apt to go off
on mystical tangents of his own. Charles Wheeler, the brilliant
young classicist who lived in a hut on the shore of Flint's Pond
out in Lincoln, was apt to dispute Margaret's statements. Jones
Very, the poet who had passed through Harvard, the Divinity
School, and the MacLean Asylum, was sometimes trying with
his constant religious exaltation. He considered himself the
organ of the Divine Spirit, directed by God in his every action.
Such diverse minds could not always meet upon a common
level, and sometimes Mrs. Dall was obliged to comment that
"we were all dull this evening." There is little evidence in her
record of the significance which the Conversations must have
had, to achieve the wide influence that they did. Of course,
good conversation is a notably perishable thing, difficult to
record and fix for posterity in all its momentary brilliance. And
then Margaret obviously regarded the mixed gatherings as a
failure, for she never repeated them. Her classes for women
must have been more successful, for all her contemporaries are
agreed that the Conversations did far more to bring her fame
than anything she ever wrote. They certainly made a host of
friends for her. Mrs. Dall's book, published fifty years after
the last Conversation, was called simply *Margaret and Her
Friends,* and it was a somewhat ungracious critic of it who
felt obliged to say that now one should speak of Miss Fuller,
though Margaret was sufficient identification to all who had
known her.

Today it is a little difficult to appreciate the importance of the
Conversations to those who took part in them. They seem more
than a little silly and ridiculous, a homespun imitation of the

salon without its social charms and amenities. The very notion
of paying for the right to share in conversation seems absurd.
But to the intellectual New Englanders of the forties conversation was indispensable and a weighty matter. Conversation was
the method of Transcendentalism, the animating spirit of the
age, and a great conversationalist was as manifestly a genius as
a great writer, preacher, or orator. It was through conversation
that Coleridge and Carlyle disseminated the new ideas in England, and Emerson, Alcott, Parker, and Margaret did the same
on this side of the Atlantic. The other great talkers of the age
left a sufficient volume of writings to insure their lasting fame;
alone among them Margaret has tended to become a shade, for
the vital spark of her conversation is seldom found on the
printed page of the books she wrote, and the spoken word dies
with the wind that utters it.

The real lasting importance of the Conversations was the
stimulus they gave to feminine intellectual activity. They did
much to make it respectable rather than eccentric in public
opinion. Condorcet and Mary Wollstonecraft had made their
pleas for women's rights in the closing years of the eighteenth
century, but their words had been largely disregarded in
America. Emma Willard had opened a boarding school for girls
at Middlebury, Vermont, in 1814, and the Troy Female Seminary was established in New York in 1821. Mary Lyon founded
Mount Holyoke College, the first institution of higher education for women, in 1836. But these were isolated pioneer efforts,
and at first bore little fruit.

The Grimké sisters and those Quaker women who were
active in the anti-slavery cause had caused grave scandal.
Margaret herself felt some of the stern disapproval and contempt which had earlier been visited on Fanny Wright and
Lucretia Mott for venturing beyond the conventional sphere
of feminine activity. But the increasing success of her Conversations and the support given to them in influential quarters of
the Boston world altered the lot of women who ventured to

question the inhibitions laid upon them by tradition. Many of her pupils became active in the Feminist movement, and the way was paved for Elizabeth Cady Stanton, Susan Anthony, and Lucy Stone. Though even in the sixties and seventies the appearance of women on the platform aroused disapproval, the right of women to take part in intellectual activities had come to be more or less generally accepted. The Conversations served as a model for the later women's clubs and helped to assure support for the new colleges. Many years before, Abigail Adams had said: "If we mean to have heroes, statesmen, and philosophers, we should have learned women." With her Conversations Margaret won the reputation of being the most learned woman in the country, and inculcated her love of learning, her intellectual curiosity, and her aspiration to creative expression in her adoring and impressionable circle. She probably did more to alter the status of her sex for the better than any other woman of the period.

For all her success in a cause that was dear to her, and for all the adulation she received from her circle, Margaret was not very happy during the years of the Conversations. The emotionalism of her nature had no profound fulfillment, and sometimes the agony she felt within broke out in her journal: "With the intellect I always have, always shall, overcome; but that is not half of the work. The life, the life! O, my God! shall the life never be sweet?" For all her masculine mind, she had a woman's heart to which little court was paid. She felt herself to be a mutilated being, unable to arouse or experience the love she longed for. This very self-consciousness frightened off the young men attracted to her, for there were some who detected the passionate woman beneath the somewhat grim exterior of the learned lady. To one of the most persistent among them, Samuel Gray Ward, Julia Ward Howe's brilliant brother and Longfellow's chosen intimate as a student in Tübingen, she wrote somewhat inconsistently in September 1839:

You love me no more. . . . At an earlier period I would fain have broke the tie that bound us, for I knew myself incapable of feeling or being content to inspire an ordinary attachment.

The handsome, quick-witted Samuel, whose promise was never fully realized, finally grew weary of a love that blew hot and cold in the same breath, and married an Astor in his native New York. But it is interesting to speculate on what might have resulted for both if this early love-affair had not been so abortive. Ward was the heir to a New York banking fortune, and had enjoyed an excellent education at the Round Hill School in Northampton, at Columbia, and some years at the German universities. When he returned to America in 1835, speaking French and German as fluently as English and bearing with him Lafayette's library from La Grange, literature was his ruling passion and he devoted his best energies to it rather than to his father's business. Before going abroad he had already contributed twice to the *North American Review;* he corresponded with Emerson, translated Goethe, and kept Longfellow in touch with such New York wits as Fitz-Greene Halleck. His means could have spared Margaret some of her hardest years, and her intellectual passion would never have allowed him to deteriorate into the King of the Lobby at Washington, an occupation that he eventually found more congenial than the banking business to which family pressure forced him to sacrifice his literary dreams.

Margaret believed that in marriage "regions of her being that else had lain in cold obstruction would burst forth into leaf and bloom and song." She blamed her lack of looks for her failure to hold the interest of those attracted to her. In May she would write: "When all things are blossoming, it seems so strange not to blossom too. I hate not to be beautiful, when all around is so." She came to think that as an artist she must put aside all thought of the happiness that fell to other women.

She loved children and longed for one of her own. But there was consoling reflection that accompanied this longing:

No one loves me.

But I love many a good deal, and see some way into their eventual beauty. I am myself growing better, and shall be a worthy object of love. . . . I have no child, and the woman in me has so craved this experience that it has seemed the want of it must paralyze me. But now, as I look upon these lovely children of a human birth, what slow and neutralyzing cares they bring with them to the mother. The children of the muse come quicker, with less pain and disgust, rest more lightly upon the bosom and have not on them the taint of earthly corruption.

She subdued the longings of her heart, although they continued to trouble her until they were finally gratified. The debate in her mind whether she should be woman or artist was settled in favor of the latter, for "womanhood is at present too closely bounded to give me scope." She determined upon literature as a profession, though she loved best to be a woman.

❖ CHAPTER VI ❖

The "Dial" and Emerson

The pen is a much less agreeable instrument of communication than the voice, but all our wishes will not bring back the dear talking times of Greece and Rome. And believe me, you cannot live, you cannot be content, without acting on other minds.—M. F.

DURING the first winter of Margaret's Conversations, the Transcendentalists had evolved their plans for a journal which was to be the organ of the movement and a reproof to the unenlightened Harvard cult which dominated the *North American Review* and filled its pages with unreadable trivialities. As the younger generation's break with the Unitarian tradition grew sharper, the *Christian Examiner* closed its pages to those tainted with "this new form of philosophy which is turning the heads of our American scholars, inflating some and dementing others." It thundered against those who would "dethrone prudence and reason and worship an indefinable spontaneity," for this revolt against the letter and glorification of the spirit brought in a mass of errors, and substituted the dark guesses of man for the word of God. So in July 1840, the Transcendentalists launched their new quarterly magazine, which was christened the *Dial*, in order to have a place to express their ideas in print. It was the first really independent and original journal to be published in America; it lacked the imitativeness of its predecessors, and was free of academic tastes and pedantic methods. Its chief emphasis was literary, as opposed to the historical bent

RALPH WALDO EMERSON

of the *North American* and the theological of the *Christian Examiner*.

Margaret was chosen as the chief editor of the new publication, both because of her ability to harmonize the disparate talents of the group and because her background was recognized to be more purely literary than that of any of the others. George Ripley was the nominal business manager, and Emerson was associated with Margaret in the editorial direction. It was really a joint editorship, although both Emerson and Ripley were willing to allow the bulk of the work to fall upon Margaret's sturdy shoulders. For she thought that her new role might permit her to be a Boston Pericles, adorning her city with monuments of the intellect. What she liked most about "that peculiarly nervous sect called Transcendentalists" was their view of man as "an immortal soul, and not as a mere comfort-loving inhabitant of earth, or as a subscriber to the social contract." Here was a way to bring their principles to wider notice, and she set to work with enthusiasm. Her nature always demanded a cause to fight for, and her struggle with the *Dial* helped to satisfy the energies smoldering within her. It was largely a labor of love, for the editor's salary was set at two hundred dollars a year, and actually Margaret never received anything like this sum during her two years of editorship.

There were to be four numbers a year of the new journal, published in January, April, July, and October, and each was to contain 136 octavo pages. At the outset, it seemed a tremendous task to Margaret to gather sufficient contributions to fulfill this scheme. To Henry Hedge in his Bangor parsonage went this appeal:

Henry, I adjure you in the name of all the Genii, Muses, Pegasus, Apollo, Pollio, Apollyon, to send me something good for this journal before the first of May. All mortals, my friend, are slack and bare; they wait to see whether Hotspur wins before they levy aid for as good a plan as was ever laid. I know you are plagued and it is hard to write; just so it is with me, for I am also a father.

As she thus wheedled contributions, she suffered misgivings about the success of the new journal. "We cannot show high culture, and I doubt about vigorous thought. But we shall manifest free action, as far as it goes, and a high aim." When she assumed the editorship, she had thought her role would be a passive and supernumerary one. "I do not expect to be of much use except to urge on the laggards and scold the lukewarm; and act like Helen McGregor to those who love compromise by doing my little best to sink them in the waters of oblivion." But she had to ply her own pen to fill the closely printed pages, and the first issue contained no less than eight contributions from her. Since the magazine was at first conceived as the means of exchanging thought among a small circle of friends, and its chief readers were to be the writers themselves, the contributions were either unsigned or only initials were used, and Margaret was able to veil in anonymity her major share of the authorship. But the first number established the magazine as the rallying ground of the younger generation, and thereafter Margaret had less trouble in obtaining contributions. It was a time when there was, as Lowell put it, "no brain but had its private maggot," and under Margaret's editorship contributors to the *Dial* were allowed to follow their individual bent to the ultimate limit.

The first number had the stamp of the "Newness" sharply marked upon it, from Emerson's introductory editorial on the new spirit at work in New England, to which the magazine was to give expression, to the prospectus on the back cover which stated that the *Dial* "aims at the discussion of principles, rather than the promotion of measures. It will endeavor to promote the constant evolution of truth, not the petrification of opinion." Margaret's most important contributions were a "Short

Essay on Critics," which was a plea for the establishment of criteria and fixed values in a field too much dominated by subjectivism, and her "Record of Impressions of Mr. Allston's Pictures." There was a discussion of Orestes Brownson's writings by George Ripley, and a collection of Bronson Alcott's "Orphic Sayings," which Margaret considered "quite grand, though oft-times too grandiloquent." The rest of the contents was a literary miscellany. The appearance of the magazine created a stir which its founders were at a loss to account for, since to Ripley it was "not *prononcé* enough" and Emerson judged that the initial number contained "scarcely anything considerable or even visible." All the sins of the Transcendentalists in the eyes of the conventional world were visited upon the *Dial's* tender head, and it drew the fire of almost every magazine and newspaper. But the new publication flourished in this atmosphere of controversy, for the Transcendentalists united to defend their cause in its pages.

The *Dial*, during the four years of its existence, may have been deemed unreadable by those untouched by the new spirit, but it cannot be accused of having been either trifling or unrepresentative. Margaret had a singular success in getting much of the best of contemporary New England writing into its pages, even though the magazine never paid its contributors. The original 136-page format swelled to include long, earnest discussions from the pens of Parker, Channing, Ripley, Clarke; Emerson's essays and poems; Margaret's pieces on art and literature, with especial attention to new and foreign books; Thoreau's nature studies and scholarly doggerel; the first translations in America of the great Oriental sacred writings; John Sullivan Dwight's papers on music; notes on archaeology, architecture, and travel sketches; and verse of varying merit from the pens of Christopher Cranch, the younger William Ellery Channing, James Russell Lowell, Ellen Sturgis, Jones Very, and Margaret herself. Then, too, there was a surprising amount of contributions from unknown young writers who swarmed upon the new magazine in numbers embarrassing to the editors, who at first had thought of the *Dial* as their private organ. Margaret sympathized with their aspirations, and by her influence brought many a thin talent to bear a blossom or two for a brief moment. In after years it seemed rare to find a New Englander who had not had a poem or an essay, often one and then no more, in the pages of the *Dial*.

The generally high quality of the contributions is impressive, although Margaret, never a stylist herself, often opened the editorial gates to loosely written, if profoundly serious, articles. Her momentary enthusiasms were apt to lead her better judgment astray and involve her in later difficulties. It became necessary for her to indicate gently to Alcott that the whole of an issue could not be devoted to his misty "Orphic Sayings," which incited more ridicule than anything else that ever appeared in the *Dial*. Alcott took the suggestion in bad part, and withdrew himself in lofty disappointment that once again his dream of an organ of free expression had not been realized. Poor Alcott suffered additional woe at this time, for Christopher Cranch, a clever caricaturist as well as a poet, depicted him lying on a sofa, with a copy of the *Dial* on the floor and his wife engaged in blacking the boots of the recumbent sage. The sketch was widely circulated as indicative of the ethereal concerns of the *Dial's* readers and writers.

The *Dial* aroused a storm of criticism; this was the surest sign of its vitality. Many of the Transcendentalists themselves were disappointed with it. George Ripley noted this reaction in his remark: "They expected hoofs and horns, while it proved as gentle as any sucking dove." Its tone was so eclectic and miscellaneous that each of its audience valued only a small portion of its contents. Possibly the fault lay with Margaret's editorial policy:

There are no party measures to be carried, no particular standard to be set up. I trust there will be a spirit neither of dogmatism nor of compromise, and that this journal will aim, not at leading public opinion, but at stimulating each man to judge for himself.

She differed with the opinions of many of the leading Transcendentalists, and was obliged to publish much of which she did not wholly approve. Alcott's mind was not the only one she distrusted, and she possessed a more practical bent than many of her collaborators. To her it seemed impossible to build up a Utopia, and her hopes for the future of man on this planet were more limited than those of most of her friends. Yet Carlyle wrote to Emerson after seeing the first numbers of the *Dial:* "Of course, I read it with interest; it is an utterance of what is purest, youngest in your land. . . . And yet . . . for me it is too ethereal, speculative, theoretic." He constantly restated his original objections during the course of the magazine's life, but he brought the publication to the attention of his English friends and made familiar the name of its editor, whom he referred to as a disciple of Emerson's "who goes into very high flights about Art, self-sacrifice, Progress, etc., etc." With his distrust of femininity, he constantly urged upon Emerson the *Dial's* need of a "stalwart Yankee *man* with color in the cheeks of him and a coat on his back" to give body to its spirit-like, aeriform tendencies. The vigorous Theodore Parker echoed this criticism with his comment that the *Dial* needed a beard, and after it ceased publication, he launched the *Massachusetts Quarterly Review* as a revised model of its predecessor. But as Thomas Wentworth Higginson remarked, this journal turned out to be "the beard without the *Dial*" and had an even shorter life.

Besides these charges of a feminine slant in the editorial policy, there were many others: the magazine lacked a definite aim; it was too conservative and conventional; it thought too much of style and literary matters; or, on the other hand, its plans of practical reform were poorly expressed. Margaret had the idea of representing many shades of opinion, often widely divergent, in the pages of the *Dial,* in the same way that she welcomed different points of view in her Conversations. But the policy was less successful in print than in talk, and there was little opportunity for her to harmonize the discussion. Finally, after two years of editorship, she gave up the onerous and unrewarded task. Emerson took over the editorship, somewhat reluctantly, for while he wished the magazine to live, he did not wish to be its life. Yet he did not want it to fall into the hands of the "Humanity and Reform men, because they trample on letters and poetry; nor in the hands of the Scholars, for they are dead and dry." Since George Ripley was now preoccupied with Brook Farm, Elizabeth Peabody was to manage the magazine's affairs, and Thoreau undertook to canvass for subscribers. For all the *Dial's* influence and the wide recognition it received, its circulation under Margaret's editorship was only a little more than 100 copies, while under Emerson it attained its high point of some 250. These figures seem appallingly small today, but this was an age of small circulations. Horace Greeley's *New York Tribune* had an average circulation of only 15,000, and it was one of the most potent mediums of expression in the country. As for the other magazines which resembled the *Dial* in character, the *North American* reached a bare 3000, for all the weight of tradition behind it, and the *Southern Literary Messenger's* 5000 for a brief period under the editorship of Edgar Allan Poe was regarded as phenomenal. The *Dial's* appeal was by intention restricted to certain quarters.

Aside from the slight increase of circulation which seems to have been due more to Thoreau's efforts than Emerson's, the magazine seemed to fare no better under the new direction than it had under Margaret's. Carlyle put his finger on the trouble in a long exhortation to Emerson:

I love your *Dial,* and yet it is with a kind of shudder. You seem to be in danger of dividing yourselves from the Fact of this present universe, in which alone, ugly as it is, can I find

any anchorage, and soaring away after Ideas, Beliefs, Revelations, and such like—into perilous altitudes, as I think. . . .
Alas, it is so easy to screw one's self up into high and ever
higher altitudes of Transcendentalism, and see nothing under
one but the everlasting snows of Himmalayeh . . . easy . . .
but where does it lead? Well, I do believe, for one thing, a
man has no right to say to his own generation, turning quite
away from it: "Be damned!" It is the whole Past and the
whole Future, this same cotton-spinning, dollar-hunting, cant-
ing and shrieking, very wretched generation of ours. Come
back into it, I tell you.

The high aspirations of the Transcendentalists led them into
excesses of sentimentalism and mysticism, and the public recognition of the absurdity of some of these manifestations hamstrung the practical efforts of the adherents of the new gospel.
The movement was essentially a wave of enthusiasm, doomed
to be short-lived. The *Dial* died with the ebb of the tide in 1844.
In its four years it had made its mark here and abroad: it had
achieved a *succès d'estime* and revealed the literary resources
of the new age in New England. It was the forcing-bed of many
a talent.

Margaret's connection with the *Dial* made her ply her pen to
more purpose than before, and she contributed at least once
to almost every number, and usually had a good many more than
one piece in an issue. One of the reasons behind her resignation of the editorship, in addition to her need for money and her
ill health, was the disagreeableness of this forced literary appli-
cation. When her work was criticized, she expressed her feelings
in the matter:

These gentlemen are surprised that I write no better, because I talk so well. I shall write better, but never, I think, so
well as I talk; for then I feel inspired. The means are pleasant; my voice excites me, my pen never.

She was impatient of details, and begrudged the labor necessary for finished literary expression: "I am delighted with my sketch, but if I try to finish it, I am chilled." She lacked confidence in her writing, and judged that there was scarcely a line of poetry in her impassioned and rhetorical verses. Her prose papers seemed devoid of notable thoughts, and her confidence returned only when in talk she discovered that she had something new to offer people. In such a state of mind, when even criticism seemed to demand a creativeness that it was difficult for her to muster, she turned naturally to translation.

The most notable of her translations was of Bettina von Arnim's *Günderode*, which she published in 1842, only two years after the book appeared in Germany. In Bettina, who had corresponded as a child with Goethe and was the sister of one notable Heidelberg romanticist and the wife of another, Margaret discovered a fellow soul, who shared her deepest feelings. The book, considered one of the most beautiful products of the sentimentalism which flourished in the romantic era, is a record of the author's passionate friendship for Karoline von Günderode, the unhappy intimate of Wilhelm von Humboldt, who killed herself in 1806. In it Margaret found many echoes of the emotional relationships she had had herself with other girls and young women. There was something of a vogue for such affairs between members of the same sex during this period. There was an undercurrent of homosexuality in them, though they were harmlessly platonic. Margaret's masculinized personality tended to attract her to girls instead of to the opposite sex, particularly when they possessed the beauty and feminine charm which she wholly lacked. They in turn were drawn to her by her superior intelligence and firmer will power. She did not realize how much Timothy Fuller's upbringing was to blame for this tendency of hers, and wrote:

It is so true that a woman may be in love with a woman, and a man with a man. It is pleasant to be sure of it, because it is undoubtedly the same love that we shall feel when we are angels, when we ascend to the only fit place for the Mignons, where *sie fragen nicht nach Mann und Weib*. It is regulated by the same laws as that of love between persons of different sexes, only it is purely intellectual and spiritual, unprofaned by any mixture of lower instincts, undisturbed by any need of consulting temporal interests; its law is the desire of the spirit to realize a whole, which makes it seek in another being that which it finds not in itself. Thus the beautiful seek the strong, the mute seek the eloquent; the butterfly settles on the dark flower. Why did Socrates love Alcibiades? Why did Kaiser so love Schneider? How natural is the love of Wallenstein for Max, that of Madame de Staël for Récamier, mine for ——! I loved —— for a time with as much passion as I was then strong enough to feel. Her face was always gleaming before me; her voice was still echoing in my ear. All poetic thoughts clustered around the dear image. . . . She loved me, for I well remember her suffering when she first could feel my faults and knew one part of the exquisite veil rent away—how she wished to stay apart and weep the whole day.

Such sentiments and experiences, coupled with the disadvantages of her background, long prevented her from fulfilling the true nature of a woman. It is doubtful whether she fully realized this twist in her nature before her marriage.

Lacking such fulfillment at this period, she experienced "terrible seasons of faintness and discouragement." Her activities in connection with the Conversations and the *Dial* did not prevent her from brooding morbidly on religious subjects and falling into excesses of mysticism and sentimentalism of an esoteric sort. Caught up in the Transcendental ferment as she was, yet wanting the solid theological or philosophical background that most of her associates possessed, she was an easy victim to these tendencies of the movement. Better than any of the other

Transcendentalists, she understood the mysterious allegories of
Goethe and Novalis, and as she translated them, her enthusiastic fancy led her to evolve a demonology of her own. Socrates
and Goethe had had their demons, and so did she. She blamed
her misfortunes on this spirit of her own creation: "With me,
for weeks and months, the daemon works his will. Nothing suc-
ceeds with me." She developed a taste for talismans, omens,
coincidences, and dreams. She chose the carbuncle as a stone
emblematic of her nature, for she had read somewhere that this
stone is either male or female, the female casting out light and
the male having his own within himself. Her carbuncle was
male. She hatched a dream personality, with whom she com-
muned in the lonely hours of the night, and published an
account of this phantom in the *Dial:*

> I did not love thee, Leila, but the desire for love was
> soothed in your presence. . . . At night I look into the lake
> for Leila. If I gaze steadily and in the singleness of prayer,
> she rises and walks on its depths. Then know I each night a
> part of her life; I know where she passes the midnight hours.
> In the day she lives among men; she observes their deeds, and
> gives them what they want of her, justice or love. . . . In
> the night she wanders forth from her human investment and
> travels amid these tribes, freer movers in the game of spirit
> and matter, to whom this man is a supplement. I know not
> then whether she is what men call dreaming, but her life is
> true, full, and more single than by day. . . .
>
> They say that such purity is the seal of death. It is so; the
> condition of this ecstasy is, that it seems to die every moment,
> and even Leila has not force to die often; the electricity ac-
> cumulates many days before the wild one comes, which leads
> to these sylph nights of tearful sweetness. After one of these,
> I find her always to have retreated into the secret veins of the
> earth. Then glows through her whole being the fire that so
> baffles men, as she walks the surface of the earth; the blood-

red, heart's blood-red of the universal heart, with no care except to circulate as the vital fluid; and it would seem waste, then, for her to rise to the surface.

Such visions clearly stem from a disordered sexuality. Emerson distrusted all this talk of demons and visions as unhealthy, with good reason, and adjured Margaret: "Let us hold hard to the common sense, and let us speak in the positive degree."

It was fortunate for Margaret that she had so good a friend to offer her sensible advice. Their collaboration on the *Dial* had brought about a closer relationship between them than Margaret had previously been able to achieve, for all her zealous pursuit of him since 1834, when she had written to Mrs. Barlow of "that only clergyman of all possible clergymen who eludes my acquaintance." He first heard of her in that same year from Frederick Henry Hedge, who lent him her manuscript translation of Goethe's *Tasso*. In the following year Harriet Martineau introduced Margaret to Emerson with warm praise for her young friend, upon the occasion of a visit paid by the Emerson brothers to the Englishwoman staying at the Farrars' home in Cambridge. It was probably as an aftermath of this meeting that Margaret was invited to Concord for a fortnight in July 1836. For all the high impression that Emerson formed of her intelligence and accomplishments during this visit, he had been repelled by her extreme plainness, her trick of incessantly opening and shutting her near-sighted eyes, and the nasal tone of her voice. He had said to himself: "We shall never get far," and the common report that came to him of her sneering, critical, disdainful ways confirmed his impression that she was personally unprepossessing. But he found himself unable to hold out, like many another whose first impressions of her were unfavorable, against the court she paid to him:

> Margaret, who had stuffed me out as a philosopher in her fancy, was too intent on establishing a good footing between us, to omit any art of winning. She studied my tastes, piqued

and amused me, challenged frankness by frankness, and did not conceal the good opinion of me that she had brought with her nor her desire to please.

Her rich and entertaining conversation made him laugh more than he liked, for to the solitary stoic of Concord there was something profane in hours given to amusing gossip. But he discovered that there was a strength of character behind the eloquence, and the broadest good sense. Her temperamental ups and downs, her craving for a larger atmosphere than was offered to her by her surroundings and circumstances, her interest in a wide range of topics strange to Emerson, made him "sensible of some barrier, as if in making up a friendship with a cultivated Spaniard or Turk." A more unlikely pair of friends it is hard to imagine: Emerson determined to maintain at all costs the peace and serenity which were essential to his work and to his temperament, in order to avoid the fate of insanity which overtook two of his brothers; Margaret needing to be called out by other minds, energetic in both speech and action, with a volatile nature much given to enthusiasm. Yet somehow they became intimates and continued so until Margaret went abroad. She came as close as anyone outside his family circle to this man who by his own confession was born cold, who lacked the kind affections of a pigeon, who found not one being in the whole wide universe to whom he could be attached with warm and entire devotion.

Their relationship was in many ways a curious one: Emerson always retreating before Margaret's friendly onslaughts, yet delighting in them; Margaret always dissatisfied with the inadequate capacity for friendship that she found in him. It was a friendship slow in ripening. Emerson distrusted the violence of her nature, her pagan preoccupations, and the evident presence in her of a "rather mountainous ME," revealed in such remarks as "God forbid that any one should conceive more highly of me than I myself." But gradually he came to feel that her real tal-

ents gave her a right to such complacency, that she was a soul
capable of greatness, struggling against the handicaps of unfortunate circumstances. He valued highly the love of truth which
dominated her life, and considered her conversation the most
entertaining in America. He found her an inspiring companion:
"All the art, the thought, and the nobleness in New England
seemed, at that moment, related to her, and she to it." But just
as he was congratulating himself on the good understanding
that existed between himself and Margaret, she told him it was
superficial and "commercial," that he valued her only for the
thoughts and things she brought him and failed to meet her
magnanimity. To this Emerson could only reply: "We use a different rhetoric. It seems as if we had been born and bred in
different natures. . . . I honor you for a brave and beneficient
woman."

On Margaret's side the progress of esteem was less marked,
mainly because from the first she had had a high opinion of
Emerson. Before she knew him, she had kept his image bright
in her mind. She felt that "his influence has been more beneficial
to me than that of any American, and that from him I first
learned what is meant by an inward life." Several of his sermons
were landmarks in her spiritual history. But as her acquaintance
with him ripened, the disciple tended to become a critic. After
a visit to Concord, she wrote that she found him a much better
companion than formerly, "for once he would talk obstinately
through the walk, but now we can be silent and see things together." She did not approve of his self-chosen isolation in Concord, where life slumbered and stole on like the river itself: "A
very good place for a sage, but not for the lyrist or the orator."
She longed to "teach this sage all he wants to make him the full-
fledged angel, to make him forego these tedious, tedious attempts to learn the universe by thought alone." Her nature demanded action, as his did passivity, in order to bear fruit, and
she did her best to convert him to her way. But he refused to be
roused from his treasured calm, and finally she accepted his

notion of their different natures with: "I will never do as Waldo does, though I marvel not at him."

Emerson's influence was of vital importance in these years much given to introspection and pondering of religious questions. He acted as a check and a curb to the excesses of her nature as she struggled with herself, and she was conscious of "how invaluable is a cool mind, like his, amid the warring elements round us." She felt him to be an equal who recognized her true spirit beneath her defects of personality and manner and the extravagances of sentiment into which her high aspirations led her. He could understand the spiritual insight she displayed when she wrote:

> I think this is the great step of our life—to change the *nature* of our self-reliance. We find that the will cannot conquer circumstances . . . the mode of our existence is not in our own power; but behind it is the unmutable essence that cannot be tarnished; and to hold fast to this conviction, to live as far as possible by its light, cannot be denied us if we elect this kind of self-trust.

If she had felt all her life the need to hitch her wagon to a star, Emerson understood, for he devoted his life to consideration of the stars. If he felt that her fancy or her pride had tampered with her religion, he was not unsympathetic to the credo she drew up for herself:

> For myself, I believe in Christ because I can do without him; because the truth he announces I see elsewhere intimated; because it is foreshadowed in the very nature of my being. But I do not wish to do without him. He is constantly aiding and answering me. Only I will not lay any undue and exclusive emphasis on him. When he comes to me I will receive him; when I feel inclined to go by myself, I will.

Emerson gave her assurance and sweet serenity when feeling

replaced intellect as the ruling force within herself, and she was conscious of "all Italy glowing beneath the Saxon crust." Sometimes she felt as if she would burn to ashes if the smoldering fires within did not burst forth in genius or heroism, but he stopped her from doing anything and made her think. She did not wish to be like him, a "calm observer of the courses of things," and she was conscious of his life stealing gradually into hers, so that she wrote to another friend: "I sometimes think that my work would have been more simple, and my unfolding to a temporal activity more rapid and easy if we had never met." She rebelled against his influence as she had against Timothy Fuller's, but she valued it as highly.

Perhaps their friendship is best explained by Miss Katharine Anthony's hypothesis that Margaret replaced Emerson's Aunt Mary in his life as he replaced Timothy Fuller in hers. Mary Moody Emerson was as perfect a type of the female Puritan as Timothy Fuller was of the male; they were both purely original fruits of the meeting of Calvinism and New England. Van Wyck Brooks has drawn a fine portrait of this strange dwarf:

> She was poor, obscure, uncomely, but an Emerson still, of the seed of the ruling caste, the child of six generations of a ruling priesthood. . . . Night and day she wrote, wrote, wrote. Letters, interminable diary, prayers, ejaculations, mystical dreams, asseverations exalted and melancholy of her submission to the Eternity. . . . She was thought to have the power of uttering more disagreeable things in twenty minutes than any other person living. She kept pace with nobody; she had received, she said, the fatal gift of penetration, and her mission was to undermine the vanity of the shallow. . . . She loved life, she loved manners, beauty, distinction, genius. She was born to command, dictate, to inspire. "For the love of superior virtue," she said, "is mine own gift from God." And who could have numbered the waste places of her journey, "the secret martyrdoms of youth, heavier than the stake,

the narrow limits which knew no outlet, the bitter dregs of the cup"?

This woman said: "I never expected connections and matrimony. . . . I knew I was not destined to please." She contented herself with scholarship and the faith that some day she would know true friendship. She was a father to her fatherless Emerson nephews, and her favorite Waldo in later life called her the "true aunt of genius." To him she had the great misfortune of "spinning with a greater velocity than any of the other tops" of her day. And there is a singular likeness between his accounts of her and of Margaret. It is certain that Emerson early noted traits in Margaret which reminded him of Aunt Mary. After Margaret's first visit to Concord he wrote in his journal:

> How rarely can the female mind be impersonal. Sarah Ripley is wonderfully free from egotism of place and time and blood. Margaret F. is by no means so free, with all her superiority. What shall I *say* of Aunt Mary?"

Again, in the following year, he coupled them in his thought:

> The fine women I think of who have had genius and cultivation, who have not been wives, but muses, have something tragic in their lot and I shun to name them. Then I say, Despondency bears no fruit. . . . It is ignoble also to owe our success to the coaxing and the clapping of society, to be told by the incapable, "That's capital. Do some more."
>
> Therefore I think a woman does herself injustice who likens herself to any historical woman, who thinks because Corinna or de Staël or M.M.E. do not satisfy the imagination . . . none can. It needs that she feel that a new woman has a new, as yet inviolate, problem to solve.

In 1841, when their common labors on the *Dial* had brought them closer together intellectually and Margaret had fallen into the habit of visiting him in Concord every three or four months, he noted the paradoxes in her character which were so reminiscent of Mary Moody Emerson:

> Margaret is a "being of unsettled rank in the universe." So proud and presumptuous, yet so meek; so worldly and artificial and with the keenest sense and taste for all pleasures of luxurious society, yet living more than any other for long periods in a trance of religious sentiment; a person who, according to her own account of herself, expects everything for herself from the Universe.

He puzzled over the course of their "strange, cold-warm, attractive-repelling conversations." He always felt admiration for Margaret, revered her most when he saw her closest, and sometimes his feeling for her amounted almost to love. Yet he froze her, and she him, into silence, when there was promise of a nearer intimacy. Perhaps the fault lay in the fact that he always seemed to be on stilts, as Sarah Shaw said; perhaps that their natures were so different.

In March 1843, Emerson wrote in his journal the fullest estimate of Margaret that he ever made, except for his memoir of her after her death. It is more interesting than the latter, as less affected by the sentimentalism about a dead friend to which even the cold nature of Emerson capitulated in accordance with the manner of the age and his own real sense of bereavement:

> A pure and purifying mind, self-purifying also, full of faith in men and inspiring it. Unable to find any companion great enough to receive the rich effusions of her thought, so that her riches are still unknown and seem unknowable. . . . We are taught by her plenty how lifeless and outward we were, what poor Laplanders burrowing under the snows of prudence and pedantry. Beside her friendship, other friendships seem trade, and by the firmness with which she treads her upward path, all mortals are convinced that another road exists than that which their feet have trod. . . .

She excells other intellectual persons in this: that her sentiments are more blended with her life; so the expression of
them has greater steadfastness and clearness. I have never
known any example of such steady progress from stage to
stage of thought and character. An inspirer of courage. . . .
Her growth is visible. . . . She rose before me at times into
heroical and godlike regions, and I could remember no superior women, but thought of Ceres, Minerva, Proserpine.
. . . She said that no man gave such inspiration to her mind
as to tempt her to full expression; that she felt a power to en-
rich her thought with such wealth and variety of embellish-
ment as would, no doubt, be tedious to such as she conversed
with. And there is no form that does not seem to wait her
beck. . . .

She has great sincerity, force, and fluency as a writer, yet
her powers of speech throw her writing into the shade. . . .
You cannot predict her opinion. She sympathizes so fast with
all forms of life, that she talks never narrowly or hostilely,
nor betrays, like all the rest, under a thin garb of new words,
the old droning, cast-iron opinions or notions of many years'
standing. What richness of experience, what newness of dress,
and fast as Olympus to her principles. And a silver eloquence,
which evermost Polyhymnia taught. Meantime, all this pathos
of sentiment and riches of literature and of invention, and this
march of character threatening to arrive presently at the
shores and plunge into the sea of Buddhism and mystic
trances, consists with a boundless fun and drollery, with light
satire, and the most entertaining conversation in America.

Such was the judgment of one who knew her well. Those who
did not railed against her as the most arrogant of mortals, a
compendium of pedantries. For herself, she considered that she
lacked the force to be either a genius or a character, that she
was dumb and ineffectual when it came to expressing the tides
of life that flowed within her, that she had not learned to think

to any depth, and the utmost that she had done was to give her character a certain consistency, cultivate her tastes, and learn to tell the truth with a better grace than at first. She struggled to learn patience and gentleness, though those traits were not natural to her. In her journal she prayed for strength to endure the slow agonies of the devouring wants of her nature. In outward action she never found refuge or rest, and sought peace in deepening the fountains of the spirit. She died daily within herself, longing for the fertilizing leaven that would enable her to rise heavenward. She cried out upon her fainting heart that would not allow her to taste the fruits of the worlds of art, science, and nature that were spread out in vain before her. She felt within herself the genius of a god, wanting only the full breath of love to call it into conscious existence and pining for fulfillment. Such was her inner life during these years of outward activity, and it was from Emerson that she drew the philosophic calm which characterizes this summary of her own nature made in 1844 and contrasts it with an earlier violence of emotion:

Mine is a great nature as yet in many regions an untrodden wild, full of wild beasts and reptiles not yet tamed and classed, but also of rare butterflies, exquisite and grand vegetations respondent to the sun and stars. Its dynamics reveal not yet their concords—as yet it energizes more than harmonizes. It has much superficial, much temporary tragedy. The woman kneels and weeps her tender raptures, finds no echo, but snowdrops and violets spring from her tears. The man rushes forth and is baffled, but returning lame a blinded Oedipus.

CHAPTER VII

Brook Farm and Hawthorne

It is a constellation, not a phalanx, to which I would belong.—M. F.

SOME of the Transcendentalists were not content to realize their dreams of a better life and social order for man only in talk or in the pages of the *Dial*. They were Puritans as well as Platonists, doers as well as thinkers, and the Puritan emphasis on the practical and moral was so strong in some of them that they felt action was necessary. Henry Hedge, George Ripley, and William Henry Channing were the leaders in the movement whose thought had certain elements of socialism in it. To George Ripley, in particular, there was an urgent necessity to cut himself off from the old and evil commonplaces of life, and to set up an ideal community where the human spirit might expand unchecked by the conventions of State Street. Ripley was a man who acted on his intellectual convictions, and so he gave up the Unitarian ministry after fourteen years of it, and laid the plans of his Utopia while he occupied himself with literary enterprises. He and his wife spent a considerable part of their time on a farm in West Roxbury, now that there were no duties to demand his presence in Boston, and found that they enjoyed farm life. In 1840 Albert Brisbane published *The Social Destiny of Man,* a book which introduced the social ideas of the Frenchman Charles Fourier to an America which was already familiar with the communities of the Owenites and other associationists. Most of these experiments had been launched by Europeans in other quarters of the country than New England. George Ripley's

NATHANIEL HAWTHORNE

Engraving by T. Phillibrown,
from the painting by C. G. Thompson

Brook Farm owed something to them, but it was decidedly native, and the Transcendental principle of plain living and high thinking, the Yankee gospel of manual labor, a revolt against the accepted Boston way of life, and the Ripleys' pleasure in farm life gave birth to it.

The Ripleys broached the idea of establishing a community to Emerson, Margaret, and Alcott on October 17, 1840. Emerson, as perhaps was expected, showed no enthusiasm for the scheme. For all his interest in manifestations of the "Newness," the proposed community seemed to promise no fulfillment for the deepest impulses of his nature:

> I wished to be convinced, to be thawed, to be made nobly mad by the kindlings before my eye of a new dawn of human piety. But this scheme was arithmetic and comfort . . . a rage in our poverty and politics to live rich and gentleman-like, an anchor to leeward against a change of weather; a prudent forecast on the probable issue of the great questions of Pauperism and Poverty. . . . It was not the cave of persecution which is the palace of spiritual power, but only a room in the Astor House hired for the Transcendentalists. I do not wish to remove from my present prison to a prison a little larger. I wish to break all prisons. I have not yet conquored my own house. It irks and repents. Shall I raise the siege of this hencoop and march baffled away to a pretended siege of Babylon? It seems to me to do so were to dodge the problem I am set to solve, and to hide my impotency in the thick of the crowd. Man is stronger than a city . . . his solitude is more prevalent and beneficent than the concert of crowds.

Margaret considered the experiment interesting, but ill-timed and premature. It is surprising that her enthusiastic mind did not take fire at the proposal, but perhaps Emerson's view dampened her natural optimism about schemes destined to better man's lot. More probably the memory of her difficulties with another farm in Groton was lurking at the back of her mind. That venture had also been painted in terms of great promise before it was begun. At any rate, she refused to join the community on any terms, even if she should be exempted from manual labor and allowed to devote herself solely to teaching— for a school was an important part of Ripley's plans. Alcott, too, was interested in the scheme, as he was in any idealistic experiment, but Ripley's community was too worldly for his taste. His own notion of a community was to achieve realization two years later in the seven months' wonder of Fruitlands.

The Social Plans were discussed among the Transcendentalists all that winter, but only John Sullivan Dwight accepted the Ripleys' scheme without reserve. The others were less willing to translate talk into action, or they were prevented from lending themselves to the enterprise by personal considerations. Hedge, for all his intellectual radicalism, was ecclesiastically conservative and fond of his Bangor pulpit. William Henry Channing longed to throw in his lot with Ripley, but his wife was opposed. Parker was enthusiastic but engrossed with his own work at his church, two miles from the proposed site of the new community. He promised to visit the colonists often and lend them a hand when he could. There were many who thought like Emerson that the soul could best be cultivated in more individualistic fashions. Many already practiced by themselves the gospel of manual labor which was to be followed by all at Brook Farm: Thoreau in Concord, young Ellery Channing splitting rails in Illinois, Charles Wheeler in his hut in Lincoln. But Ripley was not to be daunted by lack of support, and in April of 1841 the experiment was begun. In its six years of existence it probably excited more attention than any other of the Transcendentalists' activities.

At first the community consisted only of Ripley and his wife Sarah and his sister Marianne, Warren Burton, who had left the ministry almost as soon as he entered it, and a printer named Minot Pratt and his wife and three children. Nathaniel Hawthorne and George Bradford soon joined them. A Vermont farmer named Allen and a neighbor, Frank Farley, supplied the practical knowledge of farming which the others lacked. Soon the little colony swelled its numbers, as it attracted many of the rebels in the younger generation who would have none of trade or the conventional ways of society. The venture was organized as a joint stock company, with shares at five hundred dollars apiece. Ripley, his sister, Pratt, Dwight, and young Charles Dana each held three shares, while Mrs. Ripley, her niece Sarah Stearns, and Mrs. Pratt had two each. The shares were put on public sale at Elizabeth Peabody's bookshop, and to many they were an attractive investment in a time of crumbling values, though Emerson for one found Concord investments more secure. Most of the investors were more motivated by their idealism than by any hope of profit; Hawthorne, for example, put almost all his savings into the shares and so did other young intellectuals. It has never been difficult to raise funds for an idealistic cause in Boston, and soon sufficient capital was available to insure the continuance of the farm.

As the community grew in numbers and succumbed more fully to the doctrines of Fourier, as amplified by Brisbane, the organization became more formal and the Farm less of the perpetual picnic that Emerson saw in it, and more of a French Revolution in small and an Age of Reason in a patty-pan—which were other ways in which he described it. The membership rose to over a hundred—at one time, that is, for many more were members for a month or two or longer—and the Association became a phalanx after Fourier's pattern. Some of the lighter-hearted rebels were driven out by the advent of the sterner and more industrialized system. The school flourished, and Harvard recognized it by sending young men who lacked sufficient preparation for college or were "rusticated" from the academic body. The women cooked and baked and sewed; the men worked in the fields or pursued their trades. Ripley himself was dismayed to find that his administrative tasks took more and more of his time, and left him little opportunity to make use of his fine library.

Margaret was a constant visitor, though she had set herself against becoming a member of the community and never regretted her decision. She held a number of Conversations at the Farm and gave lectures on various subjects to the community. She was one of the most highly honored guests among the swarm of visitors attracted to the Farm—in one year four thousand registered in the visitors' book at the Hive, as the main building was called. Some of the young people and many of the elders regarded her as a prophetess, and her visits were events for which special preparations were made. Georgianna Bruce, an English girl who had resigned her post as a governess in Dr. Ezra Gannett's household to join the community, was delighted to give up her room to the visitor, and burnt pastilles so that it might be properly perfumed. In the morning she brought Margaret's coffee to her in the Farm's only decorated china cup. There were others who paid the visitor the adoring respect that she always seemed to arouse in young women. It is curious how firmly Margaret's name is associated with Brook Farm, although she never was as close to it as many other individuals of reputation. One of the original buildings, still standing today, though rapidly falling apart, is often called the Margaret Fuller Cottage, although it is the only place where Margaret did not stay on her visits to the Farm. Hawthorne's Transcendental Heifer, which was supposed to belong to her, has become a byword, but the legend is mythical, for Margaret never had any property at the Farm. She has been identified with Zenobia, the heroine of Hawthorne's thinly disguised tale of life at Brook Farm, although both Hawthorne and Margaret's friends rejected the identification on the publication of *The Blithedale Romance*. This book has kept alive the association of Margaret with the Farm, though actually she shared Emerson's position toward the experiment. For all that Brook Farm grew out of Transcendentalism, its attempt at collectivism contrasted sharply with the extreme individualism of the movement, which was reflected in both Emerson's and Margaret's lives. She was interested in self-culture and the formation of the spirit and in artistic expression, and hard necessity had made her sufficiently practical to support a family with her earnings. Ripley's experiment was at once too materialistic and too impractical in her view; it offered satisfaction of neither her spiritual nor her material needs. She had no high opinion of Fourier's doctrines, and disliked the utilitarian emphasis they gave to the Farm's life when they were put into practice there in 1844. She did not wish to be regimented in a phalanx; she wanted to soar to the heavens.

In the early years of the Farm began her acquaintance with Hawthorne, which was to follow a curious course. Elizabeth Peabody had come upon his stories in the magazines and tracked him to his solitary garret in Salem, where he had spent most of the fourteen years since his graduation from Bowdoin, writing constantly but without recognition. She brought him into the Transcendentalist circle of Salem and encouraged an intimacy which soon sprang up between the shy solitary and her witty invalid sister Sophia. Sophia was something of an artist, and drew pictures in Flaxman's style for one of Hawthorne's stories. Elizabeth published his *Grandfather's Chair* in her series of juvenile books which were "to make artists of children from the beginning." When the Peabodys moved to Boston, leaving their native Salem which had become desolate in its decaying years, deserted by its great families and brooding over its past as a thriving port, she got an appointment for him as a clerk in the Boston Customs House, from her friend George Bancroft, who combined his historical studies with his duties as collector of customs. Margaret was apt to find this romantic and picturesque young man hanging about the West Street bookshop as he waited for Sophia, or to notice his magnificent eyes when he took time off from his coal-measuring at the Customs House to attend a Transcendentalist meeting. At this period she had an eye for young men, particularly if there was a romantic or pathetic air about them. She wrote to her friend Caroline Sturgis of one youth who had attracted her notice because "he talked of the Lady of Shalot and looked as if he might have lived as she died." But Hawthorne had no eyes for any woman but Sophia, and seems to have shunned opportunities to meet Margaret, who was regarded as a paragon among her sex. In November 1840, he wrote in his notebook: "I was invited to dine yesterday at Mr. Bancroft's, with Miss M. F.; but Providence had given me some business to do, for which I was very thankful."

He disliked consciously intellectual women and judged them unfit for authorship: "There is a delicacy . . . that perceives, or fancies, a sort of impropriety in the display of woman's natal mind to the gaze of the world." It may well have been that her frank expression of her thoughts, her vigorous egotism, her passionate Feminism, grated on his own shyness, reticence, and shrinking fascination with sexual matters. Or it may have been irritating to him to see a woman six years younger than himself receiving wide recognition of her talents when he was yet unknown. It would be natural, too, for him to resent the admiration that his Sophia paid the Sibyl of the Conversations, although the witty Sophia was not uncritical of "Queen Margaret" and thought that married women might not be such impassioned Feminists as she.

When the spoils system cost Hawthorne his job at the Customs House and he threw in his lot with the Brook Farmers in the spring of 1841, he soon came into closer contact with Margaret. His earlier vague feelings about her no doubt gained force from a weariness with hearing her praises sung by the Ripleys, and he seems to have transferred them to the heifer whose troublesome nature bothered the amateur farmers. He grew interested in the Transcendental Heifer, as the beast was dubbed, and recorded a series of observations on her which clearly show what was passing in his mind:

She is very fractious, I believe, and apt to kick over the milk-pail. Miss F.'s cow hooks the other cows, and has made herself ruler of the herd, and behaves in a very tyrannical manner.

The herd has rebelled against the usurpation of Miss F.'s heifer; and, whenever they are turned out of the barn, she is compelled to take refuge under our protection. . . .

She is not an amiable cow; but she has a very intelligent face, and seems to be of a reflective cast of character. I doubt not that she will soon perceive the expediency of being on good terms with the rest of the sisterhood.

This innocent *jeu d'esprit* and the earlier note have been taken as evidence that from the first Hawthorne was contemptuous of Margaret, and that his dislike steadily grew until it exploded in the almost hysterical outbursts of malignity which he directed against her late in life. But the evidence that Hawthorne and Margaret felt friendship for each other, once he, like all her friends, had passed through the avenue of sphinxes which led to the inner temple where she was truly revealed, is far more weighty than any that can be mustered in support of this commonly held view.

Late that summer, when he had grown rather weary of the Farm, he noted his pleasure in a talk with Margaret and Emerson, who came "dressed like Christians" to a fancy dress party at the Farm. On another visit that she made to hold a Conversation for the Farmers, she found him suffering from a severe cold and insisted on making some gruel which she brought to him herself. If the gruel was unsatisfactory, he found her vivacious conversation more pleasant, though he was startled by her willingness to overset all human institutions and scatter them as with a wave of a fan. He began to respect her intellect, and she had made evident her good opinion of his writing in a review of his *Grandfather's Chair* tales in the *Dial* for January 1842. When Hawthorne finally mustered up his courage to propose to Sophia in May 1842, after three years of mute adoration, Sophia confided the secret of their engagement to Margaret on the day after she made her decision to accept him. In Margaret's reply, which offered her congratulations, she foresaw great happiness for the couple, since "if ever I saw a man who combined delicate tenderness to understand the heart of a woman, with quiet depth and manliness enough to satisfy her, it is Mr. Hawthorne."

The marriage took place that summer and the young couple established themselves in the Old Manse at Concord. Margaret had given them a bronze jar, which they kept filled with ferns and admired, as it set off the yellow paper which Sophia had put upon the walls to make their new home less dim and dismal. Even the music box to which Sophia danced, lent to them by Thoreau, had been given to the naturalist by Margaret's brother when he was being tutored for Harvard in Concord. Margaret was often there herself this summer, for her sister Ellen had just married the poet Ellery Channing and they had installed themselves in the red cottage on the turnpike. Ostensibly Margaret came to visit her good friend Emerson, but at heart she was worried about Ellen's marriage and wished to watch over it, for Ellery was something of a scapegrace and fell easily into lax, poetical ways. Margaret admired his poems, but as a member of the family he was to be as much of a thorn in her flesh as he had been in the Channings'. She was on friendly terms with the Hawthornes, and Nathaniel recorded a long account of a pleasant afternoon spent in her company that August. He had just returned a book he had borrowed from her to Emerson's house, when he came upon her reading in the Sleepy Hollow cemetery:

She said that no inhabitant of Concord ever visited Sleepy Hollow, when we saw a group of people entering the sacred precincts. Most of them followed a path which led them away from us; but an old man passed near by and smiled to see

HENRY DAVID THOREAU

Portrait by his sister Sophia

Margaret reclining on the ground and me sitting by her side. He made some remark about the beauty of the afternoon, and withdrew himself into the shadow of the wood. Then we talked about autumn, and about the pleasures of being lost in the woods, and about the crows, whose voices Margaret had heard; and about the experiences of early childhood, whose influence remains upon the character after the recollection of them has passed away; and about the sight of mountains from a distance, and the view from their summits; and about other matters of high and low philosophy. In the midst of our talk we heard footsteps above us, on the high bank; and while the person was still hidden among the trees, he called to Margaret, of whom he had gotten a glimpse. Then he emerged from the green shade, and behold! it was Mr. Emerson. He appeared to have had a pleasant time; for he said that there were muses in the woods today, and whispers to be heard in the breezes. It now being nearly six o'clock, we separated—Margaret and Mr. Emerson toward his home, and I toward mine.

Surely this is the record of a friendly and even affectionate relationship, since the old man was led to suppose that here was a pair of lovers and the staid Emerson to make jesting remarks. It would seem that Hawthorne had fallen somewhat under Margaret's spell, if he could spend an afternoon in philosophizing with her while his loving Sophia awaited him at home. There is evidence that he found her deeply sympathetic, because a few days later he wrote to her: "There is nobody to whom I would more willingly speak my mind, because I can be certain of being thoroughly understood." Margaret had talked with Sophia, suggesting that she and he might be willing to take Ellery and Ellen Channing under their roof, for the poet showed no signs of making any substantial effort to maintain a home. Hawthorne found Ellery a good companion for a fishing or boating expedition on the river, and he appreciated Margaret's good-hearted motive in making the suggestion, but he liked to preserve his solitude, with only Sophia at hand when he wanted a companion. In the following year, when she proposed Charles Newcomb as a boarder, he was far from being outraged by Margaret's meddling in his domestic matters, as many have thought, and wrote a most friendly refusal of her plan:

> How strange, when I should be so glad to do everything that you had the slightest wish for me to do, and when you are incapable of wishing anything that ought not to be! Whether or no you bear a negative more easily than other people, I certainly find it easier to to [sic] give you one; because you do not peep at matters through a narrow chink, but can take my view as perfectly as your own.

The remainder of the letter shows that the relations between the Hawthornes and Margaret were both close and intimate at this time. Several critics have blamed the break that was later made evident by Hawthorne's reflections on Margaret's European career on his resentment at this proffering of a busybody's good offices. But this letter of February 1843 offers no support to such a theory, nor do Hawthorne's references to Margaret in the notebooks of the following April. During the course of as good a talk as he ever had with Emerson, Margaret was discussed and Emerson remarked that she had "risen perceptibly into a higher state since their last meeting." And again, in commenting on the new issue of the *Dial*, he found the satisfaction in Margaret's article on Canova, "which is good," that was lacking in the discussion of Alcott. Their ways seem to have drifted apart after this, as Margaret became involved in activities outside the Boston world, but there was no conscious break in the goodwill that bound them together, for when her *Woman in the Nineteenth Century* was published two years later as a brochure in New York, the Hawthornes wrote a letter to her about it, and she replied from New York that at the moment she was weary of discussing it, but soon hoped to give them a viva-voce reply.

When she was in Concord at her sister Ellen's during 1844, she was a daily visitor at the Hawthornes' and had much to say about Sophia and little Una in her accounts of her doings there. As to Nathaniel, she wrote: "I feel more like a sister to H., or rather more that he might be a brother to me, than ever with any man before. Yet with him it is, though sweet, not deep kindred; at least, not deep as yet."

Margaret's own view of the relationship seems nearer the truth than the legend of enmity which sprang up after both of them were dead. For if there were any two beings in New England at this era who should have felt akin, they surely were Margaret Fuller and Nathaniel Hawthorne. The Puritan had set his stamp on both of them, and they were deeply idealistic, conscience-ridden, self-torturing, and introspective. They both had had lonely childhoods and adolescences, and the solitary hours that Hawthorne devoted for years to unsuccessful attempts at writing were in some measure matched by those Margaret gave to her studies and self-culture. Hawthorne remained a solitary all his life, but Margaret's drive to action and the recognition paid to her erudition brought her out into the world. The unhappiness which preyed on both of them throughout their lives was in large measure due to the struggle between the Puritan and the artist in their natures. They both felt a compelling urge to self-expression, although Margaret's found vent in several ways, while Hawthorne's was concentrated upon the literary. They both fought to escape from the bonds of their native Calvinism, although Hawthorne dwelt on it in his work after he had rejected it for himself, while Margaret escaped from it more fully and found other influences to replace it. They both had a great love of mystery, visions, dreams, symbols: the Gothic residue of Calvinism was strong in them. They both sought to escape from a land which offered little comfort to the artist, and Hawthorne may well have envied Margaret her earlier success in making good this escape. Their aesthetically starved natures both found comfort and delight in

Rome, although Hawthorne was perhaps too old, when he finally reached the Eternal City, to absorb its spirit as fully as Margaret did. Yet he may have been fortunate in this, for he did his best work before he left the America that he longed to escape from, while Margaret never did hers. They were both neurotic if brilliant personalities, and it is not surprising that there should have been a clash between them, although Margaret was never conscious of any such conflict. For all their similarities, there were nevertheless wide differences, and it may well have been that some of these grated unconsciously on Hawthorne as he worked and brooded in prosaic Massachusetts while she soared in the company of the great abroad. His fundamental melancholia was opposed to her alternate moods of ecstasy and depression; his inbred reticence to her yearning for self-revelation; his dislike for intellectual and Feminist-minded women to her idealization of them and to her struggle to approximate herself to the ideal. He may have been jealous of the fame which came so much more easily and earlier to her than it did to him, for he denied her talent, while she early recognized his. Somehow he never achieved fulfillment and with it happiness, while she did for a brief moment at the close of her life. He won in the end, although he never knew it, for she is remembered largely by his slanders, and his fame totally eclipses hers. His books were cast in the classic mold and lived; hers sprawled and died.

But Hawthorne did not fall into the mood to slander a dead friend until the dark years at the end of his life when his mind began to fail. His *Blithedale Romance* was published in 1852, five years after Brook Farm broke up and two years after Margaret's death. Its heroine, Zenobia, is as clearly drawn from Margaret as Blithedale is from Brook Farm, despite Higginson's protest that Margaret "had neither the superb beauty of Zenobia, nor her large fortune, nor her mysterious husband, nor her inclinations to suicide; nor was she a member of Brook Farm." He and many others among Margaret's friends denied the identification which leaps to the reader's mind, perhaps because the portrait is not uncritical of its original and because they felt that a decent reticence should be preserved about their dead friend, if it were not possible to heap praise upon her as her biographers did in the *Memoirs* published in this same year. But they did not read Hawthorne's preface to *Blithedale* carefully enough. He disclaimed any intent to criticize the Brook Farm experiment, but avowed his use of "the most romantic episode of his own life—essentially a day-dream and yet a fact"— as a theater in which the creatures of his brain could play their antics in a world between fiction and reality. He deliberately sought to avoid the contrasting of his characters with living mortals, and claimed the poetic license permitted to the romancer in Europe. But his memories of his life at the Farm were still lively, and were much invoked in the writing of his tale. Coverdale, who tells much of the story in the first person, is Hawthorne with a difference; and Zenobia is Margaret, with certain characteristics of Fanny Kemble, whom he had known in the Berkshires, and perhaps of Mrs. Barlow, whose physical charms threw a spell over most of the men at the Farm. As for Higginson's objections, Zenobia's beauty may have derived from either of these two women who had attracted Hawthorne, or it may be symbolic of the transfiguration that Margaret's friends noted in her when she was in an inspired mood. In any case, beauty was a conventional and necessary attribute for the heroine of a novel. Both Fanny Kemble and Mrs. Barlow were separated from their husbands, and both may be said to have enjoyed large fortunes by Hawthorne's standards. A mysterious husband and a large fortune are also romantic attributes for a heroine. Margaret's depressions were so severe as to suggest to her friends the possibility of her suicide, and if she was not a member of Brook Farm, she was much in evidence there and bound up with Hawthorne's memories of the place.

But there are many positive bits of evidence for the identification scattered through *Blithedale*. Early in the tale Coverdale is

asked whether he knows Zenobia. He replies that he expects to
meet her on the morrow, and asks whether his questioner is
interested in the advocacy of women's rights, or whether he has
a literary turn of mind. Later on, Coverdale remarks on "something imperial which her friends attributed to this lady's figure
and deportment," and on her "noble courage, conscious of no
harm and scorning the petty restraints which take the life and
color out of other women's conversation." When the waif
Priscilla joins the community, she has eyes only for Zenobia
and begs to be always near her. Noting this slavish adoration,
Coverdale remarks that "a brilliant woman is often the object
of the devoted admiration—it might almost be termed worship
or idolatry—of some young girl, who has perhaps beheld the
cynosure only at an awful distance and has as little hope of
personal intercourse as of climbing to the stars. . . . There
occurred to me no mode of accounting for Priscilla's behavior,
except by supposing that she has read some of Zenobia's stories
. . . or her tracts in defence of her sex, and had come hither
with the sole purpose of being her slave." Zenobia, who wore
an exotic hothouse flower in her hair as a symbol of the luxuriant
pride and pomp of her character, brought gruel made by her
own hands to Coverdale's sick chamber and quickened his pulse
with her vivacious conversation. He judged that:

> Her poor little stories and tracts never did justice to her
> intellect. It was only the lack of a fitter avenue that drove her
> to seek development in literature. She was made (among a
> thousand other things she might have been) for a stump
> oratress. I recognized no severe culture in Zenobia; her mind
> was full of weeds. It startled me sometimes, in my state of
> moral as well as bodily faint-heartedness, to observe the
> hardihood of her philosophy. She made no scruple of over-
> setting all human institutions, and scattering them as with a
> breeze of her fan. A female reformer, in her attacks upon
> society, has an instinctive sense of where the life lies, and

is inclined to aim directly at that spot. Especially the relation between the sexes is naturally among the earliest to attract her notice.

Later on, the reader is thrown off the scent for a moment by a reference on Coverdale's part to Priscilla's resemblance to Margaret, "one of the most gifted women of the age," in a certain curve of the shoulders and in a "partial closing of the eyes, which seemed to look more penetratingly into my own eyes through the narrowed aperture, than if they had been open at full width." Zenobia reads the romances of George Sand; her "inequalities of temper had been rather difficult for her friends to bear." She declaims against the world's injustice to women, and cries out: "If I live another year, I will lift up my own voice in behalf of woman's wider liberty!" She mourns that the pen is not for woman: "Her power is too natural and immediate. It is with the living voice alone that she can compel the world to recognize the light of her intellect and the depth of her heart!" She appears at a masque in the character of a queen, in a fanciful costume, bejeweled, with her eyes on fire and a crimson spot on either cheek, so that Coverdale "at first doubted whether it was not artificial." She was truly a magnificent woman, and the stage would have been her proper sphere. And in the end Zenobia drowns herself.

No other woman of Hawthorne's acquaintance but Margaret Fuller could have supplied the original of Zenobia. These small details add up to a vivid and faithful portrait of Margaret, more complete in some respects than that supplied by her professed biographers. The sympathetic yet penetrating picture of Margaret, based upon her life and works as they had been revealed to Hawthorne and reflected on by him, supplies evidence that he too had felt that kinship of their minds of which Margaret was conscious. Two of the details are particularly interesting: the mention of Margaret's name with reference to Priscilla and the manner of Zenobia's death. No other person

connected with Brook Farm is mentioned in the book by his
right name. Hawthorne may have introduced the reference
purposely because the Zenobia-Margaret identification was too
evident as his portrait grew more faithful than he at first intended, or it may have slipped in unconsciously because his
thoughts were much concerned with Margaret as he wrote the
book in the year following her death. Then the germ of the
scene in *Blithedale* in which a search is made for Zenobia's
drowned body is to be found in a real incident of this sort in
which Hawthorne took part in Concord and which stamped on
his brain the horror of death by water. It is curious that he
should make his heroine perish as Margaret had, when the
resemblance was already so marked. He did full justice to his
dead friend in this fiction, and it seems a pity that the records
of their friendly relationship did not close upon this note. His
reputation did not gain by the revelation after his death that
he was capable of slandering the name of a woman, long dead,
who had been his friend and had helped to build that reputation with her pen. To be sure, it was recorded in his private
journal, and not destined for publication, and made just as the
world which he had always seen in a distorted way was beginning to go completely out of focus for his eyes. And so that
story is told elsewhere in this book.

CHAPTER VIII

The West and Feminism

Say, is it not deeper and truer to live than to think? These chasings up and down the blind alleys of thought neither show the centre nor the circumference.—M. F.

IN THE spring of 1843 Margaret felt crushed by the burden of her activities. She became increasingly dissatisfied with her Boston life, and desired some change. Just as she was conscious of this desire, her old friend James Freeman Clarke, with whom she had first studied German, asked her to join him and his sister Sarah in a trip to the West. With the invitation he sent her—delicately, with a poem—fifty dollars, which would make the trip possible for her. The prospect of such a tour, in the company of close friends—for Sarah Clarke, who was beginning to show promise as a painter, had been a faithful follower of the Conversations and shared Margaret's interest in Dante—was too much for Margaret's pride, and she accepted the gift and the invitation. She was curious to see the region into which so many New Englanders were pouring at this time, in search of richer farm land than the rocky hillsides at home. Her uncle William Williams Fuller had practiced law for many years in the town of Oregon in northern Illinois. The Clarkes were now half Westerners, for James had occupied a pulpit in St. Louis soon after he entered the Unitarian ministry, and his mother and sister lived with two of his brothers, who had settled in Chicago in 1835. So the travelers had a personal interest in the frontier region they were to visit, in addition to the attractions of the trip and the opportunity to satisfy their curiosity about the land which was beginning to depopulate New England.

They went first to Niagara Falls and thence by water to Chicago. Margaret was struck by the absence of mountains and valleys; everywhere she looked there was rolling prairie. It was all new to her, for in previous summer excursions she had got no farther from her native parts than Nahant or Newport or Trenton Falls, and it was exciting:

> I would ascend the roof of the house where we lived and pass many hours, needing no sight but the moon reigning in the heavens or starlight falling upon the lake, until all the lights were out in the island grove of men beneath my feet, and felt that nearer heaven there was nothing but this lovely, still reception on the earth; no towering mountains, no deep tree-shadows, nothing but plain earth and water bathed in light.

Soon a party consisting of Margaret and Sarah Clarke, with William Clarke as guide and companion, set off on an expedition through northern Illinois. They traveled in a large wagon, well stocked with all manner of provisions and drawn by two strong horses who could overcome the mudholes and stumps which were to be encountered. They headed west from Chicago toward the Fox River, and at the end of the first day reached the little town of Geneva. Here they visited the Reverend Augustus Conant, who had come to the West before he was twenty-one. Later in his life he became interested in Unitarianism through reading an article of Clarke's in the *Western Messenger,* and had gone back east to Cambridge to study for the ministry. Upon his ordination he had returned to Geneva, where he was pastor of a little group of Boston Unitarians. As befitted a pioneer minister, he was a man of his hands, a carpenter and hunter, as well as a preacher and student. Margaret found him "just such a teacher as is wanted in these regions." Whether because of the charms of Mr. Conant or the rich booty of fish which the gentlemen found in the Fox, the party lingered in Geneva a day or two, before continuing southward along the river. Once they resumed their journey, they spent a night with a cultivated Englishman, whose home boasted a large library and whose convent-bred daughters somewhat awed Margaret by combining a knowledge of French and music with the ability "to take care of the milk-room and kill the rattlesnakes that assailed their poultry-yard." Here they found the melting-pot at work, for settled near their English host were Norwegian peasants, still wearing native costumes, and a Welsh family.

They turned away from the river and put up the next night at a tavern·in one of the groves of great trees which stood out like islands in the sea of prairie. The tavern was crowded and the ladies were obliged to sleep in the bar-room, Margaret making her bed on the table that had been used for supper. There was an Englishwoman who found it difficult to adapt herself to such indecorum and sat up all night:

> . . . wrapped in her blanket-shawl and with a neat lace cap upon her head—so that she would have looked perfectly the lady if anyone had come in—shuddering and listening. . . . She watched, as her parent country watches the seas, that nobody may do wrong in any case, and deserved to have met some interruption, she was so well prepared. However, there was none, other than from the nearness of some twenty sets of powerful lungs.

The following day they crossed the Rock River and reached the property of an Irish gentleman named Alexander Charters, who had put his home at their service for as long as they wished to linger. They stayed three days here, and Margaret wrote some verses entitled "The Western Eden," which describe the charms of the spot. Then they journeyed on to Oregon, where Margaret's uncle lived until his death later in this same year. Here there is a high bluff, known as the Eagle's Nest, which towers above the Rock River. The beauty of the countryside was making Margaret brim over with poetic impressions, and as she sat on this height she composed the stanzas of "Ganymede to His Eagle." The Fourth of July fell during their stay in Oregon, and the happiness of the pioneers in their celebration of the holiday aroused Margaret to an appreciation of the advantages of Western life. She found little to criticize, except for the lot of women, who were unfitted by education as ornaments of society for the harsh realities of frontier life. Margaret railed that "methods copied from the education of some English Lady Augusta are as ill suited to the daughter of an Illinois farmer as satin shoes to climb Indian mounds!" Her mind was still at work on the Feminist ideas which she had just expressed in her article for the July *Dial*, "The Great Lawsuit: Man vs. Men, Woman vs. Women." After leaving Oregon behind, they continued on through the Black Hawk country to Belvidere. They did not pause in this small town for any length of time, but it must have impressed Margaret favorably, for it was here that her brother Arthur came in the following October to conduct an academy, and Margaret's aid helped to make this venture possible. From Belvidere they returned to Chicago.

In Chicago Margaret reread *Philip van Artevelde*, and as she watched the Hoosier wagons coming and going and the great lake boats bringing hordes of German, Dutch, and Irish immigrants to the new farm country, she began to speculate about the future of America. This land, "still nearer the acorn" than her native New England, which was so self-conscious about its youth in comparison to the old world across the sea, teemed with life and energy that promised great things if properly directed. She wondered when America would have such a man as the Hollander of her book:

It is what she needs; no thin Idealist, no coarse Realist,

but a man whose eye reads the heavens while his feet step firmly on the ground and his hands are strong and dexterous for the use of human implements. A man religious, virtuous, and sagacious; a man of universal sympathies, but self-possessed; a man who knows the region of emotion, though he is not its slave; a man to whom this world is no mere spectacle or fleeting shadow, but a great, solemn game, to be played with good heed, for its stakes are of eternal value, yet who, if his play be true, heeds not what he loses by the falsehood of others; a man who hives from the past, yet knows that its honey can but moderately avail him; whose comprehensive eye scans the present, neither infatuated by its golden lures, nor chilled by its many ventures; who possesses prescience, the gift which discerns tomorrow—when there is such a man for America, the thought which urges her on will be expressed.

It would seem that her first impression of the bustling West had made her somewhat skeptical of the Boston and Concord scale of values.

After a brief period of rest, her party journeyed to Milwaukee, which was then filled with immigrants, like Chicago, but was much more of a frontier town. Wisconsin was still a territory and Indians were much in evidence, although they had already been enfeebled and degraded by contact with white civilization. A day's drive in the country here prompted Margaret to remark that "it was pleasant, but almost as tame as New England." Here, too, she met a contented woman, "the only one I heard of out there." This was an Englishwoman, who said that she had endured so much suffering in her own country that the trials of the new land seemed trivial. But Margaret found that it was not so with others, who were confined to a "comfortless and laborious indoor life," and felt moved to remark darkly: "But it need not be so, long!"

In search of contact with a wilder West, Margaret went on

from Milwaukee to the island of Mackinaw, where many members of the Chippewa and Ottawa tribes were assembled at
this time to receive their annual payment from the United
States Government. She was greatly interested in the Indians
and their picturesque manners; she only wished that a Walter
Scott were there to draw inspiration from these "weather-
beaten, sullen, but eloquent figures." But the condition of
women in most of the tribes was revolting to her Feminist
mind, and she was dismayed by the low state to which the
Indian had already been reduced by the white man. The
strange alliance of trader and missionary was a blasphemous
mockery of Christianity in her eyes, and she was moved to
plead that steps be taken to save the fast dying savage culture
before it disappeared entirely. She passed some ten days here
alone, making excursions in the company of Indian guides. She
endured the hazards of shooting rapids in a canoe with a calm
not to be expected in one who had led so sheltered a life. Reluctantly she returned to Chicago and traveled back over the
lakes to Buffalo, where the account of this trip given in her
first original book, *Summer on the Lakes,* concludes.

As soon as she got home, she began to revise her journal of
the excursion for publication. She found it necessary to consult
reference works, and for this purpose was the first woman
reader admitted to the library of Harvard College. Her visits
there revived the memory of Hannah Adams working in the
sacred precincts of the Athenaeum, where the disturbed authorities had been obliged to lock her in because it was not
polite to lock her out. Though that had been some time before,
the sight of literary ladies at work in libraries was unfamiliar
enough to cause a stir among the faculty and students. Miss
Fuller's absent-minded ways may have made the visits more
notable than they otherwise would have been, for she was so
concerned with lofty matters that everyday things were apt to
escape her attention. On her return from the West she had
stayed with Emerson's brother William at Staten Island, and

visited the fort there in company with Thoreau, who was acting as a tutor to the family during his only period of residence outside of Concord. But Margaret forgot to pay the driver of her carriage, and was obliged to write and ask Henry to do it for her after she returned home. The work on the book, which was to be only a short one, went slowly, and it was not finished until the following spring. Margaret wrote the last line on her birthday, May 23, and was glad to reach the end. Writing was always tedious to her, and at this period still positively painful. It had been trying, too, to come back into the old narrow world of Boston after her escape from it had provided contact with a less circumscribed life, to be beset by family difficulties, and to exert once more the energy necessary to conduct the Conversations and provide a living for those dependent on her. But the little book, born after such labor, was to release her from the world which now seemed like a prison to her, though once she had longed to be a member of it. For the book caught the eye of Horace Greeley, who shared the enthusiasm for the West that its author displayed. It reinforced the high opinion of her talents that he had formed during his visits to Brook Farm and from his wife's praises of this new goddess of the intellect who held sway over her Boston friends. Shortly after the book's publication in the summer of 1844, Greeley offered Margaret the post of literary critic on his *Tribune* and a place in his New York home. Margaret was to see little more of Boston, the battlefield of her early struggles and the scene of her first triumphs.

Orestes Brownson wrote a fitting epitaph for her Boston career in a review of *Summer on the Lakes* in the October number of his quarterly:

Miss Fuller is a woman of more than ordinary abilities, and, we are told, of rare attainments. She is said to possess remarkable conversational powers, and her conversations are represented by her friends to be in the highest degree brilliant, instructive, and inspiring. . . . Her writings we do not like. We dislike them exceedingly. They are sent out in a slipshod style, and have a certain toss of the head about them which offends us . . . wholly deficient in a pure, correct taste, and especially in that tidiness we always look for in women. . . . She is a heathen priestess, though of what god or goddesses we will not pretend to say. She is German, heart and soul. . . .

No person has appeared among us whose conversation and morals have done more to corrupt the minds and hearts of our Boston community. For religion she substitutes art; for the Divinity . . . she would give us merely the Beautiful. This high-priestess of American Transcendentalism has read much . . . but the materials she has connected lie fermenting in her intellectual stomach, and generate all manner of strange and diseased fancies. She is ill at ease. . . . She now reminds us of the old heathen Euripides, now of the modern skeptic Byron, and finally of the cold indifferentism of Goethe dashed on the warm woman's heart of Bettina Brentano. We see in her a melancholy instance of the fate which awaits a gifted woman in an age of infidelity. All she needs, to be the ornament of her sex, and a crown of blessings to her country, to be at peace with herself and the world, is the firm, old-fashioned Catholic faith in the Gospel. Her soul would then burst its fetters, and her powers would find free scope, and her heart the rest after which it yearns.

But for all his truculent criticism and his advocacy for Margaret of the Catholicism which he himself embraced in this same month, the journalist in Brownson recognized "flashes of a rare genius," "uncommon and versatile powers" in her book. The review is extraordinarily just and penetrating.

The book had been written during a winter of tedious toil. But in the spring Margaret was able to congratulate herself that she had done all she could during the past months, for she was now free of debt. She intended to remain so, for she dreaded debt as much as a Dutch burgomaster might. Her plans for her family had worked out as she wished, and the little household went smoothly as a wheel under her management. Ellen was safely married, even if Ellery was a none-too-reliable husband. Arthur had given up his school-teaching and had entered the Cambridge Theological Seminary; and Richard was attending the Harvard Law School and working in his uncle's law office. Eugene and William had long since left the family nest and established themselves elsewhere. Only Mrs. Fuller and the youngest son, Lloyd, who was somewhat unbalanced and had been a constant source of trouble at the Brook Farm school where Margaret sent him, was left to be taken care of. Margaret thought that it was time that she should be free of the burden she had carried since her father's death, and found her older brothers sympathetic to her desire.

You wish . . . that I was not obliged to toil and spin, but could live for a while like the lilies. I wish so, too, for life has fatigued me, my strength is little, and the present state of my mind demands repose and refreshment, that it may ripen some fruit worthy of the long and deep experiences through which I have passed. I do not regret that I have shared the labors and cares of the suffering million, and have acquired a feeling sense of the conditions under which the Divine has appointed the development of the human. Yet, if our family affairs could now be so arranged that I might be tolerably tranquil for the next six or eight years, I should go out of life better satisfied with the page I have turned in it, than I shall if I must still toil on. A noble career is yet before me, if I can be unimpeded by cares. I have given almost all my young energies to personal relations; but at present I feel inclined to impel the general stream of thought. Let my nearest friends also wish that I should now take share in more public life.

So it was determined to break up the home which Margaret had maintained, leaving her free while Mrs. Fuller could visit in turn her scattered children. After Margaret went to New York, Richard headed the family and acquired a home on Prospect Street in Cambridgeport, in exchange for the old house on Cherry Street. Greeley's offer promised to give realization to Margaret's dream of a more public life and an opportunity to impel the general stream of thought. It was to lead to that noble career of which Margaret was so sure, but the toil it demanded interfered with her other plans. And the six years she had left to live were anything but tranquil, though she was free of family concerns at last.

Once the work on her book was over, Margaret realized just how exhausted she was and feared that she might not be able to accept Greeley's offer, despite the attractions it offered of an assured position, good pay, and a chance to see how the world went outside Boston. She wrote: "I am so unwell that I can scarcely keep up the spring of my spirits, and sometimes fear that I cannot go through with the engagements of the winter. But I have never stopped yet in fulfilling what I have undertaken, and hope that I shall not be compelled to now." In order to build up her health for her new post in New York, she spent seven weeks that autumn at Fishkill on the Hudson with her friend Caroline Sturgis. Here, amid the glorious scenery of the Highlands, which is at its best in Indian summer, Margaret had leisure to recruit her strength and to think calmly about her life. She realized that she must strive "to be patient to the very depths of the heart, to expect no hasty realizations, not to make her own plan her law of life, but to learn the law and plan of God," for otherwise she would wear herself out uselessly. She saw clearly that her moments of intense passion must be modified into a gentler, steadier energy. One night she lay on a sofa and watched the fire:

. . . and saw how the flame shot up from beneath, through

the mass of coal that had been piled above. It shot up in wild beautiful jets, and then unexpectedly sank again, and all was black, unsightly and forlorn. And thus, I thought, is it with my life at present. Yet if the fire beneath persists and conquers, that black mass will become all radiant, life-giving, fit for the altar or the domestic hearth.

For all her realization that she thought and felt too much for her own good and her intention to drift along lazily, gathering force slowly, during these vacation weeks, she could not silence the ceaseless eloquence of her nature. On the first rainy day at Fishkill she began to revise and expand her *Dial* article, "The Great Lawsuit," into book form. Her head began to teem with other plans, "of which there will be time for very few only to take form," despite the almost platitudinous good sense with which she had written in her journal of her object in spending these weeks in relaxation.

Her reading during this "vacation" consisted of the four books of Confucius, the *Desatir,* some of Taylor's translations from the Greek, a book on Scandinavian mythology, Möhler's *Symbolism,* Fourier's *Nouveau Monde Industriel,* and Landor's *Pentameron.*

Despite all these serious occupations, Margaret managed to recruit new strength during these weeks at Fishkill, and when she returned to Boston for a brief stay before going to New York, she was able to finish the job of revision and expansion more easily and rapidly than she had expected. When she finished the book in November, she felt "a delightful glow, as if I had put a good deal of my true life into it, and as if, should I go away now, the measure of my footprint would be left upon the earth." Her feelings about writing were changing:

> Formerly the pen did not seem to me an instrument capable of expressing the spirit of a life like mine. An enchanter's mirror, on which with a word could be made to rise all the apparitions of the universe grouped in new relations; a magic

ring, that could transport the wearer, himself invisible, into each region of grandeur or beauty; a divining rod, to tell where lie the secret fountains of refreshment; a wand, to evoke elemental spirits—only such as these seemed fit to embody one's thought with sufficient swiftness and force. In earlier years I aspired to wield the sceptre or the lyre; for I loved with wise design and irresistible command to mold many to one common purpose, and it seemed all that man could desire to breathe in music and speak in words the harmonies of the universe. But the golden lyre was not given to my hand, and I am but the prophecy of a poet. Let me use, then, the slow pen. I will make no formal vow to the long-scorned Muse; I assume no garland; I dare not even dedicate myself as a novice; I can promise neither patience nor energy —but I will court excellence as far as a humble heart and open eye can merit it, and if I may gradually grow to some degree of worthiness in this mode of expression, I shall be grateful.

There is a deal of good sense in this manifesto to herself, despite its bombast. It was high time she put aside her romantic notions and stopped thinking of herself as a queen and a sibyl, if she were to earn her living by her pen. The ex-editor of the *Dial* had to reconcile herself to writing for the daily press, and could no longer afford to find a certain vulgarity in writing for the multitude. She was right about being "only the prophecy of a poet": her lyrics are stillborn and for the most part completely devoid of true poetic feeling. They are largely set pieces, like those she included in *Summer on the Lakes,* and are labored productions, overburdened with tags of learning. She badly needed the training in simple, straightforward writing that she got from her work on the *Tribune,* and it made her a far better writer than if she had continued to produce rather precious pieces when she felt in an inspired mood. It gave her the facility of expression that she had lacked before, and that she only began to experience at this time.

Her book was called *Woman in the Nineteenth Century,** although Margaret preferred the title she had given to the original version when it appeared in the *Dial*, "The Great Lawsuit: Man vs. Men, Woman vs. Women." But her friends had persuaded her to abandon this resounding mouthful, with its echo of the language of her father's profession. Even in its final, expanded form, *Woman* is little more than a pamphlet, and today its theses seem curiously mild and it is difficult to understand the furor it aroused. But it was full of intellectual dynamite at the time it was published, and for some decades thereafter. Julia Ward Howe, an ardent Feminist herself, wrote forty years after Margaret's book was published: "Nothing that has been written or said in later days has made its teaching superfluous." It was the first considered statement of Feminism to be made by an American. Its only predecessor was Mary Wollstonecraft's *Vindication of the Rights of Woman*, which had appeared some fifty years before. The two women had much in common in their personal circumstances, but the emphasis of their books is different. Mary Wollstonecraft, as a member of the Godwin-Paine group, was concerned with the abstract rights of woman, as the men of that circle were concerned with the abstract rights of man. The battle for these rights had largely been fought and won during the following half-century, and now the struggle was for a different goal. Margaret belonged to a group much influenced by socialism, and her discussion of the condition of woman turns upon the ideas of "attractive industry" and "liberty of law," notions borrowed from Fourier as Mary Wollstonecraft borrowed hers from Rousseau. Margaret's book was a broad and sweeping treatment of the question of feminine shortcomings and the reasons for them. The arguments against the emancipation of woman are refuted, with illustrations

* See Appendix, p. 289.

drawn from the careers of prominent women in history and from the general condition of woman at various times and in various cultures. In the preface to the book, which is dated November 1844, Margaret lays down her fundamental proposition:

> . . . while it is the destiny of Man in the course of the ages to ascertain and fulfill the law of his being, so 'that his life shall be seen as a whole to be that of an angel or messenger, the action of prejudices and passions which attend in the day the growth of the individual is constantly obstructing the holy work that is to make the earth a part of heaven. By Man I mean both man and woman; these are two halves of one thought. I lay no especial stress on the welfare of either. I believe that the development of one cannot be effected without that of the other. My highest wish is that this truth shall be distinctly and rationally apprehended, and the conditions of life and freedom recognized as the same for the daughters and the sons of time; twin exponents of a divine thought.

And she blamed the present conditions of women on their own willing subserviency; the epigraphs of her book were: "Frailty, thy name is Woman" and "The Earth Waits for her Queen."

Margaret preached no mere Feminist version of the prevailing perfectionism of her day, for she felt that "never were lungs so puffed with the wind of declamation, on moral and religious subjects, as now," and that "hypocrisy is the most hopeless as well as the meanest of crimes." What she wanted to do was to

> ascertain the true nature of woman; give her legitimate hopes, and a standard within herself; marriage and all other relations would by degrees be harmonized with these . . . as a nature to grow, as an intellect to discern, as a soul to live freely and unimpeded, to unfold such powers as were given her when we left our common home.

Woman's customary domestic occupations were worthy of

WOMAN

IN THE

NINETEENTH CENTURY.

BY S. MARGARET FULLER.

"Frei durch Vernunft, stark durch Gesetze,
Durch Sanftmuth gross, und reich durch Schatze,
Die lange Zeit dein Busen dir verschwieg."

"I meant the day-star should not brighter rise,
Nor lend like influence from its lucent seat;
I meant she should be courteous, facile, sweet,
Free from that solemn vice of greatness, pride;
I meant each softest virtue there should meet,
Fit in that softer bosom to reside;
Only a (heavenward and instructed) soul
I purposed her, that should, with even powers,
The rock, the spindle, and the shears control
Of destiny, and spin her own free hours."

NEW-YORK:

GREELEY & McELRATH, 160 NASSAU-STREET.

W. Osborn, Printer, 88 William-street.

1845.

WOMAN IN THE NINETEENTH CENTURY

Title-page of Greeley's first edition

respect, but "these 'functions' must not be a drudgery or enforced necessity, but a part of life. . . . Penelope is no more meant for a baker or weaver solely than Ulysses for a cattleherd." But women did not want any more idolization than they received from their lovers; more power than they could gain as coquettes, shrews, or good cooks. They did not envy men the wealth, fame, and authority which were largely denied them. What they wanted was something more fundamental and the "birthright of every being capable of receiving it: the religious, the intelligent freedom of the universe to use its means, to learn its secret, as far as Nature has enabled them, with God alone as their guide and judge."

Margaret felt that such beings as Mary Wollstonecraft and George Sand—and perhaps herself—"rich in genius, of most tender sympathies, capable of high virtue and a chastened harmony, ought not to find themselves, by birth, in a place so narrow that in breaking bonds they become outlaws." The harsh reception they received from the world might be laid to man's refusal to consent to improvement of the condition of woman, but these women of genius were also in some measure to blame. They were enslaved by a passionate sensibility; they fed on flattery and wished to win admiration as women as well as minds. To Margaret, "the intellect . . . is not to be cultivated merely that Woman may be a more valuable companion to Man, but because the Power who gave a power by its mere existence signifies that it must be brought out toward perfection." She would have Woman dedicate herself to the Sun of Truth, "free from compromise, from complaisance, from helplessness, because I would have her good enough and strong enough to love one and all beings, from the fullness, not the poverty of her being."

Margaret wrote much of herself into this book. She made free use of incidents from her own life to illustrate her points, and the general emotional feeling is her own at this stage in her life. There is a rather passionate defense of old maids and bachelors, with emphasis on the former, whom she terms "mental and moral Ishmaelites," on the ground that they have the same advantages as the saints and geniuses of the past who chose solitude that their lives might be richer. To her the only remedy to evil institutions and external ills lies within the individual character, and she painted a picture of the ideal Feminist:

> Those who would reform the world must show that they do not speak in the heat of wild impulse; their lives must be unstained by passionate error; they must be severe law-givers to themselves. They must be religious students of the divine purpose with regard to man, if they would not confound the fancies of the day with the requisitions of eternal good. Their liberty must be the liberty of law and knowledge.

In Swedenborg's view of women, and in that of Quakerism also, she found no obstacle offered to woman's progress, though she found that despite the original purity of thought in Quakerism, its scope was too narrow. Fourier she judged to have a superficial mind, preoccupied with the outward needs of man and neglectful of the more important inward needs. Goethe's view of woman was to her the most satisfactory offered by the moderns, and the Natalia of *Wilhelm Meisters Lehrjahre* the most perfect embodiment of the wisdom that arises from serenity. Not content with discussing these views, which came from sources regarded with strong disfavor by the conventional, Margaret dared to deal with such matters as prostitution, the double standard, passion, and the true nature of marriage. Such topics were taboo even in conversation, much less in print, in those days, and Margaret's rebellious boldness in airing them was regarded as highly shocking.

Woman in the Nineteenth Century was published in New York early in 1845. It was a tract for the times, and it caught on. Copies of the book reached remote spots on the expanding frontier, and it was pirated in London. It was praised and denounced on all sides, until Margaret grew weary with it and all that had been said and written about it. The book served her as introduction to the intellectual circles of New York and later of England and the Continent. It is the only one of her works which is generally remembered, although it is little read today. It was the fundamental text of the early Feminists, and the later Declaration of Sentiments stems directly from it. It brought Margaret recognition as the most distinguished advocate of the Feminist cause in America and established her as a writer. Her place was made, and the long struggle for fame was over. But she had only six more years left to live and enjoy that hard-won place, and these years were to be stormy ones for her.

When she left Boston for New York, Margaret gave her journals to her mother. On the leaf that contained the last entry before her departure to begin her public life, Mrs. Fuller wrote:

> I commend my first-born child to the guidance of her Father and mine . . . with many acknowledgements for the love and tender care I have experienced at the hands of my dear daughter, praying God to do more and better for her than I can ask or think, and to return her again to me in his good time.

The brief, crowded span of years that remained to Margaret held many things for her, but she was not to be restored to her mother.

III

FEMINISM AND FRUSTRATION

1844–1847

CHAPTER IX

Horace Greeley's "Tribune"

> *I have no real hold on life—no real permanent connection with any soul. I seem a wandering Intelligence driven from spot to spot that I may learn all secrets and fulfill a circle of knowledge.* —M. F.

THE *New York Tribune* was in its fourth year of existence when Margaret joined its staff in December 1844. It was a one-man paper: Horace Greeley was the soul and body of the *Tribune* and gave it his own crusading and reforming bent. He had made it a Liberal Whig paper in general policy, and strove particularly to reach the feminine audience to which none of the other newspapers catered. Its columns brimmed over with articles designed "to advance the interests of the people and to promote their moral, social, and political well-being." More space was devoted to literary topics than in any other journal, and the *Weekly Tribune* provided Margaret with one of the best mediums of criticism then available, from the point of view of circulation and remuneration. Greeley's own interest in social and economic reforms was mirrored in lively discussions of such matters in the pages of the *Tribune*. He had a large circle of friends, most of whom shared these interests and contributed to the *Tribune* on such subjects. The group included Albert Brisbane, the American apostle of Fourierism; Marcus Spring, a philanthropic merchant; and Margaret's friend William Henry Channing, the young socialistic minister. Brisbane wrote articles on Fourierism which appeared on the front page of the *Tribune*, although he paid Greeley for the space he used. Both Marcus

Spring and Greeley were deeply interested in the North American Phalanx at Red Bank, New Jersey. This community was
one of the most notable of the social experiments, and survived
for twelve years while the average life of these ventures was
only two. Channing and Margaret collaborated on a survey of
the New York public institutions which launched the *Tribune*
on another reforming campaign. Since Greeley devoted himself
passionately to one cause after another, it was fortunate that he
had a silent partner, a Mr. McElrath, who had a practical bent
and kept the *Tribune's* wheels going round during the editor's
idealistic crusades.

Greeley's home, for all intents and purposes, was the *Tribune*
office, although he had recently acquired a spacious old house,
with some eight acres of land about it, on the shores of the
East River at Turtle Bay. He had exhausted himself in the
campaign which resulted in the election of Polk to the Presidency, and his friends had advised him to move away from
his work. For thirteen years he had lived only a few yards from
his office, and like most country boys who come to New York,
he had loved the sensation of being in the midst of the city's
hubbub. He had followed his friends' advice, however, and
acquired this place in the country, which he called the Farm
(he never forgot that he had been a Vermont farmer's boy,
particularly in campaign years). He found it hard to accustom
himself to the peace and quiet of Turtle Bay, and spent so
much of his time at the office that Margaret and he "scarcely
met save at breakfast," although she was a member of his
household. Mrs. Greeley, who had been left much alone because
of her husband's preoccupation with his work, was delighted
at the new addition to the family. She had a great admiration
for Margaret, who privately observed that her hostess was "a
typical Yankee schoolmistress, crazy for learning." To have this
paragon of feminine intellect in her home was enough for Mrs.
Greeley, and the housekeeping was allowed to go on, as Margaret remarked, in "Castle Rackrent style." The new member of

HORACE GREELEY

Engraving by J. C. Buttre

the household soon gave up trying to better matters, when she discovered that "things would not stay put" despite her efforts. The prophet of feminine emancipation was the staid domestic influence in this odd home.

Margaret liked both the Greeleys and found the Farm very much to her taste. In a letter to a Boston friend she described her new home:

> This place is to me entirely charming; it is completely in the country and all around is so bold and free. It is two miles or more from the thickly settled parts of New York, but omnibuses and cars give constant access to the city, and while I can readily see what and whom I will, I can command time and retirement. Stopping on the Harlem road, you enter a lane nearly a quarter of a mile long, and going by a small brook and pond that locks in the place, and ascending a slightly rising ground, get sight of the house, which, old-fashioned and of mellow tint, fronts on a flower garden filled with shrubs, large vines, and trim box borders. On both sides of the house are beautiful trees standing fair, full grown, and free. Passing through a wide hall, you come out on a piazza stretching the whole length of the house, where one can walk in all weathers; and thence, by a step or two, on a lawn with picturesque masses of rocks, shrubs, and trees overlooking the East River. Gravel paths lead by several turns down the steep bank to the water's edge, where round the rocky point a small bay curves, in which boats are lying. And owing to the currents and the set of the tide, the sails glide sidelong, seeming to greet the house as they pass by. The beauty here, seen by moonlight, is truely transporting. I enjoy it greatly, and the genius loci receives me as to a home.

She enjoyed the Farm so much that she was apt to remain there, pleading a headache, when she should have been at the *Tribune* office. Margaret's periodic inability to write her three

columns a week was strange to Greeley, who thought nothing
of filling ten columns daily, regardless of nerves or moods. He
blamed her frequent indispositions on her lavish use of tea and
coffee, both of which he himself refused to touch as a matter of
principle. But at their meetings at the breakfast table, Margaret
"declined being lectured on the food or beverage she saw fit to
take," when Greeley suggested that the cause of her headache
was "her strong potations of the Chinese leaf the night before."
He found her "mentally the best instructed woman in America;
while she was physically one of the least enviable—a prey to
spinal affliction, nervous disorder, and protracted, fearfully tor-
tured headaches."

It was distinctly annoying to him to discover that these ail-
ments, which often kept her from the office, did not interfere
with tea parties at the Farm, where Margaret held court for
feminine admirers, like an empress receiving her subjects. Besides, he disliked the atmosphere of "Oriental adoration" which
prevailed on these occasions. Her Feminism was a bit too much
for him, although he was the declared friend of the movement.
He found her inconsistent in asking equal rights with men in
the affairs of the world, while she wished to retain all the little
courtesies that men pay to women as the weaker sex. He soon
fell into the habit of repeating one of her ringing phrases from
Woman in the Nineteenth Century, "Let them be sea captains
if they will!" whenever Margaret waited for him to open a door
for her.

But the reception given to her book when it appeared in
New York that February, and fuller acquaintance with its
author, allayed Horace Greeley's early misgivings about the
new member of his staff and household. The storm of praise
and criticism which arose brought the *Tribune's* new literary
critic into prominence and gave her an open sesame to the
intellectual circles of New York. Greeley himself judged
Woman in the Nineteenth Century thus: "No woman, no man,
ever read it without profit; but many have closed it with but

vague and dim ideas of what ought to be done." Margaret he deemed to be "a philanthropist, a critic, a relentless destroyer of shams and traditions; not a creator, a legislator." His opinion of Margaret rose steadily as he came to know her better; what at first seemed to him blemishes in her character were seen in "new and brighter aspects in the light of her radiant and beautiful soul." He found much to say of "her wonderful range of capacities, of experiences, of sympathies . . . adapted to every condition and phase of humanity." To him Margaret was "the most remarkable and in some respects the greatest woman whom America has yet known . . . the loftiest, bravest soul that has yet irradiated the form of an American woman." Her inability to labor as incessantly as he did, her need for attendance and care, could be excused in one who, "had she condescended to appear before the footlights, would soon have been recognized as the first actress of the nineteenth century." And he very shrewdly observed that "noble and great as she was, a good husband and two or three bouncing babies would have emancipated her from a deal of cant and nonsense."

Without consciously realizing it, Margaret put aside much "cant and nonsense" in her first few months away from the idealism and mysticism which were then so prevalent in Boston. Here in New York she felt that she stood on no pedestal and breathed no incense of adulation, but mixed in common life and breathed the same air as others. The Greeleys were interested in matters that affected the whole of America, rather than in the doings of a small group of chosen spirits, and under their healthy influence she came to take an interest in the political and social topics which she had previously neglected. Her work on the *Tribune* turned her concern to the main stream of contemporary thought and life, and away from the back currents which had previously occupied her attention. She no longer found any vulgarity in writing for the multitude, and paid little attention to those who thought that journalistic employment was "unwomanly" and enough to blacken the reputation of any female who dared to practice it. Her reviews for the *Tribune*, a paper known for the excellence and freedom of its criticism, deal with the work of Carlyle, Browning, Landor, Elizabeth Barrett, Shelley, Crabbe, Tennyson, Longfellow, Hawthorne, Poe, Emerson, and Lowell, rather than with such Transcendental poetic sprigs as Jones Very. Her critical essays and reviews were collected in 1846 in a volume called *Papers on Literature and Art,* which was impressive and attracted attention even in London. When she began her work for the *Tribune,* she was close to intellectual maturity and reaching the end of the mystical sentimentalism that had vitiated her early work. In the twenty months that she devoted mainly to criticism —"the first period in my life when it has been permitted me to make my pen my chief means of expressing my thoughts"— she established herself as one of the leading American critics, with Poe the only rival claimant to notice today. Her criticism was penetrating and original. Although often clumsy, it stands so far above the standards of the day as to be notable. Critically, the age was given to puffing and pussyfooting. Margaret naturally was frank and outspoken, and her forthrightness was sometimes too great for the subjects of her critical attentions. But her verdicts are on the whole amazingly just, and anticipate in many instances the opinions not generally held until many years after she wrote.

Journalism was a dangerous occupation in this era, and it took courage to speak out honestly without regard for possible consequences. Horace Greeley had recently been horsewhipped in Washington by a political antagonist, and forced to pay James Fenimore Cooper damages of two hundred dollars for libel as a result of reviewing one of the Leatherstocking Tales unfavorably. It was probably something of a relief to Greeley to turn over the duties of literary critic to Margaret, with the thought that a woman's gentle pen would be less likely to involve the *Tribune* in such difficulties. But Margaret promptly proceeded to raise storms of indignation by her fearless plain-speaking. Several of her reviews started feuds which were vigorously waged by the victims of her critical attentions for years after her death. American literature was young and very sensitive, and any unfavorable comment on the budding promise of the new writers was apt to be resented more or less violently. Margaret was no respecter of persons. Her standards were high, if romantic rather than classical. She judged the grist which came to her critical mill by comparison with the achievements of her literary idols: Dante, Shakespeare, Cervantes, Molière, and Goethe. She had a genius for classification, as her friend James Freeman Clarke knew well: "The God Terminus presided over her intellect. . . . No sophist could pass on her a counterfeit piece of intellectual money; but also she recognized the one pure metallic basis in coins of different epochs, and when mixed with a very ruinous alloy." This ability, coupled with her familiarity with a wide range of literature, made her critical mind operate to the embarrassment and fury of some of the newly canonized saints of American letters.

In reviewing Longfellow's *Poems* in 1845, Margaret summarily dismissed the most esteemed American poet of the day:

We must confess a coolness towards Mr. Longfellow, in consequence of the exaggerated praises that have been bestowed upon him. When we see a person of moderate powers receive honors which should be reserved for the highest, we feel somewhat like assailing him and taking from him the crown which should be reserved for grander brows. And yet this is, perhaps, ungenerous.

Mr. Longfellow has been accused of plagiarism. We have been surprised that anyone should have been anxious to fasten special charges of this kind upon him, when we had supposed it so obvious that the greater part of his mental stores were derived from the work of others. He has no style of his own, growing out of his own experiences and observation of nature. Nature with him, whether human or external, is always seen through the windows of literature.

This want of the free breath of nature, this perpetual borrowing of imagery, this excessive, because superficial, culture which he has derived from an acquaintance with the elegant literature of many nations and men, out of proportion to the experience of life within himself, prevent Mr. Longfellow's verses from ever being a true refreshment to ourselves.

Mr. Longfellow presents us not with a new product in which all the old varieties are melted into a fresh form, but rather with a tastefully arranged Museum, between whose glass cases are interspersed neatly potted rose trees, geraniums, and hyacinths, grown by himself with the aid of indoor heat. Twenty years hence, when he stands upon his own merits, he will rank as a writer of elegant, if not always accurate taste, of great imitative power, and occasional felicity in an original way, where his feelings are really stirred.

Longfellow was a mild-mannered man and made no public rejoinder to this devastating criticism, much of which rings true to us today. He contented himself with describing Miss Fuller's "furious onslaught upon me" in his journal as "a bilious attack." But when Margaret treated James Russell Lowell in similar fashion, she caught a Tartar who never forgave her for humiliating him. She wrote of his work:

> Lowell . . . we must declare it, though to the grief of some friends and the disgust of more, is absolutely wanting in the true spirit and tone of poesy. His interest in the moral questions of the day has supplied the want of vitality in himself; his great facility at versification has enabled him to fill the ear with a copious stream of pleasant sound. But his verse is stereotyped; his thought sounds no depth, and posterity will not remember him.

JAMES RUSSELL LOWELL

Engraving by H. B. Hall

This was a bitter pill for Lowell, and he did not take it well. In his letters he made unfriendly references to Margaret, describing her as a "very foolish, conceited woman, who has got together a great deal of information, but not enough *knowledge* to save her from being ill-tempered." More than two years after Margaret's review he vented his spite by giving her a prominent part in his *Fable for Critics*, where she appears in the role of Miranda. He labored the satire so much that their mutual friend William Wetmore Story reproached him for having driven his arrow "so sharply through Miranda." Lowell replied that the poem had been the work of but a few days and was done without any malice. Actually, the composition of the *Fable* took most of a year, and Lowell's literary agent, Mr. Briggs, had urged that the lines about Margaret be modified. Lowell dismissed the suggestion with the comment: "With her I have been perfectly good-humored, but I have a fancy that what I say will stick uncommonly." It did stick, but with no particular credit to Lowell. The relevant lines of the poem run thus:

> But there comes Miranda, Zeus! where shall I flee to?
> She has such a penchant for bothering me too!
> She always keeps asking if I don't observe a
> Particular likeness 'twixt her and Minerva;
> She tells me my efforts in verse are quite clever;
> She's been travelling now, and will be worse than ever.
> One would think, though, a sharp-sighted noter she'd be
> Of all that's worth mentioning over the sea.
> For a woman must surely see well, if she try,
> The whole of whose being's a capital I:
> She will take an old notion and make it her own,
> By saying it o'er in her sibylline tone,
> Or persuade you 't is something tremendously deep,
> By repeating it so as to put you to sleep;
> And she well may defy any mortal to see through it,

When once she has mixed up her infinite *me* through it.
There is one thing she owns in her own single right,
It is native and germane—namely, her spite.
Though, when acting as censor, she privately blows
A censer of vanity 'neath her own nose.

Here Miranda came up and said, "Phoebus! you know
That the Infinite Soul has its infinite woe,
As I ought to know, having lived cheek by jowl,
Since the day I was born, with the Infinite Soul;
I myself introduced, I myself, I alone,
To my land's better life authors solely my own,
Who the sad heart of earth on their shoulders have taken,
Whose works sound a depth by Life's quiet unshaken,
Such as Shakespeare, for instance, the Bible, and Bacon,
Not to mention my own works; Time's nadir is fleet,
And as for myself, I'm quite out of conceit ——"

I'm as much out of salt as Miranda's own writings
(Which as she, in her own happy manner, has said,
Sound a depth, for 't is one of the functions of lead).
She often has asked me if I could not find
A place somewhere near me that suited her mind;
I know but a single one vacant, which she,
With her rare talent that way, would fit to a T.
And it would not imply any pause or cessation
In the work she esteems her peculiar vocation—
She may enter on duty today, if she chooses,
And remain tiring-woman for life to the Muses.

Miranda meanwhile has succeeded in driving
Up to a corner, in spite of their striving,
A small flock of tearful victims, and these,
With an I-turn-the-crank-of-the-Universe air
And a tone which, at least to *my* fancy, appears
Not so much to be entering as boxing your ears,

Is unfolding a tale (of herself, I surmise,
For 't is dotted as thick as a peacock's with I's).

Her judgments of other contemporary literary figures are
penetrating. Of Emerson she remarked that he "raised himself
too early to the perpendicular, and did not lie along the ground
long enough to hear the secret whispers of our parent life." She
found evidence of greater power than had before been attained
in Poe's 1845-collection of poems: "With the exception of *The
Raven*, which seems intended chiefly to show the writer's artistic skill, and is in its way a rare and finished specimen, they are
all fragments. . . . We would wish to see Mr. Poe engaged in
a metaphysical romance." Margaret did not hesitate to rank
Elizabeth Barrett "in vigour and nobleness of conception, depth
of spiritual experience, and command of classical allusion, above
any female writer the world has yet known." But she observed
that the "great book culture of this mind is too great in proportion to that it has received from actual life." Browning's *Paracelsus* led her to remark that "he who means nobleness, though he
misses his aim, cannot fail to bring down a precious quarry
from the clouds," and his *Sordello* she described as "a work
more thickly enveloped in refined obscurities than ever any other
that really had a meaning." William Cullen Bryant's "range is
not great, nor his genius fertile." Hawthorne seemed to her the
best writer of the day in his field.

These opinions were not random intuitions, but sprang from
a critical system, perhaps the first evolved in America. Margaret
established three categories for the flood of new books which
claimed her attention: the work of genius, the work of scholars,
and the work of vigorous minds who had something of importance to say to their own generation. In reviewing books which
fell in the last two classes, she merely listed their interesting
ideas and did not attempt formal criticism. In dealing with
works of genius, or works that aspired to that rank, she criticized
by comparison with her chosen immortals. Since many did not

understand her system, she was thought to praise mediocrity and condemn talent. Her fundamental aesthetic principle was that "a great work of Art demands a great thought, or a thought of beauty adequately expressed." Beauty was something that had not been taken into account in previous American criticism, for Puritan dogma allowed no merit to it, and confused aesthetics and ethics. Margaret protested against the prevailing tendency to draw a moral at all costs:

> It is always a mistake to try and force a meaning from a tale. As long as it is to your mind a piece of life, it exercises a living influence. A correct picture from nature is always instructive in proportion to the power of the mind which looks in it to receive instruction, but the attempt of any one person to get from it a formal moral for all is distasteful and dissuades from a natural surrender to the charm of facts.

Such standards as hers were European rather than American, and it is not surprising that she attained her critical zenith in considering German and French literature. Her writings on Goethe did much to rouse American interest in him, and she awoke appreciation of George Sand, Balzac, and Eugène Sue. During her association with the *Tribune*, she was able to keep in close touch with European literary developments, for it was part of her duties to go through the foreign newspapers and magazines in search of items of political interest for Greeley's editorials. Occasionally she ran a column called "Items of Foreign Gossip," made up of material which her employer did not use. In the preface to the collection of her *Tribune* papers, she wrote:

> It has been one great object of my life to introduce here the works of those great geniuses, the flower and fruit of a higher state of development, which might give the young, who are soon to constitute the state, a higher standard in thought and action than would be demanded of them by their own time. . . . I feel with satisfaction that I have done a good deal to

extend the influence of the great minds of Germany and Italy among my contemporaries.

She was an apostle of the foreign literatures, and through her conversation and writing did much to spread the movement launched twenty years before by George Ticknor and Edward Everett. Until 1817, when Harvard established the Smith Professorship of the French and Spanish Languages and Belles Lettres, no college in the United States had concerned itself with the modern literatures. Ticknor, the first holder of the new chair, did much to make these literatures part of the living tradition of his students. Margaret and the young men returning from years of study at the German universities introduced German literature to America, and the large colony of American artists and sculptors who studied in Rome did much for the cause of Italian. The fresh worlds of thought revealed in the classics of these countries helped to make the second quarter of the century an Elizabethan age for America.

With this discovery that there were other literatures than English and Greek and Roman, that most nations had their own literatures, there arose the question of whether there was an American literature, distinct from the English, and if not, why not? Margaret wrote a historical sketch of American letters, the first ever attempted from this point of view, for original publication in her *Papers on Literature and Art*. This survey is a hasty but suggestive and interesting piece of work. As she wrote it, she was pressed for time, for she was winding up her career in New York and preparing to go abroad. Her space was also limited, for many of the papers which were to be included in this volume were radically abridged or dropped entirely to meet the exigencies of the press; much of her criticism is buried in the *Tribune's* files. It is certain that she felt that this essay was too much given to generalization, for she added at its end several of her *Tribune* reviews of authors mentioned in it, "to eke out the statements as to the merits of these authors."

The essay opens with the remark that "some thinkers may object to this essay, that we are about to write, of that which has as yet no existence. For it does not follow because many books are written by persons born in America that there exists an American literature." Before it can exist, "an original idea must animate this nation and fresh currents of life must call into life fresh thoughts along its shores." Margaret professes no disdain for those who write "in the methods and of the thoughts of Europe," for these are "useful schoolmasters to our people in a transition state." She confesses that she herself has been accused of "undue attachment to foreign continental literature," but what drew her to it was the "range and force of ideal manifestations in forms of national and individual greatness." She is confident that a genius "wide and full as our rivers, flowery, luxuriant and impassioned as our vast prairies, rooted in strength as the rocks on which the Puritan fathers landed" will rise up in America, but equally sure that "scarce the first faint streaks of that day's dawn are yet visible." That day will not come until the fusion of the many races here is accomplished; until moral and intellectual freedom are prized as highly as political freedom; until the work of knitting the country together physically is finished. But already a general longing for that day is felt, and much attempted, despite the meager rewards of authorship in America.

After this introduction, Margaret makes a rapid survey of what has already been accomplished. She singles out Prescott and Bancroft among the historians, and Channing and Emerson among the theologians and philosophers. As for novelists, she gives notice to Irving, Cooper (she avenged Greeley by writing: "His fellow citizens, in danger of being tormented by suits for libel if they spoke freely of him, have ceased to speak of him at all"), and the budding regional writers—these last being highly commended. She dismisses the general run of magazine fiction as "flimsy beyond any texture that was ever spun or dreamed of by the mind of man in any other age and country

. . . calculated to do a positive injury to the public mind, acting as an opiate, and of an adulterated kind, too." Among the poets she selects Bryant, Halleck, Willis, Longfellow, Emerson, Lowell, Ellery Channing, and Cornelius Matthews (these last two being unknown young Transcendentalists, Margaret's notice of them furnished Lowell with a point for his *Fable*). As for the drama, she holds that its day is past—not a bad conclusion in view of its state in her time—and that various substitutes will meet "the need of some kind of spectacle and dramatic representation . . . absolutely coincident with an animated state of the public mind." She acclaims the arrival of the first "Yankee novel," Sylvester Judd's *Margaret, or the Real and Ideal*. Then she turns her attention to periodical literature, "the only efficient instrument for the general education of the people." She has little use for the light magazines. She finds that the reviews are hamstrung by a "fear of censure from their own readers," and takes advantage of this occasion to read a sermon on the necessity of fearlessly pursuing truth:

> Publishers are afraid; authors are afraid; and if a worthy resistance is not made by religious souls, there is some danger that all the light will soon be put under bushels, lest some wind should waft from it a spark that may kindle dangerous fire.

The weekly and daily papers seem to her to be in a better state, and she suggests that "this mode of communication is susceptible of great excellence in the way of condensed essay, narrative, and criticism, and is the natural receptacle for the lyrics of the day." Her interest in her new occupation is evident, for she devotes several paragraphs to the rights and privileges of the journalist, and observes that "newspaper writing is next door to conversation and should be conducted on the same principles." Then she hurriedly winds up her essay, regretting that she has not had time to speak of Brockden Brown, "a novelist by far our first in point of genius and instruction as to the soul of things," or of Hawthorne, "the best writer of the day, in a similar range with Irving, only touching many more points and discerning far more deeply." And she concludes by saying that "the subject, even in this stage, lies as a volume in our mind, and cannot be unrolled in completeness unless time and space were more abundant." It is a pity that Margaret went no further with this plan for a book devoted to American literature, for her essay suggests that the book would have been extremely interesting. The ideas that animate the essay and the reviews of Brown, Hawthorne, and Longfellow which she appended to it are largely those which supplied the basis for the revaluation of American literature which began fifty years after her death.

Edgar Allan Poe, the only other critic of any lasting consequence in this period, made a just estimate of Margaret's literary work in *The Literati*. He had little use for her early productions, and spoke of her contributions to the *Dial* as "the most forcible and certainly the most peculiar papers." Her poetry was "tainted with the affectations of the transcendentalist . . . but is brimful of the poetic sentiment." He judged that "*Woman* is a book which few women in the country could have written, and no woman in the country would have published, with the exception of Miss Fuller," and commented on her excessive subjectiveness and earnest, declamatory style. But he had a high opinion of her criticism, which he found "nervous, forcible, thoughtful, suggestive, brilliant, and to a certain extent scholar-like." Her much discussed review of Longfellow seemed to him "frank, candid, independent," and revealed the "most thorough capacity to appreciate and the most sincere intention to place in the fairest light the real and idiosyncratic merits of the poet." And he, a stylist if there was one in this age of American literature, considered her style "one of the very best with which I am acquainted. In general effect, I know of no style which surpasses it. It is singularly piquant, vivid, terse, bold, luminous— leaving details out of sight, it is everything that a style need be." The "details" included Margaret's tendency to write with as fine

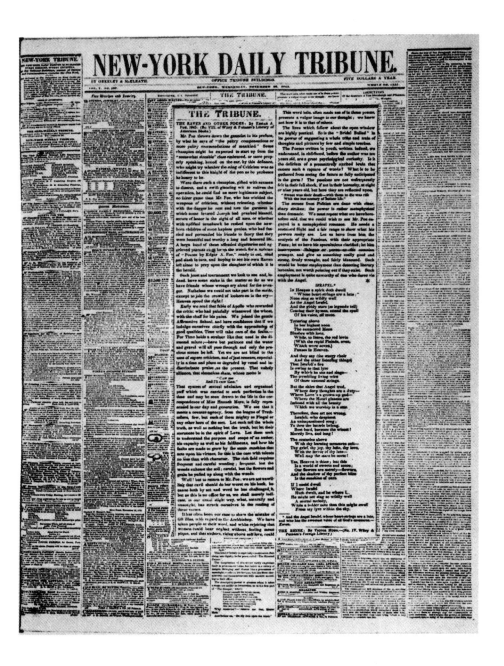

MARGARET'S REVIEW OF *THE RAVEN*

From the *New York Daily Tribune*, November 26, 1845

a disregard for the niceties of grammar and construction as Carlyle himself. Poe amused himself by making a list of "a few, very few, instances taken at random from among a multitude of *willful* murders committed by Miss Fuller on the American of President Polk." He also observed that "her personal character and her printed book are merely one and the same thing. Her acts are bookish, and her books are less thoughts than acts." Thus she was judged by a discerning contemporary, and today it is clear that her articles for the *Tribune* from December 1844 to August 1846 are one of the highwater marks of American criticism before 1850.

It gave Margaret considerable satisfaction to be able to say in her preface to *Papers on Literature and Art:* "I have written enough, if what is afloat, and what lies hid in manuscript, were put together, to make a little library, quite large enough to exhaust the patience of the collector, if not of the reader." She had learned to use the slow pen, in spite of her early misgivings, during her twenty months on the *Tribune.* But Horace Greeley, with his great facility in expression, thought: "While I never met another woman who conversed more freely or lucidly, the attempt to commit her thoughts to paper seemed to induce a singular embarrassment and hesitation." He considered that "she wrote always freshly, vigorously, but not always clearly," and he valued the "directness, terseness, and practicality" of her writings. These qualities were new in her work and doubtless the conditions of her employment had done much to develop them. There is a remarkable difference between her early productions and those of this period and thereafter. The fact that she lived among actualities, and no longer in an ideal world of her own, affected her style as much as her personality. The broadening of her interests is evident in her articles for the *Tribune,* for these are by no means confined to literary and aesthetic matters.

Before she came to New York, while she was staying at Fishkill with Caroline Sturgis, Margaret had visited Sing Sing one

Sunday to observe the condition of the women prisoners there. The humane theories of penology formulated by Judge Edmonds had been adopted and applied at this institution by the matron, Mrs. E. W. Farnum. Margaret, full of the thoughts which were going into *Woman* as she revised it during these vacation months, found support for her notions in the way the women prisoners responded to the new system:

> They showed the natural aptitude of the sex for refinement. These women were among the so-called worst, and all from the lowest haunts of vice. Yet nothing could have been more decorous than their conduct, while it was also frank; and they showed a sensibility and a sense of propriety which would not have disgraced any society. All passed, indeed, much as in one of my Boston classes. I told them I was writing about Woman; and as my path had been a favored one, I wanted to gain information from those who had been tempted and afflicted. They seemed to reply in the same spirit in which I asked. Several, however, expressed a wish to see me alone, as they could then say all, which they could not bear to do before another. I shall go there again, and take time for this. It is very gratifying to see the influence these few months of gentle and intelligent treatment have had upon these women: indeed, it is wonderful.

Margaret kept her resolve to revisit Sing Sing, and spent her Christmas at the prison. She made an address to the women in their chapel, and took as her text the wonted remark of the outside world when it had heard of the riotous women prisoners under the old system of administration: "Women once lost are far worse than abandoned men, and cannot be restored." She showed the falsity of this belief by using her audience as an illustration, and she preached the gospel of self-regeneration. The sympathetic hopefulness and good sense of her talk had a pleasant effect upon an audience accustomed to either righteous denunciation or pious sentimentalizing.

Upon her arrival in New York, a few weeks before she gave this Christmas talk at Sing Sing, Margaret had found the problem of public institutions almost on her new doorstep. For the Greeley Farm was opposite Blackwells Island, and Margaret wrote:

> Seven hundred females are confined in the Penitentiary opposite this point. We can pass over in a boat in a few minutes. I mean to visit, talk, and read with them. I have always felt great interest in those women who are trampled in the mud to gratify the brute appetites of men, and wished that I might be brought naturally into contact with them. Now I am.

With William Channing as a collaborator, Margaret did more than merely visit Blackwells Island; she made a thorough survey of all the public institutions of New York and reported her findings in the *Tribune.* The condition of these "benevolent" institutions was shocking at this time, and her exposé was very much to the taste of the crusading Horace Greeley. It created discussion, and discussion sold newspapers. But the articles on the prisons and hospitals of New York were not mere calculated sensationalism; Margaret hoped to spur into action the powerful audience at which Greeley aimed the *Tribune:* the women of substance who interested themselves in public affairs without caring much about politics. They could do much to remedy the conditions that Margaret had exposed, if only they could be swayed into action. Margaret attacked the problem with a zeal that had not marked the timid and tentative attempts that had been previously made to remedy matters. Mrs. Marcus Spring told how Margaret, on one of her visits, was urged to go away because the women she came to see had smallpox. But Margaret would not leave until she had found out all about it and had given encouragement and advice. It was sufficient reward to be told as she finally left: "You are the only one that is not afraid of us: how good you are!"

One of the fruits of Margaret's revelations about the institutions was a scheme for a house of refuge, to which released women convicts could turn if they were unable to make a place for themselves in the respectable world. She used her column in the *Tribune* to appeal for funds to expand the work of the ladies of the Prison Association. It was difficult to raise money for such a cause, because the line was sharply drawn between good and bad women in that day, and the established view was that the line could be crossed only one way. In fact, it was dangerous for a woman to interest herself in the plight of the less fortunate members of her sex, as Horace Greeley noted in his account of Margaret's social work:

I have known few women, and scarce another maiden, who had the heart and courage to speak with such frank compassion in mixed circles of the most degraded and outcast portion of the sex. The contemplation of their treatment, especially by the guilty authors of their ruin, moved her to a calm and mournful indignation, which she did not attempt to suppress or control. Others were willing to pity and deplore; Margaret was more inclined to vindicate and redeem. She did not hesitate to avow that on meeting some of these abused, unhappy sisters, she had been surprised to find them scarcely fallen morally below the ordinary standard of Womanhood—realizing and loathing their debasement; anxious to escape from it; and only repelled by the sad consciousness that for them sympathy and society remained only so long as they should persist in the ways of pollution. Those who have read her *Woman* may remember some daring comparisons therein suggested between these pariahs of society and large classes of their respectable sisters; and that was no fitful expression—no sudden outbreak—but impelled by her most deliberate convictions. I think if she had been born to large fortune, a house of refuge for all female outcasts desiring to return to the ways of Virtue would have been one of her most cherished and first-realized conceptions.

And Greeley had elsewhere observed how keenly Margaret appreciated rank, riches, power, and luxury, yet how cheerfully she would have surrendered them all if "the well-being of our Race could thereby have been promoted." Generosity was a large element in her nature, as was love for all about her.

✦ CHAPTER X ✦

Mr. James Nathan

Woman is born for love, and it is impossible to turn her from seeking it.—M. F.

THOUGH her duties on the *Tribune* and her own interests consumed most of Margaret's time in New York, she occasionally moved in the circles of that "good society" to which she was so indifferent. Her reputation as a writer and talker opened any door she desired to enter, and her position as the wielder of the *Tribune's* critical accolade assured her welcome to literary gatherings. People came out to the Farm to see her, and she held court behind the tea table. She visited various families in the city—her old friend Lydia Maria Child, the Christopher Cranches, and the Marcus Springs were her chief intimates— though only rarely did she accept invitations for evening parties. Those she attended most frequently were the soirees of Miss Lynch, where the authors, artists, critics, wits, and dilettanti of New York forgathered. Edgar Allan Poe christened this group the Literati, and wrote a book about them under this title. Amid this distinguished company Margaret held a position similar to that which had been hers among the Transcendentalists of Boston, with the difference that she made no close friends among them. She felt that in Boston she had known the noblest souls that America had to offer, and did not trouble to make intimates out of her new acquaintances. Since her manner was one of grave thoughtfulness and absorption in serious matters, and many of the group already disliked her sectarian and reformative tendencies, she made a poor impression on the more frivolous intelligentsia of New York. "Conceit, pedantry, a harsh spirit of criticism" were detected in her nature, just as they had been when she first entered Boston society; and she was characterized as "cold, abstracted, and scornful." Only a few among the Literati discovered her capacities as a confidante and a conversationalist, felt her social magnetism, and became her friends. She commanded respect rather than admiration, and although all were eager to see her and noticed how her fine head and spiritual expression marked her out in a crowded room, the majority were repelled by a way she had of making those around her seem frivolous, superficial, and conventional. For her part, Margaret found more satisfaction in good music than in any other form of entertainment at this time. The only society that she delighted in was that of small children, and the unloved, unmarried woman of thirty-five carefully cultivated her acquaintance with several youngsters—Pickie Greeley and Eddie Spring were two of them—"in whom I always find more genuine sympathy than in their elders." The affection was returned, for little Eddie Spring sent her a rose he had managed to grow by himself, for her desk at the *Tribune*.

The truth was that Margaret was going through a difficult phase of psychological development and readjustment. She was striving to fight down her private feelings and emotions—her longings for love, marriage, and children of her own—and to devote herself wholly to her professional career. At the very time she was criticized for being cold and scornful, she was writing this obviously sincere prayer in her private journal:

Father, let me not injure my fellows during this period of repression. I feel that when we meet my tones are not as sweet as I would have them. O let me not wound! I, who know so well how wounds can burn and ache, should not inflict them. Let my touch be light and gentle. Let me keep myself uninvaded, but let me not fail to be kind and tender where

need is. Yet I would not assume an overstrained poetic magnanimity. Help me to do just right, and no more. O make truth
profound and simple in me!

She felt that she had no real hold on life, no permanent connection with any other soul. She thought of herself as a wander-
ing intelligence roving homeless in search of knowledge, and
the thought oppressed her: "I do not see how I shall go through
this destiny. I can, if it is mine; but I do not feel that I can."
It is no wonder that she seemed sad and abstracted in manner
to casual acquaintances of this period; that when asked why
she sighed so deeply at the close of a Valentine's Day party, she
replied: "I am alone, as usual." Nor is it surprising that she fell
head over heels in love, for the first time in her life, during the
spring which followed on this winter of depression.

One of the many presentiments of Margaret's mystical period
was that some day she would know intimately a member of the
Jewish race, "who would show me how the sun of today shines
upon the ancient Temple." In February 1845, there was a plastic
model of the city of Jerusalem on exhibition in New York, and
a Mr. James Nathan, whom Margaret had met at a soiree, asked
her to go and see it in his company. Something very much like
love at first sight—at least, on Margaret's part—flared up on that
occasion, and the following spring was spent in secret meetings,
exchanges of notes, and all the accepted rigmarole of a romantic attachment.

James Nathan, who had been born a year after Margaret in
Holstein, had come to America in 1830 as a penniless immigrant.
He had managed to establish himself in the commission business by the time he met Margaret, and despite his professed
distaste for buying and selling—for he had a poetic nature—was
a prosperous young man. His somewhat feminine temperament,
his love of music, and his freely expressed disdain for her intellect made him attractive to Margaret. She saw in this gentle,
civilized, and blue-eyed young man, who called her "a foolish

little girl," a personification of all the romance of the East. By his own account he was attracted by her "high intellectuality, purity of sentiment, and winning conversation," but he was clever enough to realize that the New England Sibyl might prefer to be admired as a woman rather than as an intellect. No one had paid court to Margaret on these grounds before, and the conquest was easy. Since neither of them had much leisure, they exchanged innumerable love letters written in their few free moments late in the evening or early in the morning. The Greeleys did not accept Nathan at first, and in the necessary atmosphere of secrecy the affair flourished, fostered by meetings at Dr. Leger's or on the street in the city and by notes left at the *Tribune* office.

Margaret's dwindling faith in signs and portents was revived by this realization of her presentiment. She soon decided that Nathan had a soul deeply akin to hers and that their meeting had been destined by Providence. Nathan early overcame such reserve as she at first maintained by begging to be allowed to keep the copy of *Woman* which she had lent him. He won her completely by confessing all his troubles to her. She asked him to tea at Christopher Cranch's and to a performance of Handel's *Messiah*. Within a few days Margaret was writing to Nathan that "when I do not see you, I had rather not go out elsewhere." She stole away from the *Tribune* office to see him on the street in the morning; she asked him to meet her at the home of her friend Mrs. Child. Nathan seems to have been a little bit startled by her impetuousness, for he probably expected more reserve from a Puritan sibyl. When he allowed some expression of this to escape him, Margaret replied: "Our education and relations are so different, and those of each as yet scarcely known to the other—slight misunderstandings may arise." Soon after this, however, they agreed to use moderation about their meetings, though Margaret felt that, "it is nothing to be together in the parlour or the street, and we are not enough so among the green things."

For by this time it was spring, and the lilacs were beginning
to bloom on the Greeley Farm. Margaret felt more in tune with
the mood of the season than she ever had before; she felt herself to be for once a part of life, growing and unfolding like the
things of nature. She wrote to her lover:

I hear you with awe assert power over me and feel it to be
true. It causes awe, but not dread, such as I felt sometime
since at the approach of this mysterious power, for I feel deep
confidence in my friend and know that he will lead me on
in a spirit of holy love and that all I may learn of nature and
the soul will be legitimate. The destiny of each human being
is no doubt great and peculiar, however obscure its rudiments
to our present sight, but there are also in every age a few in
whose lot the meaning of that age is concentrated. I feel that
I am one of those persons in my age and sex. I feel chosen
among women. I have deep mystic feelings within myself,
and intimations from elsewhere. I could not, if I would, put
into words these spirit facts; indeed they are but swelling
germs as yet, and all I do for them is to try to do nothing that
might blight them. Yet as you say you need forget your call,
so have I need of escaping from this overpowering sense.
But when forced back upon myself, as now, though the first
turnings of the key were painful, yet the inner door makes
rapturous music upon its golden hinge. What it hides, you
perhaps know, as you read me so deeply; indeed some things
you say seem as if you did. Yet do not, unless you must. You
look at things so without their veils, yet that seems noble and
antique to me. I do it when you hold me by the hand, yet,
when I feel how you are thinking, I sometimes only say:
Psyche was but a mortal woman, yet as the bride of Love,
she became a daughter of the gods, too. But had she learned
in any other way this secret of herself, all had been lost, the
plant and flower and fruit.

But it is impossible to say all these things, at least for me. They are myself, but not clearly defined to myself. With you, all seems to assume such palpable reality, though you do not forget its inner sense either. I love to hear you read off the secret, and yet you sometimes make me tremble, too. I confide in you, as this bird, now warbling without, confides in me. You will understand my song, but you will not translate it into language too human. I wish, I long to be human, but divinely human. Let the soul invest every act of its abode with somewhat of it own lightness and subtlety. Are you my guardian to domesticate me in the body, and attach it more firmly to the earth? Long it seemed that it was only my destiny to say a few words to my youth's companions and then depart. I hung lightly as an air-plant. Am I to be rooted on earth, ah! choose for me a good soil and a sunny place, that I may be a green shelter to the wary and bear fruit enough to pay for staying. Au revoir! Adieu!

Misinterpreting this letter, Nathan pressed his suit with such ardor that Margaret recoiled, deeply shocked at his "lower nature." The man of the world was revealed to the "sister of his soul," and this was something that Margaret had not anticipated. She begged him to restore their relationship to its original lightness, while she realized that "now it is deeper and we cannot get out of the labyrinth, nor my heart find what it craves, sweet content with thee." To show him how she would be courted and esteemed, she sent him two poems which had been written to her by Samuel Ward and Ellery Channing. Nathan hastened to apologize, and gave her his handsome Newfoundland puppy as a peace offering. She was pleased, but noted that Josey the dog was "more affectionate than deep in his feelings" —perhaps as a hint to its owner.

All through April the letters went back and forth, echoing the lovers' quarrels and reconciliations. On a Wednesday of one

week Margaret penned a few lines to assure Nathan that her
thoughts were always with him. On the following Monday she
is magnificent in her outraged dignity:

> The last three days have effected as violent a change as the
> famous three days of Paris, and the sweet little garden, with
> which my mind had surrounded your image, lies all dese-
> crated and trampled by the hoofs of the demon who con-
> ducted this revolution, pelting with his cruel hailstones me,
> poor child, just as I had laid aside the protections of reserve
> and laid open my soul in heavenly trust. I must weep to think
> of it, and why, O God, must eyes that never looked falsehood
> be doomed to shed such tears! . . . Truth is the first of jewels,
> yet let him feel that if Margaret dared express herself more
> frankly than another, it is because she has been in her way a
> queen and received her guests as also of royal blood.

But a reconciliation was achieved before the end of the week,
and on Saturday Margaret accuses herself of vanity and arrogance, and humbles herself completely:

> It is I, who by flattering myself and letting others flatter
> me that I must act ever nobly and nobler than others, have
> forgot that pure humility which is our only safeguard. I have
> let self-love, pride, and distrust creep upon me and mingle
> with my life-blood.

The storms that April were not confined to the weather.

As the days went by Margaret became lost in her love for
Nathan. She confessed that "these times of pure soul communion
are almost too much for my strength." She exchanged books and
other tokens of affection with Nathan, but after a letter from her
Liebster she wrote: "There is no time for books and no poem
like the poem we can make for ourselves." Horace Greeley was
called out of town and she had won over Mrs. Greeley to the
lovers' cause, so she urged Nathan to come to the Farm and give

her an evening of music with his guitar. When she became ill
with lovesickness and was forced to her bed, she wrote to him:

> There is far more repose in being with you, when your look
> fills my eye and your voice my ear, than in trying to keep
> still, for then the endless thoughts rush upon me. And then
> comes, too, that tormenting sense that only a few more days
> shall we be together, and how can I rest, though indeed I am
> desirous to do as you desire.

For now it was May, and Nathan was planning a long trip
abroad. Under pressure from Margaret he put off his departure
until June. They passed the remaining days in excursions into
the country, where they could be alone in places made beautiful by spring, or stole time for rendezvous from the hours devoted to business. Evening after evening the incessant letter-
writing went on. There was some trouble with the Greeleys, for
Horace thought that Margaret was neglecting her work, although he didn't know the reason, and Mrs. Greeley, who did
know, was alarmed by the state of Margaret's health. Nathan,
who was somewhat furtive by nature, had been disturbed that
Margaret had confided in her hostess, but Margaret had scorned
his alarm as baseless and unworthy. But now she regretted that
she had been so free with her secret, for Mrs. Greeley plagued
her with well-meant advice. Also she detected an undercurrent
of coolness on Nathan's part in his letters and actions, and she
asked him to return her letters before he left for Europe, that
she might burn them. "They have been like manna, possible to
use for food in their day, but they are not immortal like their
source. Let them perish! . . . Keep my image in the soul without such aids and it will be more livingly true and avail you
more." Again she asked him to destroy some "intimately personal verses" that she had sent him. He did not answer her
requests, and she was too far gone in love to press the matter.
Early in June Nathan finally sailed for Europe. His ship was

hardly out of the harbor before Margaret sat down to write to him:

> Ever since you went, it has been the most beautiful weather, such as we never had at all. I do not think, my friend, fate smiled upon us; how much cold and storm there was, how little warm soft air when we could keep still out of doors in peace, how much interruption throughout from other affairs and relations, and the cloud of separation threatening from the distance from the very first. One good month, containing unbroken days of intercourse, and with no thought of the future, would have been worth in happiness these five that we have known each other in such a way. . . .
>
> All is full and lustrous, as it has not been and will not be again, for these first days of June are the bridal days of the year; but through all breathes to me a tone of sorrow, over all droops a veil. For I have lost my dear companion, the first I ever had who could feel every little shade of life and beauty as exquisitely as myself, whose strength gladdened and whose gentleness soothed me, and, wanting this finishing note, Nature herself pleases no more. It will not be so long, I trust, but it is so now.

She was not conscious that she had written the epitaph for her first love-affair, and that it was all over. Every two or three days she wrote to him again, describing her occupations, how Josey the Newfoundland puppy was getting along, her somewhat strained relations with Mrs. Greeley, how she was devoting all her energies to the *Tribune*, since Horace wished her to pay more attention to her work than she had during the spring. It was almost August before she heard from him, and the meager note he then sent did not satisfy her. It would seem that the trip abroad had been a convenient flight for Nathan from the too-exacting demands of a love-affair, for she received only two or three more letters from him, and these were cold in tone and devoted to requests to further his interests. Would Margaret get him a letter of introduction from George Bancroft, the Secretary of the Navy, whom she had spoken of as a Boston friend? Would she arrange to have his travel notes published, possibly in the *Tribune?* She fulfilled all these requests and could not understand why Nathan did not reply. At first she blamed the absence of letters from abroad on Horace's careless way with things he brought home from the office for her, and penned long letters to the traveler with the same zeal as before. But finally she realized that it was all over, that it actually had been over for months, and that Nathan had merely used her to promote his own welfare, long after any feeling that he may have had for her was dead.

Margaret would have been lost in loneliness after Nathan's departure if her friends, who may have heard from Mrs. Greeley of what had passed, had not rallied around her. Mrs. Fuller came to New York to visit her daughter that June, and after she returned to Boston, Marcus and Rebecca Spring asked Margaret to spend the hot weather with them at their beautiful country estate at Eagleswood. She was treated as a member of the family and consoled herself in the absence of her lover by lavishing affection on little Eddie Spring, who returned her devotion by worshiping her. There was nothing to remind her at Eagleswood of Nathan, while there was much in the city, and so she did her writing for the *Tribune* at home, pleading that the heat was too great to work at the office. Emerson paid her a visit in August, and she took a short vacation in October in Massachusetts, renewing her old friendships. When she returned to New York, she took lodgings in a boarding house, because of the coolness that had arisen between her and Mrs. Greeley. During the winter she buried herself in her work, and did her best to forget that she was a woman who had been spurned by the man she loved. Possibly she came to share the Greeleys' opinion of Nathan, for she made her peace with them and returned to the Farm in the spring of 1846. But the Castle Rackrent atmosphere of that home proved too much for her after having had her own establishment, and she soon took rooms in a house on Brooklyn Heights. Here she could look out over the harbor and see the ships arriving and departing. One of them might bring her *Liebster* back to her, full of explanations of his coldness and his failure to reply to her letters. Or some day one of them might take Margaret herself to the Europe she had longed to see for so many years.

That day came sooner than Margaret had expected. The Springs proposed that Margaret join them in a grand tour of Europe, which was to begin in the late summer of 1846. They knew how Margaret had always wanted to go to Europe, more particularly since James Nathan was to be found there. They were fond of her and she would make a good traveling companion for them and little Eddie, who was to go along. The Springs had ample means at their disposal and enjoyed using them to gratify their friends' desires. They had played the fairy godfather and godmother to many a talent. For instance, they had made it possible for William Channing to come to New York when he grew weary of the uncongenial life of Cincinnati. The temptation for Margaret to accept their offer was strong, but first she consulted Horace Greeley. Nathan's request to arrange for publication of his travel notes had given her an idea, and if Greeley would only agree to it, she need not be wholly dependent upon the Springs. He made no difficulty about her departure, and agreed that she might well act as foreign correspondent for the *Tribune* instead of as its literary critic. The rest and new experiences would do her good, and her old position would be waiting for her when she returned home from her travels. But he was sorry to part temporarily with a friend, even if he thereby gained a valuable foreign correspondent. When she paid her last visit to the *Tribune* office, Horace and Mrs. Greeley and young Pickie were all there to bid her farewell. They accompanied her to the ferry which would take her over to Brooklyn, where she had to finish her packing, and took a tender and affectionate leave of her on the dock. Pickie was inconsolable in his grief at parting with Margaret, and all the assurances that she would soon come back over the water were in vain. If Margaret still had faith in premonitions, she might have felt that there was something portentous in this incident, but she was far too excited at the prospect of going to Europe to let any dark thoughts oppress her.

❅ CHAPTER XI ❆

England and Scotland

O were life but longer, and my strength greater! Ever I am bewildered by the riches of existence.—M. F.

MARGARET sailed for Europe with her three traveling companions on August 1, 1846, on the steamer *Cambria*. She had paid a brief visit to Boston before her departure, in order to say farewell to her family and closest friends there, and she had been given all manner of opposing counsels on the relative merits of the old sailing packets and the new steamships. Though most of her friends seemed to favor the packets, Margaret found the *Cambria's* accommodations very satisfactory, and the prospect of a quick passage and the certainty as to the time of arrival were very much to her taste, for she found that she did not enjoy being at sea:

> In the evening, when the wind was favorable and the sails set, so that the vessel looked like a great winged creature darting across the apparently measureless expanse, the effect was very grand, but ah! for such a spectacle one pays too dear; I far prefer looking out upon the "blue and foaming sea" from a firm green shore.

There were moments when Margaret wished that she were enjoying the sea from the beach at Nahant, as she used to do during her summer vacations, and she found the sea air "excessively bracing" after the languorous New York summer. But the voyage seems to have been a well-nigh perfect one, for the

172

Cambria reached Liverpool ten days and sixteen hours out of Boston. This was the fastest passage yet made across the Atlantic, and caused much excitement in the press. She suffered from "the smell and jar of the machinery, or other ills by which the sea is wont to avenge itself on the arrogance of its vanquishers," but she got no sympathy from the stewardess, who observed that "anyone tempted God Almighty who complained on a voyage where they did not even have to put guards to the dishes!"

The *Cambria* had called at Halifax on its voyage, and there picked up the Governor of Nova Scotia and his lady, who were returning to England after having made themselves thoroughly unpopular in the colony. The Governor's wife was a daughter of William IV by the famous actress Mrs. Jordan, and this fact made quite a stir among the passengers. But Margaret, true to her Feminist principles, refused to attach any importance to the lady's "left-handed alliance with one of the dullest families that ever sat upon a throne" and regretted that nobody but herself respected her descent from one endowed "with genius that fascinated the attention of all kinds and classes of men, grace and winning qualities that no heart could resist."

Margaret had hardly set foot upon English soil before she was noting the differences from life at home which met her on every side. She found that things went just as well, if not better, with the traveler, though there was none of "that rushing, tearing, and swearing, that snatching of baggage, that prodigality of shoeleather and lungs which attend the course of the traveller in the United States." On the other hand, she did not enjoy being forced to wait hours at the customs, because after the tradition of an aristocratic government, the baggage of Lord Falkland, the Nova Scotian Governor, was given first attention. The travelers rested after their voyage for half a day at Liverpool, and then set out for Manchester, where they inspected one of the great warehouses and visited the Mechanics' Institute. Margaret was much impressed by this establishment and its fellow in Liverpool, where more than seventeen hundred pupils were taught. These popular schools were designed to supply instruction at a very low fee to mechanics, clerks, apprentices, and the women of their families. A wide range of studies was offered: English, mathematics, composition, French, German, fine arts, architectural drawing, and many others. Lectures and concerts were open to students at the Institutes without charge, and large libraries were at their disposal. Margaret was pleased to discover that the scheme had recently been broadened to include girls in its scope, and that they were taught, "as they ought to be in all American schools," to cut out and make dresses. She was even more pleased when the director of the Liverpool Institute quoted from the *Dial* in an address describing the purposes of this educational program. It was a strange place for the seed of the New England idealists to be found flowering; Margaret was surprised to see the Transcendentalist journal so well known in these "especially practical" regions. Later she discovered extracts from the writings of Charles Sumner and Elihu Burritt enshrined in *Bradshaw's Railway Guide*, a volume, she sagely noted, "more likely in an era like ours to influence the conduct of the day than would an illuminated breviary."

She also found a curious contradiction between the opinions expressed in conversation by her English acquaintances and the principles the English seemed to act on. Talk of the blessings of peace and the evils of war greeted her on every side, but British arms were waging war in China and Ireland. There were many schemes afoot for improving the condition of the working classes, and the reformers prided themselves on the progress already made. But Margaret and the Springs were depressed by the sight of swarming, shameless beggars in Liverpool and of Manchester mill girls seen on the streets or through the windows of the gin-shops where they sat drinking, "too dull to carouse." Margaret was particularly annoyed to find that neither the Liverpool nor the Manchester hotel boasted a bath, in this land which made much of its cleanliness as compared to the Latin countries. It was no doubt with some relief that her party left this industrial region and went on to Chester, whose romantic charms were more like what Margaret had expected to find in old England. Here there were reminders of the Roman and Welsh invasions, a fine old city wall, a ruined cathedral, and ivied ramparts. These things appealed to Margaret's imagination, although she remembered the assurances of an American fellow traveler on the *Cambria* that she would find "castles and that sort of thing all humbug" and that it would be "best to sit at home and read some handsome work on the subject."

From Chester the little party went on to the lake country, where they passed eight days in a stone cottage which had been procured for them by Margaret's old friend Harriet Martineau. At this season, the lake district was a favorite resort for people from all parts of England, and Margaret found their company almost as interesting as the excursions by carriage and boat and on foot to the celebrated beauty spots of the region. She took pains to draw out the people she met, whether they were landed proprietors, manufacturers, university teachers, or simple folk. The Reform movement was the great conversational topic of the day, and Margaret was beset by arguments for and against the new measures. Probably it was a pleasure for her to escape to the familiar company of Miss Martineau, who had recently established herself here, in a home presented to her in recognition of her achievements. Harriet had not forgotten the resentment she had felt at Margaret's candid criticism of her *Society in America*, and was somewhat cool to the visitors. In one of the most vivid portions of her autobiography, she later had much to say of Margaret's bad manners and behavior as a guest at Ambleside. To be sure, Miss Martineau was hostess to the visitors only in half-hearted fashion. The Springs paid for the lodgings she had arranged for their party in the village near her home. Her criticism of Margaret's incessant harangues during the visit is somewhat suspect, for she was a mighty talker herself, and made the most of a deafness which was convenient in disregarding interruptions. Also she was but lately recovered from five years of helpless invalidism, during which she had been prey to some baffling nervous malady which had defied the best efforts of the doctors. Much to the scandal of the medical profession, she had finally been cured by a mesmeric treatment received from a Mr. Atkinson.

Margaret was greatly taken with this Mr. Atkinson, who was known as "the prince of English mesmerizers." She saw much of him at Ambleside, and later in London, and her account of him in a letter to a friend at home is prefaced with this observation: "As soon as I reached England I found how right we were in supposing that there was elsewhere a greater range of interesting character among the men than with us." Her interest in the subject of which Mr. Atkinson was a master, and her lifelong sufferings from a malady similar to Miss Martineau's, gave them common ground on which to meet. Soon she perceived that in addition to a handsome presence and a "head for Leonardo to paint," he had the merit of a habitual mental process similar to her own: "He does not think, but perceives and acts." Perhaps Margaret's open acknowledgment of the discovery of another soul deeply sympathetic to her own—she was never one to conceal such discoveries—had something to do with Miss Martineau's ill-tempered account of the American invasion of Ambleside, for Harriet had grown quite fond of Mr. Atkinson.

The lake country boasted the presence of a still more famous personage than the redoubtable Miss Martineau, for William Wordsworth was living in retirement at Rydal Mount. He showed Margaret and Eddie Spring about his abode, quoting from his poems as he went. Margaret was a little disappointed that his home was not more wild and romantic in its setting, and also that the poet himself was not more exciting in his person, for she mentions her surprise that the little boy was not disappointed when he found "no Apollo flaming with youthful glory, laurel-crowned and lyre in hand, but instead a reverend old man, clothed in black and walking with cautious step along the level garden path." Wordsworth seemed less concerned with poetry than with the recent measures adopted about the Corn Laws; he judged that "the principle was certainly right, though as to whether existing interests had been as carefully attended to as was just, he was not prepared to say." Wordsworth at seventy-six, buried in his idyllic retreat, bore little resemblance to the young rebel of the *Lyrical Ballads*, and Margaret regretted that "his habits of seclusion keep him much ignorant of the real wants of England and the world." She found that he enjoyed high esteem in the neighborhood, and asked her landlady: "Do the people here value Mr. Wordsworth most because he is a celebrated writer?" "Truly, madam," the landlady replied, "I think it is because he is so kind a neighbor."

Leaving the lake district, the travelers went northward to Edinburgh by way of Carlisle. In the coach Margaret was lectured on the respective merits of Walter Scott and Robert Burns by a gentleman from London, who made a yearly visit to Burns's birthplace. Scott was dismissed by him as a poet of the past, wedded to the notion of a feudal aristocracy, while Burns was hailed as the democratic bard of the present and the future. Margaret admitted the truth of the argument, but said she could not "endure a comparison which by a breath of coolness depreciates either." She shared too much of the spirit of the Romantic Revival to hold a poor opinion of one of its most popular figures. She must have read all Scott's work with eager attention, for she makes frequent and familiar reference to it in her account of her three weeks in Scotland.

Edinburgh won Margaret's heart, though many of the people she wished to meet there were out of town, for it was not the season. But the beauty of the northern capital was enough to captivate her, and from the window of her hotel on Princes

Street she could catch glimpses of many a place rich in associa-
tions to her. Conscientiously she saw the sights of the city, but
she displayed real enthusiasm when she inspected the model
publishing establishment of the brothers Chambers. It was delightful to find that these gentlemen shared her view of publishing as not chiefly a business, but rather "the means of
mental and moral benefit to their countrymen." Being thus
borne out in one of her dearest opinions by these eminently
successful publishers, she took the opportunity to lecture
Horace Greeley on his own sordid views in her next letter
home. She spent several hours with De Quincey, the English
opium eater, being fortunate enough to find him in a mood
for conversation. Though he seemed to live much in the past
mentally, she was impressed by his eloquence and narrative
powers, and more particularly by his urbanity, a quality, Margaret noted, "now becoming rare in literary conversation." She
sought out such other celebrities as were in town at the time of
her visit: Dr. Chalmers, the great preacher, and Dr. Combe,
who was full of indignation at the carefree ways of his American publishers. After such a surfeit of conversation, the Springs
were no doubt glad to leave Edinburgh for the Highlands.

They went by coach, and Margaret insisted on riding on top,
even when it rained, in order to enjoy every view of the countryside that the journey offered. The ruins of Lochleven Castle
reawakened the thoughts about Queen Mary which had come
to Margaret as she looked at the blood stain and the secret stair
of Holyrood House in Edinburgh. She felt strongly the strange
attraction of Mary's tragic story, which time has not been able
to destroy. Then the party went on to Crieff, where they visited
Drummond Castle, and thence to the Trossachs, which disappointed the expectations that had been roused in Margaret by
a reading of *The Lady of the Lake:* "It is very grand, but the
grand part lasts so little while." Though a "hateful little
steamer" had already begun to ply Loch Katrine, and another
Loch Lomond, her party traveled the lakes in rowboats, and

Margaret was much taken with the boatmen's singing of Gaelic lovesongs, whose wild and plaintive airs were most pleasing to her. At Rowarden the party halted for the night, in order to ascend Ben Lomond on the following day. But the weather made them wait still another day, and then, when they arose after sleeping late, they discovered that another party had secured all the available horses.

The ascent was four miles long and by no means effortless, but Margaret and Marcus Spring decided to attempt it on foot. It was a marvelously clear day for Scotland, so they took no guide. They climbed slowly, often stopping to admire the views. The spectacle from the summit was so magnificent that they did not think of starting down until four in the afternoon. The path was not clearly marked near the summit, and they soon lost it. Mr. Spring left Margaret to rest while he searched for the track, and soon called to her that he had found it again. But because of some trick that the hills played with their voices, Margaret was not able to find him where she thought he was, and her own calls went unheard by him. She determined to make her own way down by herself, but lost much time in avoiding numerous bogs, into which she sank up to her knees when she blundered into them.

It was twilight before she got a glimpse of the lake, and a steep watercourse barred the last of her way. She was exhausted, and sank down on the ground to rest. Before she was well aware of it, darkness came, and she realized that she would have to spend the night where she was, for she dared not wander blindly among the treacherous bogs. The mist soon hid the stars, and a cold autumn wind sprang up. Since she was lightly clad and no shelter was at hand, she had to keep warm by moving about as much as she dared. There was ample time for Ossianic visions during the long night hours, before dawn broke and she was able to pick her way through the mist until she was discovered by some of the twenty shepherds who had been searching all night for her. These men, whom

Mr. Spring had sent out in his alarm for her, were rewarded
with a splendid dinner in the barn at the inn, at which he presided as host. After a day or two of rest Margaret was none
the worse for her experience. She felt that she had really come
to know the Highlands during her night on Ben Lomond, and
found that the incident "created quite an intimate feeling between us and the people there." These Highland shepherds
supplied the first instance of the higher regard that was paid to
Margaret in Europe than ever had been at home. It was to
come from higher quarters in the next four years.

Margaret had had something more to think about than her
immediate plight during her lonely night on Ben Lomond.
Just before she left Edinburgh she received a letter from James
Nathan which finally made it perfectly clear to her that the
love-affair was dead. He refused to return her letters, for which
she had asked, except for a consideration. She realized that she
had been living in a world of false hopes since his departure
from New York, and she wrote bitterly in her diary:

> I understand more and more of the character of the *tribes*.
> I shall write a sketch of it and turn the whole to account in a
> literary way, since the affections and the ideal hopes are so
> unproductive. I care not. I am resolved to take such disap-
> pointments more lightly than I have. I ought not to regret
> having thought other of "humans" than they deserve.

If she ever had any serious intention of making literary use
of her abortive love-affair, she failed to carry the scheme into
execution. It was high time, however, that she saw the true
condition of the relations between Nathan and herself, for
he was already planning to marry another woman. Margaret
spared herself the added humiliation of being recognized as the
cast-off lover, for she broke off her correspondence with Nathan.
She wrote to a Mr. Delf in London, who was Nathan's friend
and the agent there for D. Appleton & Co., and asked him to
tell Nathan that she had received his letter, "but was too

much involved in the routine of visiting and receiving visits to allow her mind a moment's repose to reply to it." In her busiest days in New York she had always been able to find time to write to her "dear friend," but now she saw that it would be well to break with a man who wanted to bargain for the return of letters which she had written without a thought of consequences. She was thoroughly disillusioned and embittered.

Fortunately she was in the company of true friends and her days were filled with pleasant distractions. After lingering a while in the Highlands, her party returned to Edinburgh by way of Dumbarton, Glasgow, and Stirling. Glasgow seemed an inferno to Margaret; she was appalled by its squalor, misery, and human degradation. But there was one consoling thought:

> The manufacturing and commercial towns, burning focuses of grief and vice, are also the centers of intellectual life, as in forcing-beds the rarest flowers and fruits are developed by the use of impure and repulsive materials. Where evil comes to an extreme, Heaven seems busy in providing means for the remedy. Glaring throughout Scotland and England is the necessity for the devoutest application of intellect and love to the cure of ills that cry aloud, and without such application erelong help *must* be sought by other means than words. Yet there is every reason to hope that those who ought to help are seriously, though slowly, becoming alive to the imperative nature of this duty; so we must not cease to hope, even in the streets of Glasgow, and the gin-palaces of Manchester, and the dreariest recesses of London.

After two or three days more in Edinburgh, the travelers headed south. They halted at Abbotsford, Walter Scott's home, and Margaret was surprised to find that no less than five hundred Americans had inscribed their names in the guestbook during the previous year.

When they reached Newcastle, Margaret's newly developed concern with economic and social conditions made her insist on being taken down a coal mine. The wet and dirt of the mine soon killed her enthusiasm, and she and Marcus Spring were brought up to the surface again "with minds slightly edified and face and hands much blackened." She seems to have felt more sympathy for the horses, who never saw the light of day again after they once had been lowered into the mine, than for the miners themselves. York Minster was a sight much more worth seeing to Margaret's mind, although she complained: "Such a church is ruined by Protestantism; its admirable exterior seems that of a sepulchre; there is no correspondent life within." Strange words for a daughter of the Puritans! From York they went to Sheffield, where they saw steel being made and visited near-by Chatsworth House, one of the great country seats of England. But the clash in England between extreme poverty and misery on one hand and wealth and grandeur on the other had already made an unpleasant impression on Margaret, and she found that she could not admire Chatsworth House, "a fine expression of modern luxury and splendor," after her visit to the steel mills. Warwick Castle was more to her taste, "a real representative of the English aristocracy in the day of its nobler life," and she thought it a fitting shrine for its famous collection of Van Dyck portraits. At Stratford she found to her surprise that Shakespeare's birthplace had only been honored for forty years, and noted that "England has learned much of her appreciation of Shakespeare from the Germans."

In Birmingham Margaret heard two speeches by George Dawson, one of the rising popular leaders of England. She thought he had a certain homely eloquence, admirably adapted to his humble audience, and that he was free of the over-intellectualism of James Martineau, Harriet's brother, whom she had heard speak in Liverpool. Shortly after this, in London, Margaret listened to another of the English reformers, W. J. Fox, and found him the most impressive of all. These three reformers reminded her of Channing and Parker, although none of them possessed the pure, extemporaneous eloquence of Channing or the full, sustained flow of thought of Parker. But they seemed more practical men than her American friends, and already they possessed more power. They won her to their cause, for a cause was always a vital necessity to Margaret. Her nature demanded that she devote herself body and soul to love for an idea or for an individual, or else be destroyed by the fire within herself. She was a born revolutionary, though she did not yet realize it.

Her party reached London at the end of September. Though the sun never shone once during the six weeks they spent there, London fascinated Margaret. The sprawling city was an inexhaustible studio to her, and she thought a lifetime not long enough to study its vast stream of life and its memorials of other ages. And within three days after she presented the letters of introduction that she had brought with her, she was taken up in such a round of social gatherings that she wrote to Emerson: "I had hardly time to dress, and none to sleep, during all the weeks I was in London." Her *Papers on Literature and Art* had just been published in an English edition, and received excellent notices. She was told by the editors of several journals that they would welcome contributions from her, but she found no time to write as she went the rounds of London's literary society. She was made welcome in the way that many English writers have been in America, but that few Americans of talent have been in England.

True to her Feminist principles, Margaret went first to pay honor to Joanna Baillie, the Scottish poetess and dramatist, who was then past eighty but still very keenly alive. Margaret had always held her and Madame Roland in particular esteem as "women of a Roman strength and singleness of mind, adorned by the various culture and capable of the various action opened to them by the progress of the Christian Idea." At Richmond she visited another well-known old lady, Miss Berry, the friend of Walpole and a famous conversationalist. She also became intimate with Mary and William Howitt, who were the main-

springs of the *People's Journal,* which Margaret thought came
"nearer being a fair sign of the times than any other publication
of England." At their home she met Dr. Southwood Smith, a
philanthropic physician then engaged in constructing model
tenements for working people. This philanthropist possessed
a still further distinction, for in his study sat the skeleton of
the great Jeremy Bentham, "dressed in the same dress he
habitually wore, stuffed out to an exact resemblance of life,
and with a portrait mask in wax, the best I ever saw." Margaret
expected to be revolted by this apparition, but found it, "on
the contrary, an agreeable sight. . . . The figure leans a little
forward, resting the hands on a stout stick which Bentham
always carried, and had named 'Dapple'; the attitude is quite
easy, the expression of the whole quite mild, winning, yet
highly individual." Bentham, in order to overcome the prejudice against dissection, had directed in his will that his body
should be used by Dr. Smith in the service of science, and that
his skeleton should be preserved as Margaret saw it, "an assistant to Dr. Smith in the entertainmemnt of his guests and
the companion of his studies!"

Visits to celebrities rather crowded out more orthodox sightseeing during Margaret's stay in London. She postponed visiting the art galleries on the ground that the absence of sunlight
would interfere with proper appreciation. She did get to see the
Murillos at the National and Dulwich galleries, but was more
impressed by Hampton Court and Kew Gardens and the Zoo
than by galleries made noisy by crowds of workingmen
"thronging to and fro on the uncarpeted floor in their thick
boots." She felt, however, despite her annoyance, that "the
sight of such objects must be gradually doing them a great deal
of good." She was taken to see the Reform Club, but it seemed
"stupidly comfortable, in the absence of that elegant arrangement and vivacious atmosphere which only women can inspire." She liked the kitchen, because there were women there,
though only as subordinates of a chef and his male assistants,

and because of its modern arrangements for large-scale cooking, which "Fourier himself might have taken pleasure in." Mr. Spring was much interested in these arrangements, and proposed to copy some of them in the home of the North American Phalanx at Red Bank, New Jersey. On the Springs' wedding anniversary the party retraced the route of John Gilpin's famous ride, but "whereas he went too fast, we went too slow," and the excursion was rather a failure. Margaret derived less enjoyment from it than from the amazement of her English acquaintances at such a mad Yankee notion.

Everywhere Margaret went in London she encountered political exiles from the European countries which were struggling to escape from the restraints laid upon them in the post-Napoleonic period by the provisions of the Congress of Vienna. She came to sympathize with their revolutionary struggles against the forces of reaction and tyranny, and in her dispatches to the *Tribune* she wished that America would "invite all genius to her arms and change her golden wheat for their green laurels and immortal flowers." Most particularly she sympathized with Giuseppe Mazzini, whom she described in a letter home as "by far the most beauteous person I have seen." She admired the way in which this homeless exile wrote stirring articles for the *People's Journal* about conditions in his native Italy, and conducted a school for poor Italian boys in London. Here was a hero who loomed as large to her as any of her beloved ancient Romans. She found him heroic, courageous, faithful, and wise; despite adversity confident, in Schiller's words, that "those who live for their faith shall behold it living." Under his influence her interest in the cause of the Italian exiles budded and then blossomed. It was to be the last and greatest cause of her life, and she was to sacrifice everything to it.

But the most eventful of Margaret's many meetings during these weeks in London—in her own view at the time—was with Thomas Carlyle, who had been admonished several months before in a letter from Emerson: "You must not fail to give a good and faithful interview to this wise, sincere, accomplished, and most entertaining of women. I wish to bespeak Jane Carlyle's friendliest ear to one of the noblest of women. We shall send you no such other." And in the letter of introduction which Emerson gave Margaret to present to Carlyle, he spoke of her as "an exotic in New England, a foreigner from some more sultry and expansive clime . . . our citizen of the world by special diploma," and urged Carlyle to introduce her to Tennyson and Browning, for "she has a sort of right to them both." Thus advised by his American friend, Carlyle called on Margaret and asked her to dinner at 5 Cheyne Row. He found her "a strange, lilting, lean old maid, not nearly such a bore as I expected." For her part, Margaret reported this visit to Emerson thus:

> That first time I was delighted with him. He was in a very sweet humor—full of wit and pathos, without being overbearing or oppressive. I was quite carried away with the rich flow of his discourse; and the hearty, noble earnestness of his personal being brought back the charm which once was upon his writing, before I wearied of it. I admired his Scotch, his way of singing his great, full sentences, so that each one was like the stanza of a narrative ballad. He let me talk now and then, enough to free my lungs and change my position, so that I did not get tired. That evening he talked of the present state of things in England, giving light, witty sketches of the men of the day, and some sweet homely stories he told of things he had known of the Scotch peasantry. Of you he spoke with hearty kindness; and he told with beautiful feeling a story of some poor farmer or artisan in the country, who on Sunday lays aside the cark and care of that dirty English world and sits reading the *Essays* and looking upon the sea.

The Sage of Chelsea was mildly pleased with the American visitor, and soon asked her to a dinner party, at which one of the other guests was George Henry Lewes. Carlyle brought them together, knowing that they were both interested in Goethe, for Emerson had assured him that Margaret was a great student of the German poet and "nobody here knows him so well." But Margaret took an instant dislike to this "witty, French, flippant sort of man, author of a History of Philosophy and now writing a Life of Goethe, a task for which he must be as unfit as irreligion and sparkling shallowness can make him." Margaret found little good to say of the man who was to attract George Eliot so greatly that she spent thirty years of her life in an irregular union with him. It was an odd trick of fate that George Eliot found comfort and encouragement in a passage from Margaret's journal, when she was about to elope with Lewes, a few years after this, and leave conventional England behind her. All that Margaret could say for Lewes was that he told stories admirably, and that she was glad of the interruptions that he made in Carlyle's discourse, which she found more acrid and brilliant than on the earlier occasion, but wearisome to one who disagreed with almost everything he said.

Carlyle held forth that evening on poetry for several hours, and to Margaret "the whole harangue was one eloquent proclamation of the defects in his own mind." Her host dismissed Tennyson as one who wrote in verse because the schoolmasters had taught him that it was great to do so; Burns as one similarly turned from the true path for a man; Shakespeare as one who had not the good sense to see that it would have been better to write in straightforward prose. This was nonsense to Margaret, amusing enough at first, but Carlyle ran the notion to death. That was bad enough, but:

The worst of hearing Carlyle is that you cannot interrupt him. I understand the habit and power of haranguing have increased very much upon him, so that you are a perfect prisoner when he has once got hold of you. To interrupt him is a physical impossibility. If you get a chance to remonstrate for a moment, he raises his voice and bears you down. True,

he does you no injustice and with his admirable penetration
sees the disclaimer in your mind, so that you are not morally
delinquent; but it is not pleasant to be unable to utter it.

The celebrated Miss Fuller, whose words had been waited
on by distinguished companies, did not enjoy being shouted
down by an "arrogant and overbearing" man, even if she considered him the "Siegfried of England." Her annoyance at this
habit of his ruined the evening for her, and may have contributed to the bad opinion she formed of George Lewes that
night.

Margaret did not allow her personal impression of Carlyle,
however, to color the account of him she wrote for the *Tribune*.
She did make much of his weakness for haranguing his listeners,
but she acclaimed him as one who bared unpleasant facts and
destroyed illusions, shattering the shams and conventions
which barred the way of progress: "He is indeed arrogant and
overbearing, but in his arrogance there is no trace of littleness
or self-love. It is in his nature, in the untamable energy that has
given him the power to crush the dragons." She summed him
up as "great and powerful, if not quite invulnerable, and of a
might rather to destroy evil than legislate for good." He seemed
to her a destructive genius, who cleared the ground for others
to build on. Carlyle was far from being immune to flattery, and
to be thus described in an influential American journal—
Emerson had posted him on Margaret's importance as a critic
—pleased his out-sized ego. He decided that she was "rather a
good woman" and regretted that he had been "somewhat loud
upon her and certain crotchets of hers." He read her new book
and found "less of that shoreless Asiatic dreaminess than I have
sometimes met with in her writings." He wrote to Emerson that
Margaret had "a true heroic mind;—altogether unique, so far as
I know, among the Writing Women of this generation; rare
enough too, God knows, among the Writing Men. She is very

narrow, sometimes; but she is truly high: honor to Margaret, and more and more good-speed to her."

Jane Carlyle was already an admirer of Margaret's work when they first met, for she had been much pleased by *Woman in the Nineteenth Century*. Margaret was quite as much charmed by her as Emerson had been. She wrote to Emerson: "I had, afterward, some talk with Mrs. C., whom hitherto I had only *seen*, for who can speak while her husband is there?" And she was not at a loss to assign a cause for the sadness of her hostess's eyes. The bond between the two women was strengthened by a little incident one evening when the Carlyles came to call upon Margaret. Mazzini, who was a close friend of Jane Carlyle's, was there, holding forth on his schemes for freeing the Italians from the Austrian yoke and for assuring European progress. Carlyle was in a surly temper, and poured forth a flood of denunciation on such "rose-water imbecilities." Mazzini tried vainly to remonstrate with him, and then became dejected. Jane noted this and said to Margaret: "These are but opinions to Carlyle; but to Mazzini, who has given his all and helped his friends to the scaffold in pursuit of such subjects, it is a matter of life and death." Margaret shared this sentiment and regretted that her last evening with Carlyle should have been thus marred.

She had tracked the last of the available literary lions to their dens, for Tennyson was away and Browning had just eloped to Italy with Elizabeth Barrett. So in November she went over to Paris with the Springs, never dreaming that her proposed return to London would not take place.

❖ CHAPTER XII ❖

France and Italy

---

*I am so constituted that it pains me to come away, having touched only
the glass over the picture.*—M. F.

MARGARET found Paris quite as absorbing as London, and regretted that so much of her time there had to be spent in
learning to speak fluent French, "without which I might as
usefully be in a well as here." She wrote home to her mother
that, "could I remain six months in this great focus of civilized
life, the time would be all too short for my desires and needs."
Here, as in London, her fame had preceded her: one of the
leading journals, *La Revue Indépendante,* had just published
a translation of her essay on American literature. The author's
name was given as Elizabeth Fuller, and Margaret asked the
editors to correct the mistake in their next issue. They in turn
asked her to become the *Revue's* American correspondent after
she returned home, for her essay had been well received, and
told her that *Woman* would be reviewed in the next number.
Margaret was greatly pleased, and thought that the offer was
"very pleasant and advantageous to me."

But somehow the printed word was not quite so serviceable
a social introduction as it had been in England and Scotland.
After two months in Paris, Margaret wrote to Emerson of her
plight:

> I need, to initiate me in various little secrets of the place
> and time—necessary for me to look at things to my satisfaction

190

—some friend, such as I do not find here. My steps have not been fortunate in Paris, as they were in England. No doubt the person exists here, whose aid I want; indeed I feel that it is so; but we do not meet, and the time draws near for me to depart.

French people I find slippery, as they do not know exactly what to make of me, the rather as I have not the command of their language. I see them, their brilliancy, grace, and variety, the thousand slight refinements of their speech and manner, but cannot meet them in their way. My French teacher says I speak and act like an Italian, and I hope in Italy I shall find myself more at home.

But she was consumed by a feverish desire to make the most of her opportunities despite all obstacles. She wanted to find out at first hand everything she could about this continent she had longed to see for so many years. She went everywhere she could, and faithfully recorded her impressions in her letters to the *Tribune*.

The theater was recommended to her as a good way to improve her French, and her first thought when she came to Paris was to see Rachel, the famous tragedienne, whose fame had crossed the Atlantic. Margaret expected to find a true genius, and for once was not disappointed in her expectations. It was the first time in her life that she had seen a play really well put on, with the lesser parts played as expertly as the leading roles, and none of the "stage-strut and vulgar bombast of tone" which had annoyed her in England. Margaret was a captious critic, but she saw Rachel seven or eight times, and only once could find fault with her performance. Rachel was now growing old and ugly, but she still had the divine force that had made her reputation. She was at her best in parts that demanded expression of the darker passions and the most desolate grief. Margaret liked her most as Phèdre: "The guilty love inspired by the hatred of a goddess was expressed in all its symptoms with a force and terrible naturalness that almost suffocated the beholder." Margaret judged her to be a "true artist, worthy Greece, and worthy at many moments to have her conceptions immortalized in marble." In the course of deploring the fact that there was no male actor fit to play with Rachel she let slip the comment that thus, besides the tragedy of the play itself, there is the additional tragedy, common in life, of "a woman of genius who throws away her precious heart, lives and dies for one unworthy of her." Margaret may have been thinking of a tragedy in which James Nathan was the inadequate foil to a woman of genius.

Another actress, almost as distinguished in lighter roles as Rachel was in tragedy, pleased Margaret a good deal. This was Rose Cheny, whom she saw play Clarissa Harlowe for the ninety-eighth time in a dramatic version of Richardson's novel. Margaret also saw her in several other parts, once in a play specially written for her by Scribe, but she was never so satisfying as in her famous role of Clarissa. There were many other plays in Paris, mostly devoted to poking fun at the personalities of the day, and Margaret found their sparkling wit and excellent acting very much to her taste. She decided that the French genius reached its inimitable best in the theater.

Then, too, there was opera galore during these months in Paris, but Margaret was disappointed in her hopes of hearing the best music well performed. She went once to the Opéra Comique, and found it no more than tolerable. She went no more, observing: "I find the tolerable intolerable in music." The Italian opera was more to her taste, but even here there was nothing truly excellent to her mind but the singing of Lablache. She deals cavalierly with the other singers, and finds the New York company preferable to that of Paris—which opinion no doubt delighted the readers of the *Tribune*. Margaret's reactions to music were sometimes rather curious, and perhaps her poor opinion of Parisian music may be discounted. She confesses that at this time she suffered miserably from toothache, both before and after going to a dentist who made an extraction with the aid of ether. The sickly after-effects of the new anesthetic and the pain continued until one night when she went to hear *Don Giovanni,* and then the music soothed her nerves and left her free from pain. In relating this experience which might have interested Mr. Atkinson, the mesmerizer, she asked pardon from the shade of Mozart, assuring him that she had "had no thought of turning his music to the account of a 'vulgar utility'!"

The French court made a great impression on Margaret, when she had the good fortune to attend the presentation of the Queen of Spain's fourteen-year-old sister, whose intended betrothal to Louis Philippe's youngest son kept the Chamber of Deputies in a tumult at this time. There was a ball after this ceremony at the Tuileries, and Margaret delighted in the picture presented by the handsome, brilliantly lit rooms filled with the flower of French society. She thought the few American women who were present carried off the honors as far as beauty was concerned, but that the Frenchwomen were better dressed and more impressive in air and manner. In this assembly she saw the astronomer Leverrier, a member of the French Academy, whose lectures at the Sorbonne she had tried to attend, only to be informed that women could not be admitted. But there were other lectures from which women were not barred, and Margaret attended these faithfully. She also visited the Academy on the day that Rémusat was inducted in the place of Royer-Collard, and was disappointed, as she had been in England, to discover that many of her literary idols were "quite old and very unlike the company on Parnassus as represented by Raphael." At the Chamber of Deputies she heard speeches for and against the Spanish marriage, and found the audience's complete disregard of a dull speaker most amusing. And in the library of the Chamber she saw Rousseau's manuscripts, which were far more eloquent to her than the most powerful orations of Berryer and Guizot from the tribune.

It was curiously exciting to her to touch these yellow, faded
papers: "I seemed to feel the fire of youth, immortally growing,
more and more expansive, with which his soul had pervaded
this century." Margaret realized how much her spirit owed to
Jean Jacques Rousseau:

> He was the precursor of all we most prize. True, his blood
> was mixed with madness, and the course of his actual life
> made some detours through villainous places, but his spirit
> was intimate with the fundamental truths of human na-
> ture, and fraught with prophecy. There is none who has
> given birth to more life for this age; his gifts are yet untold;
> they are too present with us; but he who thinks really must
> often think with Rousseau, and learn of him ever more and
> more.

It is a question whether Rousseau or Goethe had the greater
influence on Margaret's development.

Margaret owed this opportunity to inspect the Rousseau
manuscripts to the kindness of Alexandre Vattemare, who had
found her sympathetic to his scheme of an international exchange of books and documents by public libraries. She saw
and praised the collection to be sent to America from France,
and pleaded in a *Tribune* letter for an equally valuable assort-
ment to be sent in return. Through Vattemare's efforts she was
also able to visit the Imprimerie Royale and the Mint, and inspect one of the night schools for working people conducted by
the Christian Brothers. Margaret was greatly taken with the
school, and thought of starting a similar scheme when she
returned to America. In her visits to this and other institutions
she found much that might well be copied across the Atlantic,
where as yet there were no establishments for intelligent care
of the feeble-minded, or places where the poor might leave
their children in good hands during working hours. She pleaded
for these causes in her letters home.

She went one day to call upon Lamennais, to whom she had

a letter of introduction, and was disappointed to find a "citizen-looking man" with him, for she had hoped to have the apostle of democracy to herself. But her disappointment soon changed to delight when she was introduced to the other visitor, who was Béranger, the great lyric poet. She was overjoyed to be in the company of these two men, of whom she wrote:

> These are men who need no flourish of trumpets to an-nounce their coming—no band of martial music upon their steps—no obsequious nobles in their train. They are the true kings, the theocratic kings, the judges in Israel. The hearts of men make music at their approach; the mind of the age is like the historian of their passing; and only men of destiny like themselves shall be permitted to write their eulogies, or fill their vacant seats.

The obvious sincerity of her interest in social reform was suffi-cient password to admit her to Lamennais's friendship, and she later wrote to him an account of the popular movement in Italy. This meeting served to strengthen her concern with social reforms, and to give it a political bent.

George Sand, whom Margaret wanted to meet more than anyone else in Paris, was at her chateau in the country for many weeks after Margaret's arrival, but finally came to her town house late in January. Margaret wrote to her at once, asking if she might come and call, but there was no answer. After a week had passed Margaret took her courage into her hands and called at the Place d'Orléans. She wrote an account of what followed to Elizabeth Hoar:

> The servant who admitted me was in the picturesque costume of a peasant, and as Madame Sand afterward told me, her god-daughter whom she had brought from her province. She announced me as "Madame Salère," and re-turned to the anteroom to tell me, "Madame says she does not know you." I began to think I was doomed to a rebuff, among the crowd who deserve it. However, to make assurance sure,

I said, "Ask if she has not received a letter from me." As I spoke Madame S. opened the door and stood looking at me for an instant. Our eyes met. I shall never forget her look at that moment. The doorway made a frame for her figure; she is large but well formed. She was dressed in a robe of dark violet silk, with a black mantle on her shoulders, her beautiful hair dressed with the greatest taste, her whole appearance and attitude, in its simple and lady-like dignity, presenting an almost ludicrous contrast to the vulgar caricature idea of George Sand. Her face is a very little like the portraits, but much finer; the upper part of the forehead and eyes are beautiful, the lower strong and masculine, expressive of a hardy temperament and strong passions, but not in the least coarse; the complexion olive, and the air of the whole head Spanish (as indeed she was born in Madrid and is only on one side of French blood). All these details I saw at a glance; but what fixed my attention was the expression of *goodness*, nobleness, and power that pervaded the whole—the truly human heart and nature that shone in the eyes. As our eyes met, she said, "C'est vous," and held out her hand. I took it and went into her little study; we sat down a moment, then I said, "Il me fait de bien de vous voir," and I am sure I said it with my whole heart, for it made me very happy to see such a woman, so large and so developed a character, and everything that *is* good in it so *really* good. I loved, shall always love her.

She looked away, and said, "Ah! vous m'avez écrit une lettre charmante." This was all the preliminary of our talk, which then went on as if we had always known each other. She told me before I went away that she was going that very day to write to me; that when the servant announced me she did not recognize the name, but after a minute it struck her that it might be *la dame américaine*, as the foreigners very commonly call me, as they find my name hard to remember. She was very much pressed for time, as she was then preparing copy for the printer, and having just returned, there were many applications to see her, but she wanted me to stay then, saying "it is better to throw things aside and seize the present moment." I staid a good part of the day, and was very glad afterwards, for I did not see her again uninterrupted.

Margaret found George Sand's conversation as lively and picturesque as her writing, with the same undertone of deep feeling and the same skill in striking the nail on the head. She enjoyed the sense of a rich, prolific, and ardent genius, and decided that she had never liked a woman better.

She needs no defence, but only to be understood, for she has bravely acted out her nature, and always with good intentions. She might have loved one man permanently, if she could have found one contemporary with her who could interest and command her throughout her range; but there was hardly any possibility of that, for such a person. Thus she has naturally changed the objects of her affections several times. Also, there may have been something of the Bacchante in her life, and of the love of night and storm, and the free raptures amid which roamed on the mountain-tops the followers of Cybele, the great goddess, the great mother. But she was never coarse, never gross, and I am sure her generous heart has not failed to draw some rich drops from every kind of wine-press. When she has done with an intimacy, she likes to break it off suddenly, and this has happened often, both with men and women. Many calumnies upon her are traceable to this cause. I forgot to mention that, while talking, she *does* smoke all the time her little cigarette. This is now a common practice among ladies abroad, but I believe originated with her.

For the rest, she holds her place in the literary and social world of France like a man, and seems full of courage and energy in it. I suppose she has suffered much, but she has also enjoyed and done much, and her expression is one of calmness and happiness.

Mazzini had painted a glowing picture of George Sand to Margaret in London, and in Paris Margaret had found her honored and esteemed, even by American women "with the feelings of our country on such subjects." But even so, Margaret had not been quite prepared for such a woman in the person of one who "has had a series of lovers, and I am told has one now with whom she lives on the footing of combined means, independent friendship!"

Later, a mutual friend took her to see Chopin, who had lived with George Sand for the last twelve years. Margaret had heard much of his chronic ill health, and found him "as frail as a snow drop, but an exquisite genius." He played for her, but she enjoyed his conversation as much as his playing. In describing this meeting to a friend in America, Margaret mentioned one or two of the stories about Chopin and Madame Sand, but refused to commit herself as to their truth: "You cannot know much about anything in France, except what you see with your two eyes. Lying is ingrained in 'la grande nation,' as they so plainly show, no less in literature than life." Margaret's natural frankness and passion for truth made her dislike the French because of this trait of theirs.

She was glad to leave Paris when February 25, the date set for starting their journey to Italy, finally came. Just before their departure, her party enjoyed the first fine day they had had since their arrival in Paris more than two months before. The fine weather brought all Paris out on the boulevards, and Margaret confessed that she had never seen anything finer or more animated than the scene along the Champs Elysées that day, with fine carriages and riders on swift horses on the roadway, and on the footpaths groups of "passably pretty ladies with excessively pretty bonnets" accompanied by their children, whom Margaret found charming. She was not charmed, however, by the Parisian men on this spring-like day: "Their air, half-military, half-dandy, of self-esteem and savoir-faire is not particularly interesting; nor are the glassy stare and fumes of bad cigars exactly what one most desires to encounter, when the heart is opened by the breath of spring zephyrs and the hope of buds and blossoms."

Margaret had come to know too well what lay beneath the superficial gaiety and frivolity of Paris: the suffering of a famine-stricken populace and the deep unrest of the poor. She prophesied that if relief did not soon come to the masses through reforms, this unrest would burst into revolutionary flames. The explosion came sooner than she had anticipated, but she had read rightly the portent she discovered in the library of the Invalides. Seeing portraits of Napoleon and Louis Philippe facing each other, she remarked that these pictures might serve as frontispieces to two chapters of French history, in the first of which was sown the seed of all that was subsequently vital: "By Napoleon the career was really laid open to talent, and all that is really great in France now consists in the possibility that talent finds of struggling to the light."

She found further confirmation of her forebodings when her party stopped at Lyons on its way southward, to inspect the homes of the weavers who had made the city famous. Here a whole family lived and worked in one room, the looms taking up so much space that the beds were shelves near the ceiling, reached by ladders. The children were put to work at the age of nine, and once they began were allowed no time for lessons or play. The weavers were always in want, and degeneration was rife. In reporting these conditions Margaret lashed out at those who calmly accepted them and dismissed those who protested and sought remedies as visionaries and fanatics. But her indignation did not interfere with a sentimental pilgrimage on the following day to the tomb of Laura at Avignon, though this proved to be rather a dreary business, since ice coated the Rhone and there was snow. Bad weather dogged the travelers'

course southward to Arles and Marseilles, where they took ship
for Genoa and spent a wretched thirty hours making a trip
which usually took sixteen.

They did not see the end of the bitter winter weather upon
their arrival in sunny Italy, and a cutting wind spoilt the
charm of Genoa for Margaret. They hurried on to Leghorn
and Pisa, and thence by steamer to Naples. The trip was eventful, for the steamer was involved in a collision which nearly
sent it to the bottom. This incident increased the dread of the
sea which Margaret had come to feel. But after the first few days
at Naples, she forgot her fears and rejoiced that at last she had
reached the heart of the Italy of which she had so long dreamed.
But the real Italy bore little resemblance to her ideal:

> For the first week was an exact copy of the miseries of a
> New England spring; a bright sun came for an hour or
> two in the morning, just to coax you forth without your
> cloak, and then came up a villainous, horrible wind, exactly
> like the worst east wind of Boston, breaking the heart, rack-
> ing the brain, and turning hope and fancy to an irrevocable
> green and yellow hue, in lieu of their native rose.

No vagaries of the weather, however, could spoil Naples for
Margaret, for here was much that she knew of through her reading, but found heightened beyond her expectations in reality.
And "if the cold wind hid Italy, it could not hide the Italians."
She liked them at first sight as much as she had disliked the
French; in the faces she saw in the streets she found character,
dignity, and the "capacity for pure, exalting passion." The
women were charming, the men refined, eloquent, and courteous. So much of Italy was as she had dreamed it.

In April the party went on to Rome, where they took lodgings
on the Corso, since they planned a stay of some length there.
Margaret was glad to settle down; she had decided that "the
traveller passing along the beaten track, vetturinoed from inn
to inn, ciceroned from gallery to gallery, thrown through in-

dolence, want of tact, or ignorance of language too much into the society of his compatriots, sees the least possible of the country." Here, in the heart of Rome, Margaret hoped to win an intimate knowledge of Italy by abandoning herself to the spirit of the place. She felt herself no tourist in this city which had been dear to her since childhood, and she was contemptuous of the hordes of foreign invaders, particularly the English, who "seem to me the most unseeing of all possible animals." She had liked them at home on their snug little island, but here they were out of place. It was a pleasure to describe them in her *Tribune* letter as guilty of worse sins than her own compatriots:

> What is the vulgarity expressed in our tobacco-chewing and way of eating eggs, compared to that which elbows the Greek marbles, guidebook in hand—chatters and sneers through the Miserere of the Sistine Chapel, beneath the very glance of Michael Angelo's Sibyls—praises to St. Peter's as "nice"—talks of "managing" the Colosseum by moonlight— and snatches "bits" for a "sketch" from the sublime silence of the Campagna.

Margaret heard owls hooting by moonlight in the Colosseum, and found their speech more to the purpose than any guide's. She attended the Holy Week services at St. Peter's, but thought the famous pomps and shows less imposing than the quiet daily life of the great church. The richness and fullness of Roman life, the serenity of the Campagna, were equally to her taste. She no longer tried to see all the sights at once, but allowed the city to exercise its spell upon her as it would.

Political forces were stirring in Rome at this time, and Margaret heard much about them from a young Italian nobleman, the Marchese Giovanni Angelo Ossoli, whom she met by chance in St. Peter's. She had gone with the Springs to hear vespers there on Holy Thursday, and after the service had wandered alone among the chapels and failed to find her friends at the

place where they were to meet her. Her shortsighted peerings
made it evident that she was seeking someone. Ossoli saw her
searching about the church, and asked if he could help her.
They were unable to find the Springs and left the church to
seek a carriage in which Margaret could go home. But there
happened to be none that evening in the piazza before St.
Peter's, so Ossoli escorted her home on foot. As Margaret had
little command of Italian, there was not much conversation between them, but they took a fancy to each other and Ossoli
became a frequent visitor. He helped Margaret to speak Italian,
and she learned a good deal of what was going on in the political world from him.

The liberal Pope Pius IX granted the Roman populace a
representative council shortly after Margaret's arrival, and
from her room on the Corso she was able to watch the thou-
sands of torch-bearers who passed through the illuminated
streets, on their way to the Quirinal to thank the Pope for this
concession. She had never witnessed a finer spectacle than this
stream of fire, the surging crowd noises, the red and white
Bengal fires shining on the animated faces, and the impressive
appearance of the Pope on his balcony to greet the crowd,
which cheered him and then knelt to receive his blessing.
During this same week, a great dinner was given in the open
air at the Baths of Titus, in honor of the founding of Rome.
Here, in sight of the Colosseum and the triumphal arches of
the Caesars, the company rejoiced in the prospect of happier
days under the liberal rule of Pio Nono. Among the guests were
many political exiles who had been restored to citizenship by
the Pontiff. The Marchese d'Azeglio, a son-in-law of the great
writer Manzoni, spoke at this dinner and made reference to an
earlier pope's defiance of the Holy Roman Emperor as kindling
the first spark of liberty in Italy. The Austrian Ambassador took
offense at this remark when it was published in the press, and
threatened that his country would be forced to break off relations with the Papacy if such language was tolerated. So the

outspokenness of the liberal leaders was checked, and the scheme of another popular dinner on the Pope's birthday was abandoned, in order to avoid the occasion of further frankness. Margaret was annoyed at the gradualism of the Roman liberals, and noted that "the liberty of Rome does not yet advance with seven-league boots; and the new Romulus will need to be prepared for deeds at least as bold as his predecessor's, if he is to open a new order of things."

In such an atmosphere as this, the shift in Margaret's interests, which had begun in New York and continued ever since, became evident even to herself. Early that May she wrote to William Channing:

> I write not to you about these countries, of the famous people I see, of magnificent shows and places. All these things are only to me an illuminated margin on the text of my inward life. Earlier, they would have been more. Art is not important to me now. I like only what little I find that is transcendently good, and even with that feel very familiar and calm. I take interest in the state of the people, their manners, the state of the race in them. I see the future dawning; it is in important aspects Fourier's future. But I like no Fourierites; they are terribly wearisome here in Europe; the tide of things does not wash through as violently as with us, and they have time to run in the tread-mill of the system. Still, they serve this great future which I shall not live to see. I must be born again.

But she had to concern herself with the "illuminated margin" in her *Tribune* letters, and no word could now be breathed about Fourier, for Horace Greeley had been badly worsted in a debate with H. J. Raymond of the *Courier and Enquirer* on the merits of socialism and Fourierism. Mr. Raymond's presentation of the shocking views of Fourier on marriage and family life had been so telling with the public that Greeley had been forced to drop the *Tribune's* advocacy of the Frenchman's economic views.

Consequently, in order to please her employer and to gain the necessary revenue from her articles, Margaret discussed more common topics in her letters destined for publication, although her heart was not in them. She visited the studios of the foreign artists in Rome, and gave an account of each, with particular attention to the numerous Americans who had flocked abroad to study art. Few of the men she concerned herself with in these accounts won any lasting fame, and what she had written Caroline Sturgis about a young English artist: "What he does is bad, but full of great desire," is the best that can be said for many of them today. But it was an essential part of a grand tour in this era to sit for one's likeness to Macdonald, Tenerani, Wolff, Gott, Crawford, Gibson, Overbeck, Terry, Cranch, or Hicks in their studios in Rome or Florence, and to bear the finished portrait or bust home for preservation as an heirloom. Margaret herself was "done" by Thomas Hicks, and most of her friends were among the American artistic exiles.

After thus catering to national pride, Margaret dealt with the art of the past. She found herself unable to express on paper her great enthusiasm for the classic marbles: "They should not be described, but reproduced." She began to appreciate Domenichino and Titian among the great painters, but her art criticism was still puerile: "Leonardo I cannot yet like at all; but I suppose the pictures are good for some people to look at; they show a wonderful deal of study and thought." Despite her intention to keep clear of such matters, her letters to the *Tribune* begin to show the change in her interests; there is less formal description of famous places and less clumsy art criticism, more social observation and mention of political happenings. The subterranean storm which was to burst out in revolution all over Europe the following spring had caught her attention, and it fascinated her.

In June her party left Rome and went to Florence by way of

Assisi and Perugia. Here they lingered a month; and Margaret tried to rest, though she was eager to see all that the city afforded. She wrote to Emerson at this time that in Rome there had always been something that they could not bear to miss every minute, both day and night, and that once she had retired, conversation or music beneath her window on the Corso had usually made sleep impossible. Her fellow travelers' scheme was to visit the cities of northern Italy hurriedly, and then go on to Switzerland and Germany. Margaret was tired out before she started, and their sightseeing pace was too brisk for her taste, so she determined to part company with them in Switzerland, return to Florence and spend the autumn and perhaps the winter in Rome. She fell ill in Venice in July, and urged the Springs to continue their tour without her.

Before reaching Venice, they had visited Bologna, which won Margaret's heart because of the fact that "there has the spark of intellect in woman been cherished with reverend care." She saw the monument of Matilda Tambroni, who had been professor of Greek in a university which did not scorn able women. She found the statue of another woman who had taught anatomy at Bologna. And the women artists Properzia di Rossi, Elisabetta Sirani, and Lavinia Fontana were honored by the conspicuous place given to their works. In other Italian cities Margaret had seen the Casino dei Nobili devoted to masculine entertainment. But here in Bologna the women had their own casino and were "the soul of society." The Feminist found great comfort in all this, and in the reverence paid to the Madonna and saintly women, and decided that these were portents of a better state in the future for the women of Italy.

Her party had gone on to Venice by way of Ravenna and Padua. The old city drowsing on the Adriatic stirred Margaret strangely. The ramshackle palaces on the Grand Canal were being restored for the use of newcomers, for Venice was now an asylum for the deposed dynasties of the past. Margaret was one of a crowd which watched the arrival of the guests at a birthday party given by the Duchesse de Berri for her son. Her palace was so brilliantly lit that even the pictures on the walls could be clearly seen from the canal, where the splendidly dressed guests left their gondolas to ascend the great entrance stairway. A band stationed opposite delighted those who came to watch from their gondolas. For once Margaret did not mourn the past which this spectacle revived:

> I, too, amid the mob, a pleasant position in Venice alone, thought of the Stuarts, Bourbons, Bonapartes here in Italy, and offered up a prayer that other names, when the possessors have power without the heart to use it for the emancipation of mankind, might be added to the list, and other princes, more rich in blood than brain, might come to enjoy a perpetual *villeggiatura* in Italy. It did not seem to me a cruel wish. The show of greatness will satisfy every legitimate desire of such minds. A gentle punishment for the distributors of *lettres de cachet* and Spielberg dungeons to their fellowmen.

The ferment of revolution was working in Margaret's brain.

Her illness in Venice had no more serious consequence than bringing about her parting with the Springs. They were reluctant to leave her, but there was much they wanted to see before Marcus had to return to his business in New York, and the time they had allotted themselves was drawing short. Margaret lingered for a fortnight in Venice, taking particular delight in the work of the painters who had mirrored every aspect of their beautiful city in their canvases. She was so charmed by Venice that she felt as if no one had ever really seen it before, for no one had expressed what she felt about it. Finally she tore herself away, and went on to Vicenza, Verona, Mantua, Garda, and Brescia, learning "more than ever in any previous ten days of my existence." She caught a fever at Brescia, and grew alarmed when it seemed to affect her head. The two days she had spent in idleness at Lago di Garda, to rest and complete her recuperation from her illness in Venice, did not offset this new attack. She had no companions to take care of her, no medicine at hand, and hardly enough Italian to describe her symptoms to a doctor. So she resolutely refrained from food, drank much cold water, and on the second day had a bed made up in a carriage and went on to Milan. She was not the iron-willed Timothy Fuller's daughter for nothing.

Milan was as firmly associated in Margaret's mind with Manzoni, the author of *I Promessi Sposi*, as the Trossachs were with Walter Scott. He was one of the literary idols that she had long wished to worship face to face, and now her wish was gratified. Her meeting with Manzoni was described in a letter to Emerson:

> Today, for the first time, I have seen Manzoni. Manzoni has spiritual efficacy in his looks; his eyes still glow with delicate tenderness, as when he first saw Lucia, or felt them fill the image of Father Cristoforo. His manners are very engaging, frank, expansive; every word betokens the habitual elevation of his thoughts; and (what you would care for so much) he says distinct, good things; but you must not expect me to note them down. He lives in the house of his fathers in the simplest manner. He has taken the liberty to marry a new wife for his pleasure and companionship, and the people around him do not like it, because she does not, to their fancy, make a good pendant to him. But I liked her very well, and saw why he married her. They asked me to return often if I pleased, and I mean to go once or twice, for Manzoni seems to like to talk to me.

To Margaret, however, and to her friends of the revolutionary party known as Young Italy, Manzoni was a representative of a past epoch in thought. "The passive virtues he teaches are no longer what is wanted; the manners he paints with so delicate a fidelity are beginning to change." The delicate humor and satire of his work were still prized, but the new age wanted a "more fervent hope, a more active faith." And to Margaret this seemed only right.

At Milan she found rest from the fever to observe and study which had driven her through northern Italy at a whirlwind pace. The Italy she had known in books had been the south, the Roman states and Tuscany, but now she found that the north was far more absorbing. But here at Milan there was little to see, and she took her ease. She met some radicals, "young and interested in ideas," and heard the latest news of the revolutionary movement. Austrian troops were marching on Ferrara, where one of their spies had been assassinated. There were disturbances in Rome, and rumors of a republican conspiracy. A National Guard, modeled on the French pattern, was being formed in preparation for events which neither radical nor moderate dared to predict. Margaret took a keen interest in all this, for she hoped to see her London friend Mazzini's program realized at last on his native soil. She wrote: "I am yet too much a stranger to speak with assurance of impressions I have received. But it is impossible not to hope."

After a good rest, she continued her solitary travels, going to Lago Maggiore and thence to Switzerland during August. She found the glories of the Swiss landscape refreshing after her preoccupation with art and man, particularly the St. Bernard region: "It was as bracing as a cold bath after the heat of a crowd amid which one has listened to some most eloquent oration." She planned to write a separate account of her Swiss journey, but never carried the intention into execution. On her return from Switzerland, she spent a fortnight at Lake Como with the Marchesa Arconati Visconti, whom she had met in Florence in June, through a letter of introduction from a mutual friend in Paris. Madame Arconati had taken a fancy to the American visitor, and introduced her to her titled friends who had their villas on the shores of the lake. It was a new side of Italian life that Margaret saw here: an easy-going, restful life lived by charming people in beautiful houses and gardens, amid the glories of a region to which Margaret thought that neither artists nor writers had done justice. She was charmed by the "duchesses, marquises, and the like," of whom she wrote rather proudly home; particularly with a Princess Radziwill, with whom she soon became very friendly. For all her democratic sentiments, Margaret was thrilled by her tours of Lake Como in the company of these women who bore two of the great names of Europe, and to be herself mistaken for a countess by the girls of Bellagio, who greeted the visitors with flowers and good wishes. In writing of her two new friends to Caroline Sturgis, she observed: "It is rather pleasant to come a little on the traces of these famous histories; also, both these ladies take pleasure in telling me of spheres so unlike mine, and do it well."

She and her friends made excursions about the lake by boat, and climbed the mountains in search of wild flowers. She also visited the near-by Lake Lugano, and was out on it in a high gale, which she found exhilarating rather than terrifying. The wild waters and the dark clouds scudding over the neighboring peaks did not disturb her, because she had great confidence in the boatmen, whom she considered more honest and manly than the urban Italians. She listened with interest to their stories and admired their strong characters and picturesque and incisive talk. The conversation of these simple men was more to her taste than the account of Van Diemen's Land which she received at Lugano from Lady Franklin, the wife of the British polar explorer.

After her stay among the lakes, she returned to Milan to see the celebrations in honor of the Madonna on the Feast of the Assumption, and of the arrival of the new Archbishop, who did not share the Austrian sympathies of his predecessor and hence was dear to the Milanese. Margaret was greatly interested in the reaction of the Italians to their Austrian overlords; she found that the invaders had gained no knowledge of their subjects and that their rule had not succeeded in rooting out

Italian patriotism. The nobility refused to associate with the
Austrians; the middle classes provided the intellectual leadership for revolutionary effort; and only the lower classes, allowed
a degree of well-being by their rulers' policy but denied a free
press and free assembly, had been dulled into passivity. But
now even they were aroused, first by indignation at the Austrian
occupation of Ferrara, and then by the police firing on a crowd
which listened sympathetically to some young men singing the
hymn in honor of Pius IX during the Archbishop's reception.

From Milan Margaret passed on to Florence by way of Pavia,
Parma, Bologna, and Modena, seeking out artistic treasures as
she went, and finding fresh evidence of the coming political
storm. She arrived in Florence just too late for the great fete
that had been held on September 12, in honor of the Grand
Duke's granting of permission to form a National Guard in
Tuscany. Of this she gathered an account from her friends
among the American colony. But when she arrived, she was
worn out by the fatigue of her journey—she always had to pay
a heavy price for her insatiable sightseeing—and was glad to
accept the offer of a Mr. Mozier, an American merchant turned
sculptor, to stay at his house. She spent a few days in bed, and
Mrs. Mozier's care, quiet, and a regular diet soon brought about
her recovery.

Margaret had discovered how many difficulties had been
smoothed over for her when Marcus Spring made the arrangements for his party. She could linger where she willed, now
that she traveled alone, but the petty annoyances and discom-
forts which beset her took all the joy out of that. There is a note
of weariness in her *Tribune* letters, a hastiness and a tendency
to skip over portions of her journey with a never-realized promise of a fuller account at another time. And now that she had
seen so much, she knew what she had missed earlier in life. "A
little money would have enabled me to come here long ago, and
find those that belong to me, or at least try my experiments;
then my health would never have sunk, nor the best years of

my life been wasted in useless friction." She had high hopes
for what might come of her five months in Rome before she had
to return home, but she wanted to spend years there, not
months.

She had not cared much for Florence when she first saw it
in June; it was not Italian enough for her. But in her present
mood Margaret was glad enough to be among friends in a town
which, as she wrote Caroline Sturgis, "is more in its spirit like
Boston than an Italian city." She had become friendly with
Powers and Greenough, the two best-known American sculptors in the city, and Carlyle had written a letter of introduction
for her to the Brownings, describing her as one "who will really
prove worthy (when once you get into her dialect) of being
known to you." She did not see much of the newly married
couple, however, for now she was more interested in politics
than in literature. Her circle in Florence was full of the former.
The grant of a National Guard had been taken by the Italians
as the first step toward truly national institutions and representation of the people, and had been accompanied by a general
forgetting of old scores and a reconciliation of all parties. On
the twelfth, strangers and one-time foes had embraced and
kissed one another; and the various groups exchanged banners
as a token of unity. Greenough, who took a keen interest in
Italian affairs, had played a leading part in the festivities.
Margaret had nothing but praise for him and scorn for her
other compatriots who joined the English residents in an attitude typified by the remark of one of them to her that "he did
not see what the Italians wanted of a National Guard, unless to
wear these little caps." She had kind words for Crawford, too,
who joined the National Guard in Rome and cheerfully took
time from his studio to drill.

The ferment of the new era was at work in Florence this
September. Everywhere in the streets Margaret heard the
hymn in honor of the Pope, who was regarded as the apostle
of progress by the people of Florence. There were processions

singing patriotic songs. Liberal plays were performed in the theaters to vast applause. The Grand Duke was constrained by these portents to more liberal measures than he had dreamed of. Margaret pleaded with her American readers for an expression of sympathy from across the Atlantic. She urged that a cannon, purchased by American contributions and graced with the name of Cabot, Amerigo, or Columbus, should be given to the National Guard in the name of democracy, "for salutes on festive occasions, if they should be so happy as to have no more serious need."

IV

FULFILLMENT

1847–1850

❦CHAPTER XIII❧

"My Italy"

Now my life must be a failure, so much strength has been wasted on abstractions, which only came because I grew not in the right soil.

—M. F.

UPON her arrival in Rome, about the middle of October 1847, Margaret settled herself for the winter in rooms on the Corso, "where I see all the motions of Rome." It was a great relief to renounce the "restless impertinence of sightseeing," and to enjoy a quiet life after the frenzied traveling of the last year. She wrote to Emerson shortly after her return to Rome: "I shall make no acquaintance from whom I do not hope a great deal, as my time will be like pure gold to me this winter; and just for happiness, Rome itself is sufficient."

She had already had one close friend in Rome, whether or not she hoped a great deal from him. This was the young Marchese Ossoli, who made much of the devotion that he had formed for her as a result of their acquaintanceship the previous spring. After Margaret's return, she saw a good deal of Ossoli, and gradually they became inseparable companions. The intimacy began on the ground that he could help Margaret in her work, but it soon developed a more personal basis. Margaret now had a notion of writing a history of the present period in Italy, and had begun to interpret the political events of the day by means of the views she had acquired from Mazzini in London and later in correspondence with him. Ossoli came of an extremely conservative family whose sole devotion was to the Papal cause, but he himself had been affected by the new liberalism and under Margaret's influence soon espoused the cause of liberty and revolution with almost as much fervor as she did. He brought her batches of political news and the latest views of both parties, as he heard them from his family and friends and in the cafés. Together they attended meetings of the different factions, and discussed the events of the day.

It was a glorious autumn in Rome. During two whole months there were but two days of rain, and the fine weather heightened for Margaret the gorgeous spectacles of the feasts of the Trasteverini and the maneuvers of six thousand members of the Civic Guard. Margaret enjoyed herself thoroughly during these months; she felt herself "no longer a staring, sightseeing stranger, riding about finely dressed in a coach to see muses and sibyls," but a citizen of Rome, who spoke the tongue with ease, knew the message every stone conveyed, and had a Roman companion to escort her. In November, when William Wetmore Story and his wife Emelyn came to Rome, proposing to spend the winter there, she found lodgings for them near her own and got them settled in Roman life as if she were the oldest inhabitant of the city. Story had given up his career as a lawyer in Boston, where he had dabbled at writing and attended Margaret's Conversations, to become a sculptor in Italy, and he was a welcome addition to Margaret's Roman circle. In December she wrote home to her mother: "My life at Rome is thus far all I hoped. I have not been so well since I was a child, nor so happy ever, as during the last six weeks." Ossoli was her constant companion; her acquaintance with the Storys ripened into warm friendship; and on Monday evenings she received her friends and queened it in her own little flower-filled salon. She wrote and studied much, although she passed five or six hours a day exploring Rome on foot and by carriage.

Sometime during this golden autumn Ossoli became her lover. His adoration was most welcome to her in her present mood, and the Latin concept of woman as mother and wife had appealed to her frustrated femininity and sunk into her consciousness, gradually displacing her notion of herself as a Feminist consecrated to a single life. With the example of George Sand before her, Margaret at first had no serious thought of marriage, for Ossoli was ten years younger than herself, well-nigh penniless, and dependent for such prospects as he had upon the goodwill of his family, who could not be expected to look with favor upon an alliance with a Protestant who professed revolutionary opinions. He was also by no means her intellectual equal, and probably in the habit of thinking of her more as a mother than a lover, which Italians often do when they idealize a woman. He had a great respect for her intellectual powers, and the spell of her personality, embodied as it was in one so different physically from Italian women, overcame for him the barriers of her age and lack of beauty. Their relationship completed the long-delayed feminization of Margaret, and brought peace to her personality at last. It was appropriate that this second spring came to her in the city that she had always felt to be her spiritual home.

Their life together served to draw Margaret closer to Roman life, and away from her compatriots. She felt that this was her Italy and her Rome, and wrote:

> Since I have experienced the different atmosphere of the European mind, and have been allied with it, nay mingled in the bonds of love, I suffer more than ever from that which is peculiarly American or English. I should like to cease from hearing the language for a time. Perhaps I should return to it; but at present I am in a state of unnatural divorce from what I was most allied to.

She was torn by conflicting emotions, as the repressions of years gave way under Ossoli's attentions. It was strange to her that her friend the Princess Radziwill should remark at this time: "How happy you are; so free, so serene, so attractive, so self-possessed!" Margaret did not feel that she was a person to be envied; her happiness had come almost too late for her to enjoy it. She would have liked to have been completely free to make the most of it, free of all care, but the letters to the *Tribune* had to be written, if that source of income was to continue, so write them she did when she longed to be passing lazy, loving hours with Ossoli. One, designed to appear in America about the first of the year, contains an interesting amplification of her opinion of her compatriots abroad, as she saw them through new eyes:

The American in Europe, if a thinking mind, can only become more American. In some respects, it is a great pleasure to be here. Although we have an independent political existence, our position toward Europe, as to literature and the arts, is still that of a colony, and one feels the same joy here that is experienced by the colonist in returning to the parent home. What was but a picture becomes a reality to us; remote allusions and derivations trouble no more: we see the pattern of the stuff and understand the whole tapestry. There is a gradual clearing up on many points, and many baseless notions and crude fancies are dropped. Even the posthaste passage of the business American through the great cities, escorted by cheating couriers and ignorant *valets de place,* unable to hold intercourse with the natives of the country and passing all his leisure hours with his countrymen who know no more than himself, clears his mind of some mistakes—lifts some mists from his horizon.

There are three species. First, the servile American—a being utterly shallow, thoughtless, worthless. He comes abroad to spend his money and indulge his tastes. His object in Europe is to have fashionable clothes, good foreign cookery, to know some titled persons, and furnish himself with coffee-house gossip, by retailing which among those less travelled and as uninformed as himself he can win importance at home. I look with unspeakable contempt upon this class—a class which has all the thoughtlessness and partiality of the exclusive classes of Europe, without any of their refinement, or the chivalric feeling which still sparkles among them here and there. . . .

Then there is the conceited American, instinctively bristling and proud of—he knows not what. He does not see, not he, that the history of humanity for many centuries is likely to have produced results it requires some training, some devotion, to appreciate and profit by. With his great clumsy hands, only fitted to work on a steam-engine, he seizes the old Cremona violin, makes it shriek with anguish in his grasp, and then declares he thought it was all humbug before he came, and now he knows it; that there is not really any music in these old things; that the frogs in one of our swamps make much finer, for they are young and alive. To him the etiquettes of courts and camps, the ritual of the Church, seem simply silly—and no wonder, profoundly ignorant as he is of their origin and meaning. Just so the legends which are the subjects of pictures, the profound myths which are represented in the antique marbles, amaze and revolt him; as indeed such things need to be judged of by another standard than that of the Connecticut Blue Laws. He criticizes severely pictures, feeling quite sure that his natural senses are better means of judgment than the rules of connoisseurs—not feeling that to see such objects mental vision as well as fleshly eyes are needed, and that something is aimed at in Art beyond the imitation of the commonest forms of Nature. This is Jonathan in the sprawling state, the booby tyrant, not yet aspiring enough to be a good schoolboy. Yet in his folly there is meaning; add thought and culture to his independence and he will be a man of might: he is not a creature without hope, like the thick-skinned dandy of the class first specified. The artists form a class by themselves. Yet among them, though seeking special aims by special means, may also be found the lineaments of these two classes, as well as of the third, of which I am now to speak.

This is that of the thinking American—a man who recognizing the immense advantage of being born to a new world and on a virgin soil, yet does not wish one seed from the past to be lost. He is anxious to gather and carry back with him every plant that will bear a new climate and new culture. Some will dwindle; others will attain a bloom and stature unknown before. He wishes to gather them clean, free from noxious insects, and to give them a fair trial in his new world. And that he may know the conditions under which he may best place them in that new world, he does not neglect to study their history in this.

Margaret unquestionably classed herself with the third group, but she had been known to ape some of the practices of the second, of "Jonathan in the sprawling state." After this sharp analysis of her fellow countrymen—the categories are still largely valid for Americans abroad—Margaret poured forth her feelings about the present state of Europe and America and her hopes for the future, in a tremendous, impassioned flow of rhetoric, for which she begged a kind reception, for "it is, of itself, some merit for printed words to be sincere."

Nothing could be more sincere than the succeeding letters in which Margaret reports the increasing political stir and the views of those engaged in the struggle for liberty. Horace Greeley got a better bargain than he had reckoned on in his foreign correspondent, for by background, natural sympathies, and present environment Margaret was cut out for her task. In April of that year Bronson Alcott had been shown some of her letters by Emerson and wrote in his *Journals:* "A finer diplomatic influence could not have been sent across the water." For once the musings of his prophetic soul were realized more promptly and completely than he ever dreamed. The truth of his observation soon became apparent to many not so close to her as he had been.

Her fate grudged her even a few weeks of joy. Sometime in December she knew that she was going to have a child. It is thought, on the basis of Mrs. Story's account of Margaret's life in Rome, that her marriage with Ossoli took place at this time, although the date is uncertain because of the secrecy they preserved about their relationship for many months after this. She had never dreamed, as she had longed for a child of her own, that its coming might be unwelcome, but so it was at this tide in her affairs. Neither she nor Ossoli had resources or friends that they could turn to in this crisis. They felt that they must keep their love secret until events might offset his family's objections. Meanwhile he was dependent upon their bounty for his slender living, and she upon her work, whose progress the coming of their child would disrupt. Margaret was swept from the peaks of happiness into the depths of despair. She wrote to Emerson, who was at a loss to account for the sudden change of her mood:

> Nothing less than two or three years, free from care and forced labor, would heal all my hurts, and renew my life-blood at its source. Since Destiny will not grant me that, I hope she will not leave me long in the world, for I am tired of keeping myself up in the water without corks, and without strength to swim. . . . None to help me, if I am not prudent to face it—this incubus of the future.

To add to her depression the weather changed, and there was nothing now but day after day of torrential rain. She could not go out for exercise, and her rooms in the Corso, which had seemed so attractive during the fine weather, were now so dark and damp that she needed a lamp to write by even in the morning, and she soon grew ill from the effects of the dampness. Just after the New Year, she wrote to Caroline Sturgis of her woes, without revealing what caused them:

I have known some happy hours, but they all lead to sorrow; and not only the cups of wine, but of milk, seemed drugged with poison for me. It does not *seem* to be my fault, this Destiny; I do not court these things—they come. I am a poor magnet, with power to be wounded by the bodies I attract. . . .

When I arrived in Rome, I was at first intoxicated to be here. The weather was beautiful, and many circumstances combined to place me in a kind of passive, childlike well-being. That is all over now, and with this year I enter upon a sphere of my destiny so difficult that I at present see no way out, except through the gate of death. It is useless to write of it; you are at a distance and cannot help me—whether accident or angel will, I have no intimation. I have no reason to hope that I shall not reap what I have sown, and do not. Yet how I shall endure it I cannot guess; it is all a dark and sad enigma. The beautiful forms of art charm no more, and a love in which there is all fondness but no help flatters in vain. I am all alone; nobody around me sees any of this.

Margaret, whose greatest characteristic was her outspokenness, somehow managed to conceal her secret so well that not one of her friends ever guessed it. She fought out her battle with despair by herself, and continued to write her letters to the *Tribune* about the march of events without revealing her mood or allowing it to interfere with her work.

At first Margaret had been a little dismayed to discover how overjoyed the Roman people were by the Pontiff's first tentative steps toward reform. Probably her Calvinistic background protested against the ruler of the "kingdom of anti-Christ" being the idol of the forces of progress and light, to which she herself belonged. And she disliked the way the people took liberal concessions from their princes as gifts, not as their due. But as she came to know the Italians better, she began, despite her prejudices, to share their admiration for Pius IX. Her fears because all the hopes of the liberals were wrapped up in one mortal man were relieved when an Italian friend assured her: "If Pius IX be spared to us for five years, it will be impossible for his successors ever to take a backward course . . . we can learn as much in two months as other nations in twenty years." And she saw the truth of this remark borne out by the progress made toward liberty in Tuscany in a few short months. Now, in Rome, the Pope was the idol of the crowds; the streets resounded with his praises. And Margaret joined in the chorus:

The Italians have one term of praise particularly characteristic of their highly endowed nature. They say of such and such, *"Ha una phisonomia simpatica"*—"He has a sympathetic expression"—and this is praise enough. This may be pre-eminently said of that of Pius IX. *He* looks indeed as if nothing human could be foreign to him. Such alone are the genuine kings of men. He has shown undoubted wisdom, clear-sightedness, bravery, and firmness; but it is above all his generous human heart that gives him his power over this people. His is a face to shame the selfish, redeem the sceptic, alarm the wicked, and cheer to new effort the weary and heavy-laden. What form the issues of his life may take is yet uncertain; in my belief, they are such as he does not think of; but they cannot fail to be for good. For my part, I shall always rejoice to have been here in his time. The working of his influence confirms my theories, and it is a positive treasure to me to have seen him.

Such was Margaret's opinion of the head of the Catholic Church. Her sympathy for Catholicism itself, which had first become evident at Brook Farm when its influence began to be felt there, grew in this Catholic land. She gave sympathetic accounts of the ceremonies on the Feast of All Souls and on the day devoted to honoring St. Carlo Borromeo, and deplored the bad manners of the English tourists who came only to see the spectacle of Papal splendor and forgot that they were attending a religious service.

But still more to her taste than any ecclesiastical celebrations were the popular festivities in honor of the inauguration of the new popular council in Rome, another liberal measure of the Pope's. The American colony prepared to display the Stars and Stripes and an eagle, to show their country's sympathy for the cause of Italian liberty, but an ordinance was issued which prohibited the display of any but the Roman flag, in order that irritation of Austria might be averted. The new councilors paraded through the streets in carriages lent by the nobility; a circumstance which Margaret found symbolic: "Thus will they be obliged to furnish from their old grandeur the vehicles of new ideas." A ball was given that evening, attended by such notables as Lord Minto, Prince Corsini, and the Torlonias in the uniform of the Civic Guard. The Trasteverini danced the saltarello in their brilliant costumes, and to Margaret the dance had the Italian wine and the Italian sun in it.

The political excitement continued with renewed vigor during the early months of 1848. To Margaret, prisoned in her little lodging by the unceasing rain and tormented by fears for the future, the only cheering news was the spread of the revolutionary movement. There were popular uprisings on the first of the year in Rome, Leghorn, and Genoa. In Milan the Austrians provoked a disturbance among the citizens, and then killed eighty people in putting it down. Elsewhere the leaders of the people, put on their guard by this incident, counseled their followers against being thus gulled by *agents provocateurs*. Sicily flamed into open revolt, and Naples stood on the brink of it. The Neapolitan king was rumored to have sought refuge in Rome in a cheap hotel, and Margaret made fun of his parsimony: "It is said he has always a taste for economy when he cannot live at the expense of his suffering people." Metternich's death was also falsely reported in Rome, but the truth was only that his repressive system was crumbling all

over Europe and the way was being made ready for his flight
from Vienna in March. One of the most unpopular cardinals
died at this time, and was mocked in death by the Romans,
who were wont to mourn on such occasions.

Though now so closely tied to a devout Catholic, Margaret's
attitude toward Catholicism seems to have become Calvinistic
again at this time. Her account of the procession of the Santo
Bambino in the Franciscan church of Ara Coeli on the Epiphany
includes an impassioned plea for Rome to burn this jeweled
wooden figure and turn its worship to a more loving and
human Christ Child. She wondered how anyone who thought
could remain a Catholic after seeing Catholicism in Italy: to
her it was only the trappings and bare bones of a once-living
religion. Her changed attitude was no doubt in part due to her
conviction that the conservatism of the Church blocked the road
to reform and progress as she saw it; in part to the usual Anglo-
Saxon reaction to the emotionalism and sentimentalism of Latin
religion; and in part, perhaps, to the fact that Ossoli's Catholicism was one reason why their marriage had to be kept secret.
And the simple ceremony before a humble priest may not have
given Margaret the best possible impression of Catholicism.

January dragged on, and still the rain poured down and the
days were as dark as the nights. Margaret's acquaintances
dropped in to see her because they knew not what to do with
themselves; she was glad to receive them for the same reason.
New reports of the provocative tactics of the Austrians came
from the north and were discussed with indignation. The
King of Naples was said to have suffered an apoplectic stroke
at hearing of the revolt in Sicily, and then to have offered his
subjects an amnesty and reform measures. The news from
France served only to render Louis Philippe more despicable
in Margaret's eyes, and the evasive Guizot a poorer creature
than the frankly tyrannical Metternich. Margaret grew thoroughly out of sorts with Roman life. On the fortieth day of rain
she wrote complainingly of the damp and the abominable reek-

ing odors which it awoke, of the atrocious arias which drifted into her window from the Corso, relieved only by the racket of a wicked organ-grinder. Her landlady's three pet dogs exercised themselves by continual barking, which was echoed by all the dogs of the neighborhood. The doorbell kept ringing, and there was a small boy who delighted in imitating "the music of cats." Margaret thought that "nothing could surpass the dirt, the gloom, the desolation of Rome."

Such a miserable existence, coupled with her worries, was too much for Margaret and her health broke down. She did not recover until the rains ended toward the close of March, and the deep blue of the spring sky rendered that terrible Roman winter only a long dark dream in the past. It had been "the most idle and suffering season" of Margaret's life. With the spring sun came news, welcome to her, of revolutions in Austria and France. Her Italian friends took heart, and the popular celebrations far surpassed the conventional gaiety of the Roman carnival. When the news of Metternich's fall reached Rome, the arms of Austria were dragged through the streets. The double-headed eagle was pulled down from above the portal of the Palazzo Venezia, and replaced by a white and gold escutcheon bearing the words *Alta Italia*. No sooner had this been done than tidings came that the Milanese had risen against the Austrians, and that Venice, led by a descendant of the last doge, was in the hands of the republicans; that Modena and Parma were driving out the Austrians. The Roman populace went mad with joy: the men danced in the streets and the women wept in their happiness. Armed forces were raised to aid the republican cause with all the zeal of a newly launched crusade. The Roman princes gave vast sums to support and equip the new legions; the humbler folk their pennies, women their jewels and trinkets, even the street peddlers their day's earnings. On April 1, it seemed that Italy was free, but Margaret feared that success had come too speedily to be real and quoted the Pope's proclamation in her letter to the *Tribune:*

The events which these two months past have seen rush after one another in rapid succession are no human work. Woe to him who in this wind which shakes and tears up alike the lofty cedars and humble shrubs hears not the voice of God! Woe to human pride, if to the fault or merit of any man whatsoever it refer these wonderful changes, instead of adoring the mysterious designs of Providence.

During April and May the republican movement marked time, and little was done to consolidate the gains already made. The Lombard forces, swollen in numbers by the Roman regulars and volunteers, faced the Austrians in the north, but there was no decisive battle. The provisional government of Milan issued appeals to the German people and to the peoples subject to Austria, to refuse aid and assistance in repressive measures undertaken by the Austrian government against the Italian people. To Margaret these manifestoes, resounding with fine rhetoric and appeals to the brotherhood of man and the principles of justice and humanity, were refreshing and hopeful signs of progress. She was now in close touch with the revolutionary movement, for her friend, the Polish poet and patriot Adam Mickiewicz, who had been staying in the same house with her in Rome, organized a legion from his compatriots in exile in Italy, and led them first to Florence for a great popular demonstration for the cause of liberty among all oppressed peoples, and thence to the battlefield. And Giuseppe Mazzini returned from his seventeen years of exile abroad to see his hopes realized at last. Margaret knew what overpowering happiness this moment brought to him, and rejoiced with her friend.

But the republican movement received a great moral check when Pius IX disassociated himself from the popular cause at a consistory of the College of Cardinals on April 29. He was dismayed by the rapid spread of open and armed revolt all over Europe, and by certain incidents in Rome itself, where the churches had been robbed of some of their treasures. He had begun a liberal program designed to raise the Roman States gradually from their semi-feudal condition to a more enlightened situation; he had not realized that he was setting a match to a powderkeg which now threatened to blow all the old Europe into ruins. When bloodshed occurred, he drew back and lamented the outbreak of civil strife and the use of his name as a rallying cry by the insurgents. Following Gioberti's idea of the role of the Papacy with sympathy, he had seen himself as the central figure of a peaceably united Italy, but the bitter spirit of the radical exiles, who had been allowed to return under his liberal administration, had carried the liberal movement to lengths to which he was not prepared to go, either as leader or as follower. Margaret was a disciple of Mazzini, who had pleaded with the Pope six months earlier in a public letter that he should be the rallying point for the popular movement, but now she shared the ideas of hotter heads. The war with Austria was to her "dear to every Italian heart as the best and holiest cause in which for ages they had been called upon to embark their hearts." The people of the Roman States now clamored for a declaration of war with Austria, and to this Pius would not consent. Threatened with the loss of his temporal sovereignty, he consented to a new ministry headed by Count Mamiani and made up of persons opposed to his own policy. Though nominally a Papal ministry, this body amounted for a while to a provisional government, such as had arisen in the provinces formerly under Austrian control, and a collision was imminent at any time after its formation, between it and the Pontiff. The activities of the conservative cardinals soon hamstrung the activities of the liberal ministry, however, and in the fall, when the first surge of the revolutionary movement had died down, Mamiani was replaced by the reactionary Count Rossi.

Meanwhile, the political events of the spring furnished Margaret with a good excuse for prolonging her stay abroad—an excuse badly needed, as the time for the coming of her child drew nearer. She had no desire to return home now, and to the friends who wrote urging her to return to America, "the land of the future," she replied:

> It is so, but that spirit which made it all it is of value in my eyes, which gave all of hope with which I can sympathize for the future, is more alive here at present than in America. My country is at present spoiled by prosperity, stupid with the lust of gain, soiled by crime in its willing perpetuation of slavery, shamed by an unjust war. . . . In Europe, amid the teachings of adversity, a nobler spirit is struggling—a spirit which cheers and animates mine.

And in the middle of May Margaret wrote to Emerson, who was then in England for a tour of lectures and visits and had asked her to return to America with him: "I should like to return with you, but I have much to do and learn in Europe yet. I am deeply interested in this public drama, and wish to see it played out. Methinks I have my part therein, either as actor or historian." To another she wrote: "Have I something to do here? or am I only to cheer on the warriors and after write the history of their deeds? . . . My private fortunes are dark and tangled; my strength to govern them much diminished. I have thrown myself on God, and perhaps he will make my temporal state very tragical." Those who read her *Tribune* letters knew that the revolutionary cause was dear to her heart, but did not know how important a part she was beginning to play in the secret work of preparation for a Roman revolt. It was jokingly that James Russell Lowell wrote to their mutual friend William Story of what he assumed to be her activities abroad, and somewhat maliciously, for he still smarted from her criticism of three years before:

> There must be not a little of the desolate island where S. M. F. is considered agreeable. I have it on good authority

that the Austrian Government has its eye on Miss F. It would
be a pity to have so much worth and genius shut up for life
in Spielberg. Her beauty might perhaps save her.

Pio Nono also regards her with a naturally jealous eye,
fearing that the College of Cardinals may make her the suc-
cessor of Pope Joan. . . .

The American Eagle is anxiously awaiting the return of
Miss F., whom he persists in regarding as the genius of
Columbia. A public dinner is to be given her in Boston at
which the Bird of our Country will preside.

Such was Lowell's reaction to Story's good reports of Margaret
in Rome, and perhaps his apathy toward Margaret's appeals for
American aid to the Italian revolutionary movement was typical
of others when the American Eagle was busy screaming in helpless Mexico.

At any rate, Margaret could not return home, for she expected her child in August. She gave up her political work,
and planned to await the birth of her baby in some quiet country place, where she could rest from the fatigues of the winter
and spring that had been passed in Rome. Before departing
she left a bundle of papers precious to her with Mr. Hicks, the
American painter, for safekeeping and for return to her family
if death should overtake her before she came back to Rome.
She dreaded the ordeal before her and had dark fears as to its
outcome. The bundle included this letter of last wishes:

You would say to those I leave behind that I was willing
to die. I have suffered in life far more than I enjoyed and I
think quite out of proportion with the use my living here is of
to others.

I have wished to be natural and true, but the world was
not in harmony with me—nothing came right for me. I think
that the spirit that governs the universe must have in reserve
for me a sphere where I can develop more freely and be happier. On earth circumstances do not promise this before my

forces shall be too much lavished to make a better path truly avail me.

So on May 24 she left the Eternal City, going first to Aquila for a month and then to Rieti, a little village in the Abruzzi. The secret had been successfully kept, and even to so close a friend as Madame Arconati she wrote only of her plan to recoup her health after the trials of the Roman winter by a stay in the mountains, which might also give her an opportunity to write a book about her experiences in Europe. She still thought of herself as an observer in the midst of great events, not as a participant in them:

> I sit in my obscure corner, and watch the progress of events. It is the position that pleases me best, and I believe the most favorable one. Everything confirms me in my radicalism; and without any desire to hasten matters, indeed with surprise to see them rush so like a torrent, I seem to see them all tending to realize my own hopes.

The summer months went by quietly enough for her in the Abruzzi, and Margaret's only contact with the world was through the journals which Ossoli forwarded to her and through her immense correspondence—at this time she wrote regularly to at least a hundred people. Part of the day she wrote, part she spent in the open, walking or riding on a donkey. In a letter to Emerson in July she painted a pretty picture of her dwelling place among the peaks, which still were snow-covered in mid-summer. She liked the peasants of the region, who found her *simpatica* and blessed her as she passed by. "They are people whom I could love and live with. Bread and grapes among them would suffice me." She boasted that she had begun to think in Italian, now that she was so far removed from any English or Americans.

But she was not quite so peaceful and contented as this letter indicated. She dreaded the experience which lay ahead of her—as a woman of thirty-eight might well dread the coming of her first child. The loneliness of her life oppressed her, for it was impossible for Ossoli to come to Aquila to see her, and after she moved to Rieti in order that he might spend Sundays with her, the march of events kept him in Rome. Then she had financial worries. Early in the summer she had asked Horace Greeley for a remittance large enough to free her from such worries until after the birth of the child, but no draft from him came to her bankers in Rome. Richard, too, had been asked for a loan, but his reply dealt only with his plan for the two of them to live together when she returned home. She wrote him a second, stronger plea, and said she could not possibly return to America at this time.

In the middle of August Ossoli wrote to her that the Civic Guard, of which he was a member, had been ordered to Bologna to serve against the Austrians, and that he was torn between his military duty and his desire to be with her when their child came. She replied bravely that the decision was his to make, but if he must go, he was to come first and see her. August dragged on, and still there was no remittance from Richard or Greeley. In desperation she borrowed a hundred dollars from an American friend in Rome. The Pope suspended the order for the departure of the Civic Guard, but Ossoli was still detained in Rome. September came, and Margaret knew that her time was not far off. One day she could not leave her bed for pain, and then it was that her husband came to her. His tenderness was welcome, for she was experiencing such anguish as she had never known could be endured. The next day, September 5, her son was born. Ossoli could not stay on with her, for he had to hurry back to Rome and leave her to the rough attentions of the local doctor. She managed to dictate a short note to her husband the day after he departed, assuring him that all was well and begging him not to be anxious about her. Actually, she had fever and was unable to nurse her child. Slowly she recovered her strength and was able to write little notes to Ossoli describing the immensely important doings of their baby. But there were many things that disturbed her, now that she had the child to care for: the petty dishonesty of the people of the inn; the landlord's unwelcome attentions to the wet nurse; an outbreak of smallpox in the village. With no one to turn to for help, these things bothered her much. The doctor was sent for to inoculate the baby against the dreaded disease. He delayed until Margaret was nearly frantic with anxiety, and then finally promised to come immediately. In the stream of tender notes which passed back and forth between Rieti and Rome, Margaret and her husband decided that it would be best to leave the child at nurse in the village, since they still considered it essential to conceal their marriage and since Margaret must be in Rome in order to write her *Tribune* letters. It broke her heart to leave the baby, but early in November she prepared to return to Rome.

❖ CHAPTER XIV ❖

Revolution and Siege

If I came home at this moment, I should feel as if forced to leave my own house, my own people, and the hour which I had always longed for.—M. F.

THE journey back to Rome proved itself a portent of the stormy months that lay ahead for Margaret. She arranged to go in the diligence, which set out from Rieti at the unearthly hour of three in the morning, but at the last minute was offered a place in a coach hired by a Marchesa Crispoldi, which would not leave until several hours later. She rose at dawn on the day set and waited in vain for the coach to come and pick her up. Finally she learned that the coach would not be leaving at all, because the diligence had been wrecked a few miles from Rieti, where a sudden torrent from the mountains had washed away the road. The passengers had barely escaped with their lives, and Margaret was convinced that in her feeble condition she would have perished if she had been involved in the accident. The road was impassable for several days, and when the diligence finally ventured forth again on the road to Rome, all the horses available along the route were needed to pull the heavy coach through the snow-covered mountain region. As they drew near to Rome, they discovered that the Tiber was in flood and that it was doubtful if they could pass. The little inn at which they learned this bad news offered no accommodations for the party, so they continued on their way, splashing through the rising waters which covered road and plain alike,

MARGARET FULLER, MARCHESA OSSOLI
IN ROME

Engraving by M. Haider, from the painting by Thomas Hicks

and expecting to be forced to a stop at any moment. But they got through safe and sound, and Margaret had an opportunity to see the statue-filled gardens of the Villa Ludovisi by moonlight, as the diligence halted for examination at the gate of Rome.

Ossoli had found a lodging for her on the Piazza Barberini—only one room, for that was the best that they could now afford. Margaret made the most of it in describing her new quarters to her mother:

> I have only one room, but large; and everything about the bed so gracefully and adroitly disposed that it makes a beautiful parlor, and of course I pay much less. I have the sun all day, and an excellent chimney. It is very high and has pure air, and the most beautiful view all around imaginable.

If her new lodging lacked the splendor of her earlier quarters, there were compensating advantages. The landlord and his wife were kindly old people, who enjoyed mothering Margaret and her neighbor, a young Prussian sculptor. In the attic dwelt a priest, who insisted on making the fire for Margaret when the landlady was absent. The other tenants, "a frightful Russian princess with moustaches and a footman who ties her bonnet for her," and an English lady who gave most of her money for pious purposes and filled the terrace of the house with flowers, amused Margaret almost as much as the immense black cat belonging to the lady, which answered to the name of Amoretto. Best of all, the Storys were now close neighbors, for they too lived on the Piazza Barberini.

It was a different Rome that Margaret found upon her return, a Rome deserted by the crowds of foreigners. The English had fled in fear of the popular unrest; the Germans and French hurried home to their strife-torn countries; and the young Russians were denied permission to linger in this hotbed of revolution. Only the more serious artists had remained, at work in their studios or volunteering for military service. A good part of Rome's population had depended on the vanished tourists for their livelihood; and widespread suffering contributed to the unrest caused by the repressive measures of the new, reactionary prime minister, Count Rossi. His ministry was opposing the republican movement as openly as it dared; Zucchi, the minister of war, left Rome to put down popular demonstrations in the provinces and to hinder the entry into Bologna of Garibaldi's republicans. Rossi summoned soldiery from the unaffected provinces to guard the opening of the Chamber of Deputies and to offset the republican Civic Guard. The newspapers were being put under censorship once more, and there were frequent political arrests, followed by exile from the Papal States.

These repressive measures had immediate serious consequences. On November 15, just after Margaret's return to Rome, Count Rossi was assassinated as he was about to enter the Chamber. No one sought to arrest the assassin, and a play entitled *The Death of Nero* was presented that night at one of the Roman theaters and received with great applause. On the following day a large crowd assembled at the Quirinal Palace and made known their wishes to the Pope through a delegation. Their requests were denied and the crowd pressed on the palace, demanding to see the Pontiff. The Swiss guards took alarm and fired on the crowd, whose resentment flared up into violence. They broke windows and attempted to burn the doors of the palace, and they killed the Pope's confessor, Parma, when he fired on them from a window. News of this came to Margaret in her lodging, from whose window she had observed the hasty measures of defense taken at the Barberini Palace across the square, and heard the beating of the drums calling out the Civic Guard. Her landlady remarked: "Thank heaven, we are poor, we have nothing to fear!" and Margaret thought that "this is the echo of a sentiment which will soon be universal in Europe."

The Pontiff could hardly pretend to temporal rule in Rome

after such events, and he soon fled secretly to the fortress of Gaeta, near Naples, where he was under the protection of the Neapolitan king. The people of Rome were reluctant to depose him as their ruler, and Rome remained without a government until February, when the Roman Republic was proclaimed. Meanwhile delegations went to Gaeta to express their devotion to the Pope and their feeling that he had been misled by his advisers, but their efforts to bring about his return to Rome met with no success. Margaret described a popular cartoon which expressed the sentiment of Rome at this time, in her letter of December 2 to the *Tribune:*

> *Don Tirlone*, the *Punch* of Rome, has just come in. This number represents the fortress of Gaeta. Outside hangs a cage containing a parrot (*pappagallo*), the plump body of the bird surmounted by a noble large head with benign face and Papal head-dress. He sits on the perch now with folded wings, but the cage-door, in likeness of a portico, shows there is convenience to come forth for the purposes of benediction when wanted. Outside, the King of Naples, dressed as Harlequin, plays the organ for instruction of the bird (unhappy penitent, doomed to penance), and grinning with sharp teeth, observes: "He speaks in my way now." In the background a young Republican holds ready the match for a barrel of gunpowder, but looks at his watch, waiting the moment to ignite it.

To Margaret Pius IX, who had once seemed the personification of good, was now a traitor to the cause he had done much to launch and which she had made her own. In a letter to a friend in America, who had asked to have a rosary blessed by the Pope, she wrote at this time:

> None can now attach any value to the blessing of Pius IX. Those who loved him can no longer defend him. It has become obvious that those first acts of his in the Papacy

were merely the result of a kindly, good-natured temperament; that he had not thought to understand their bearing nor force to abide by it. He seems quite destitute of moral courage. He is not resolute either on the wrong or the right side. First he abandoned the liberal party; then yielding to the will of the people and uniting in appearance with a liberal ministry, he let the cardinals betray it and defeat the hopes of Italy. He cried peace! peace! but had not a word of blame for the sanguinary acts of the King of Naples, a word of sympathy for the victims of Lombardy. Seizing the moment of dejection in the nation, he put in this retrograde ministry; sanctioned their acts, daily more impudent; let them neutralize the constitution he himself had given; and when the people slew his minister and assaulted him in his own palace, he yielded anew; he dared not die, nor run the slightest risk—for only by accident could he have perished. His person as a Pope is still respected, though his character as a man is despised. . . . The common people were staring at the broken windows and burnt door of the palace where they have so often gone to receive a blessing, the children playing. *"Sedia Papale. Morte ai Cardinali, e morte al Papa!"*

Margaret was by now a complete revolutionary, who despised liberal backing and filling.

She was torn between her interest in the revolution and her desire to be with her child. She thought much of him, and debated the question of revealing her secret to her family and friends. Finally she decided against it, and contented herself with mysterious hints in her letters home, which caused more alarm than the news itself might have done. She wrote thus to her mother on November 16:

Of other circumstances which complicate my position I cannot write. Were you here, I would confide in you fully, and have more than once in the silence of the night recited to you these most strange and romantic chapters in the story of my sad life. At one time, when I thought I might die, I empowered a person who has given me, as far as possible to him, the aid and sympathy of a brother, to communicate them to you on his return to the United States. But now I think that we shall meet again, and I am sure you will always love your daughter, and will know gladly in all events she has tried to aid and striven never to injure her fellows. In earlier days I dreamed of doing and being much, but now am content with the Magdalen to rest my plea hereon, "She has loved much."

What was poor Mrs. Fuller to make of this, despite Margaret's "Do not feel anxious about me"? It no doubt disturbed her as much as a later letter from Margaret troubled Marcus Spring, when he read these words:

Of me you wish to know; but there is little that I can tell you at this distance. I have had happy hours, learned much, suffered much, and outward things have not gone well with me. I have had glorious hopes, but they are overclouded now, and the future looks darker than ever, indeed quite impossible to my steps. I have no hope, unless that God will show me some way I do not know of now, but I do not wish to trouble you with more of this.

Margaret was taking a strange way to assure her friends that all was well with her. But she was tormented by fears, and too much troubled to avoid letting some hint of her difficulties appear in her letters. Anything might happen to her baby in the rude mountain village where she had been forced to leave him; her husband was in some danger as a member of the Civic Guard; and the discovery of their relationship by his strongly Papal-minded family, in the present state of political affairs, would be fatal to their prospects of living together openly later on, on the patrimony that was to come to him.

Just before Christmas Margaret felt compelled to go up to Rieti and see how her child was doing. She was relieved to find him seemingly well and happy, but he had not grown as she had expected. Then she learned that he had had a severe case of smallpox, for the doctor, despite his promise, had never bothered to inoculate him. Fortunately the disease seemed to have done him no harm beyond momentarily checking his growth, for his face was unmarked by scars. She could stay only a few days in Rieti, for the inn seemed unbearably cold and smoky to her, though the child appeared to thrive in this rude environment. It was a great joy to her to lie in bed, with the baby's head pillowed on her arm, but she had to tear herself away and be off for Rome, where her husband anxiously awaited her and the unfolding revolutionary movement demanded her observation.

The first six months of 1849 saw the playing out of the last act of the public tragedy which Margaret had made her own. They began pleasantly enough; after her experience of the previous winter, Margaret marveled at the weather. There was no rain at all; the days were as warm as May, and moonlight excursions were delightful. The life of Rome was scarcely touched as yet, except for the absence of tourists, by what Margaret called "this most peaceful of revolutions." She enjoyed the fair held early in January in the quarter of St. Eustachio, where the streets were crowded with brightly lit toyshops set up for the occasion, and every man, woman, and child joined in a mock concert of whistles, tin trumpets, and tambourines every evening between ten and midnight. The carnival was less splendid than before, because of the absence of the nobles' coaches and fine clothes, but it was not less gay for that.

But underneath this surface life of Rome, a grimmer reality was preparing. The Pope announced on January 6 the excommunication of all who should assist in the Constitutional Assembly which had been summoned to form a new administration for the Roman States. The mob mocked his proclamation and vented its indignation by taking cardinals' hats from the shops favored by the Papal Court and throwing them into the Tiber. The opening of the Constitutional Assembly on February 5 was marked by a great public procession. All the troops in Rome figured in it; the bands played the "Marseillaise"; the flags of Sicily, Venice, and Bologna were everywhere waving triumphantly, while that of Naples was veiled with black crape. The deputies to the Assembly walked together, distinguished only by a tricolored scarf. Among them were Garibaldi and Napoleon's nephew. Margaret saw all this from a balcony in the Piazza di Venezia, and thought this procession far more impressive than the more splendid one she had seen fourteen months before, at the opening of the new council.

The Assembly wasted no time in declaring its sentiments; the Roman Republic was proclaimed at one o'clock in the morning of February 8 to the crowd gathered in the courtyard before the meeting place, the Palazzo della Cancellaria. This was the very spot where Rossi had been stabbed to death in the previous November. All through the night the bells of Rome were rung to celebrate the birth of the Republic. Early the next morning, Margaret went through the streets to the Capitol to hear the public reading of the Assembly's decree. On her way she met some English acquaintances, who dampened her joy by announcing that the Republic would not survive a month and that those who had given it birth should be shot or hanged. The Americans seemed to share such convictions, and even the less reactionary among them felt that the Roman people were unfit to be trusted with power. Margaret despised all such misgivings and listened happily as a deputy read aloud the articles of the decree:

Article I. The Papacy has fallen in fact and in right from the temporal government of the Roman State.
Article II. The Roman Pontiff shall have all necessary guar-

antees for independence in the exercise of his spiritual
power.

Article III. The form of the government of the Roman State
shall be a pure democracy, and will take the glorious name
of the Roman Republic.

Article IV. The Roman Republic shall have with the rest of
Italy the relations exacted by a common nationality.

After the reading of each article there was a pause, while the
great bell of the Capitol pealed, cannon boomed, and the crowd
shouted *Viva la Repubblica, viva Italia!* Margaret's heart quickened and her nerves thrilled; she did not see how anyone present could remain unmoved. But her companion, an American
art student, remarked that "he did not see the use of these
popular demonstrations." Nothing irritated her more, now,
than her compatriots' inability to share her passionate sympathy for the Italians—she spoke of them now as "*my* people"
—in their struggle for democracy.

Her circle of friends of the previous winter had largely been
dispersed by the march of events. Sometimes she missed them,
but more often she felt content to enjoy a full communion with
the spirit of Rome. She was much alone, for Ossoli was now a
captain in the Civic Guard and there were many demands upon
his time. Of her own life at this period Margaret wrote this
description to her brother Richard:

> I pass my days in writing, walking, occasional visits to the
> galleries. I read little, except the newspapers; these take up
> an hour or two of the day. I own my thoughts are quite fixed
> on the daily bulletin of men and things. I expect to write
> the history, but because it is so much in my heart.

It troubled her to think that her plan for a history of the Roman
revolution might distress her friend Madame Arconati, whose
background and environment made her unsympathetic to the
republican cause. She wrote to her that "there is a congeniality,

I dare to say, pure, strong, and good, at the bottom of the heart, far, far deeper than these differences, that would always on a real meeting keep us friends."

There was another Italian friend close at hand, however, with whom Margaret's republican sentiments gave her only a closer bond. This was Mazzini, now in Rome as a deputy to the Constitutional Assembly. He had been made a citizen of Rome by popular vote, and was shortly to become one of the Triumvirs who presided over the short life of the Republic. One night soon after his arrival in Rome he called to see Margaret, and spent two hours with her, talking of his hopes and fears for the newly born Republic. He came again as often as the press of his responsibilities allowed him, and sent her tickets which enabled her to hear the speeches in the Assembly. Margaret felt that she would cheerfully give her life to aid his work; she feared that his battle against foes both within and without Italy would be too much for this prince among men, who looked "as if the great battle he had fought had been too much for his strength, and that he was only sustained by the fire of the soul." She called him her "dearest, reverend friend"; he was her first Italian friend and still infinitely most prized, "a great and solid man."

The tides of the republican movement were running so fast that Margaret did not dare to discuss them too much in her *Tribune* letters, for fear that by the time the letters were published in America the tidings would be false. So she filled in her dispatches with accounts of the American artists, and lent her aid to a proposal that one of the three chief American sculptors in Italy—Crawford, Greenough, or Powers—should be commissioned to do a colossal equestrian statue of Washington. She got one of her friends in Rome to supply figures on the expense of an artist's life there, in order to justify the high prices charged by the American artistic exiles. Then, having done her best to promote a better understanding between her friends and the American public, she felt entitled to indulge herself in personal concerns once more, and stole off for a short visit to Rieti. The child's health was satisfactory and he seemed to recognize her —she had had a haunting fear that he might not know his own mother—but she found cause for new concern about him, because of an incident which occurred during her stay in Rieti. While she was upstairs watching her sleeping child, she heard the sound of a violent quarrel below. She rushed down to find the two sons of the house doing their best to kill each other. One was prevented from using his knife by the women clutching his arm, while the other was hurling great chunks of wood at his opponent, one of which just missed crushing Margaret's head. Summoning up all her strength, she stepped between the struggling peasants and commanded them to stop. They fell back, somehow awed by her, and though at first they swore to be avenged upon each other at the first opportunity, Margaret succeeded in calming them and making them promise to abandon such designs. But she could not help thinking what might have happened to her little child, if he had happened to have been in the midst of the fray, as he might well have been in her absence.

Margaret's strange power over the passion and violence of the Italian nature was noted by many of her friends. She had occasion to make use of it again on her way back to Rome from Rieti. She was resting at a wayside *osteria,* when the landlord rushed into the room in a panic and screamed that they would all be robbed and no doubt killed, for a detachment of Garibaldi's Legion was galloping down the road to the inn. Margaret feared that they might take her horses, for the Legion had earned a bad name, but she was determined to make the first move by offering them lunch at her expense. The rough troopers swarmed boisterously into the inn; at their entrance she commanded the landlord to bring bread and wine for them. Surprised by her kindness, they quieted down, gave her a respectful account of their activities, and assisted her when she made ready to leave. It was nothing short of a miracle to the landlord, and to Margaret's friends in Rome, when she told them of the incident, for Garibaldi's Legion was a notoriously hard-bitten crew.

The next three months of Margaret's life were filled with scenes of violence which made her think little of these incidents. The Catholic powers of Europe decided to intervene in Italy and restore the Pope's temporal sovereignty. Louis Napoleon, now president of the French Republic, sent a "protective" expeditionary force of twelve thousand men under General Oudinot, which landed and seized Civitavecchia near Rome in April. Oudinot issued a proclamation to the effect that he had come as a friend and a brother, for, relying on advices from Gaeta, he expected that the Papal party in Rome was in a majority and that the presence of his troops would be enough to open the gates of Rome to him. He was informed by the Triumvirs that he was neither wanted nor trusted. The city was soon put in a state of siege, and on April 30 he made his first assault, which was checked largely by a gallant sortie of Garibaldi's Legion. For some time preparations had been made in Rome to care for the wounded of the conflict that was hourly expected. On the very day of Oudinot's assault, Margaret, as an intimate of Mazzini and a warm partisan of the revolutionary cause, received this letter:

Dear Miss Fuller:

You are named Regolatrice of the Hospital of the Fate Bene Fratelli. Go there at twelve, if the alarm bell has not rung before. When you arrive there, you will receive all the women coming for the wounded, and give them your directions, so that you are sure to have a certain number of them night and day.

May God help us,
Cristina Trivulzi, of Belgiojoso

The Princess Belgiojoso, born into one of the greatest Milanese noble families, but combining, as Miss Katharine Anthony has put it, the aggressiveness of a Florence Nightingale and an Emma Goldman, was a woman after Margaret's heart. She had endangered her great wealth by participation in liberal activities, and had been forced to flee to Paris. Later she recovered her fortune and used it to promote the revolution. Until Milan fell again to the Austrians in August 1848, she had supported a company of soldiers and a newspaper devoted to the republican cause. She had been forced to leave Milan, and the Austrians confiscated her property, and she went first to Paris and then to Rome, doing any work that seemed needed in the republican movement. For two months before Oudinot's assault she had been putting the hospitals of Rome in order—most of them were ecclesiastical institutions and had been abandoned since the Pope's flight—and begging money on the streets to further her purpose. At her command, the women of Rome prepared bandages and lint, and were ready to offer their services as nurses. She had chosen Margaret to direct the second of her hospitals.

Margaret plunged into her new duties with tremendous energy. She spent the whole night of April 30 at the hospital, watching men dying and undergoing amputations, and comforting the less seriously wounded. Mrs. Story painted a picture of Margaret going her rounds:

> I have walked with Margaret through the wards, and seen how comforting was her presence to the poor suffering men. "How long will the Signora stay? When will the Signora come again?" they eagerly asked. For each one's peculiar tastes she had a care: to one she carried books; to another she told the news of the day; and listened to another's oft-repeated tale of wrongs as the best sympathy she could give. They raised themselves on their elbows to get the last glimpse of her as she was going away.

According to Mrs. Story, the prevalent impression in Rome at this time was that she was "a mild saint and a ministering angel." From the night of the first assault, Margaret spent most of her days and nights either at her own hospital or that of the Princess Belgiojoso, the Trinità dei Pellegrini. All the work of administering the hospitals fell upon the shoulders of these devoted women. They were badly handicapped by lack of funds, but they did everything for the wounded that lay within their powers. Margaret had other cares to oppress her besides these duties. Sometimes she did not hear from Ossoli, who was with the defending troops, for two or three days at a time; and there was no word at all of her child, for communications between Rome and Rieti were cut off. The city was completely isolated in a triple siege, for besides the French in Civitavecchia, the Austrians were marching down through Romagna, and the Neapolitan forces threatened Rome from the south.

Yet somehow, despite her great labors and anxieties, Margaret managed to drive her tired body and brain into writing reports of the siege for the *Tribune*. Her letters of this period are first-rate journalism: the reader is made an eye-witness of the scenes within the beleaguered city and a partaker in the emotions of the Roman people as they struggled to preserve their newly won liberty. The French, having failed in their first attempt at armed assault, now resorted to diplomacy. De Lesseps was sent to negotiate as a minister plenipotentiary. The Triumvirs rejected his proposal of a French occupation of Rome, and he then professed himself satisfied that the French troops should take up positions in the country outside the city. But while de Lesseps returned to Paris to have this agreement ratified by his government, the nettled Oudinot launched another attack on the gate of St. Pancrazio. Since this met with as little success as the first attempt, his cannon directed their fire on the city itself. Though this swelled the number of wounded within the walls, the Romans did not lose heart. As a gesture, they sent to Pius IX two of the French cannonballs that struck St. Peter's.

One of the most heartbreaking results of the siege to Margaret was the destruction of the famous villas and gardens outside the walls of Rome, in order that they might not provide shelter for the attackers. She wrote in a *Tribune* letter:

> War near at hand seems to me even more dreadful than I had fancied it. . . . Here it has produced much fruit of noble sentiment, noble act; but still it breeds vice too, drunkenness, mental dissipation, tears asunder the tenderest ties. . . . I feel what I never expected to—as if I might by and by be willing to leave Rome.

The tension within the city grew ever greater. The French pressed nearer and nearer to the walls, while Oudinot issued ultimatum after ultimatum to the inhabitants and protested his unwillingness to bring "bloody ruin to the capital of the Christian world." But the defenders paid no attention to these fair-sounding words, accompanied as they were by a vicious cannonade, and fought the French advance at every step. Ossoli's post was on the city's walls in one of the most exposed positions, and as Margaret went about her work in the hospitals, she hourly expected to find him among the arriving cartloads of newly wounded. She was staying with William and Emelyn Story now, since their home was thought to be less exposed to the French fire than hers, and they could mother her in her rare moments of leisure. When she could spare the time, she went with them to her husband's post, carrying a basket of provisions which he always shared with his men. They had time for only a few words about themselves and their child, cut off from them by war; then they returned to the duties that they had voluntarily assumed, never knowing whether this might be their last farewell.

Exhausted by her strenuous efforts and nerve-racked by anxiety about the child and Ossoli, expecting death hourly, Margaret confided the story of her secret marriage to Mrs. Story, told her of the child's whereabouts, and begged her to take the baby to Margaret's mother if both the Ossolis should perish in the siege. Certain papers were also confided at this time to this good friend, which Mrs. Story later described thus:

> The papers thus given me I had perfect liberty to read; but after she had told me her story, I desired no confirmation of this fact beyond what her words had given. One or two of the papers she opened, and we together read them. One was written on parchment in Latin, and was a certificate given by the priest who married them, saying that Angelo Eugene Ossoli was the legal heir of whatever title and fortune should come to his father. To this was affixed his seal, with those of the other witnesses, and the Ossoli crest was drawn in full upon the paper. There was also a book in which Margaret had written the history of her acquaintance and marriage with Ossoli, and of the birth of her child. In giving that to me, she said, "If I do not survive to tell this myself to my family, this book will be to them invaluable. Therefore keep it for them. If I live, it will be of no use, for my word will be all that they will ask." I took the papers, and locked them up. Never feeling any desire to look into them, I never did; and as she gave them to me, I returned them to her, when I left Rome for Switzerland.

It seems rather a pity that Mrs. Story was not less high-minded and more curious, for these papers subsequently disappeared, and a fuller account of them would not be without interest, since it would fill many gaps in the story of Margaret's Italian years. It is difficult to imagine what the paper she described actually was: it was clearly something more than baptismal certificate and hardly a marriage certificate, for as Andrew MacPhail has remarked, "the name of the heir is not usually specified in such documents." But the secrecy with which Margaret long cloaked her relationship with Ossoli has never been completely dissipated, nor is there any possibility of its ever being so.

Early in June Margaret wrote a long letter to Emerson, which must have read strangely in peaceful Concord:

I received your letter amid the round of cannonade and musketry. It was a terrible battle fought here from the first till the last light of day. I could see all its progress from my balcony. The Italians fought like lions. It is a truely heroic spirit that animates them. They make a stand here for honor and their rights, with little ground for hope that they can resist, now that they are betrayed by France.

Since the 30th April I go almost daily to the hospitals, and though I have suffered—for I had no idea before how terrible gun-shot wounds and wound-fever are—yet I have taken pleasure, and great pleasure, in being with the men; there is scarcely one who is not moved by a noble spirit. Many, especially among the Lombards, are the flower of Italian youth. When they begin to get better, I carry them books and flowers; they read and we talk. The palace of the Pope on the Quirinal is now used for convalescents. In those beautiful gardens I walk with them—one with his sling, another with his crutch. The gardener plays off all his water-works for the defenders of the country, and gathers flowers for me, their friend.

A day or two since, we sat in the Pope's little pavilion where he used to give private audiences. The sun was going gloriously down over Monte Mario, where gleamed the white tents of the French light-horse among the trees. The cannonade was heard at intervals. Two bright-eyed boys sat at our feet and gathered up eagerly every word said by the heroes of the day. It was a beautiful hour, stolen from the midst of ruin and sorrow; and tales were told as full of grace and pathos as in the gardens of Boccaccio, only in a very different spirit—with noble hope for man, with reverence for woman. . . .

Should I never return—and sometimes I despair of doing

so, it seems so far off, so difficult, I am caught in such a
net of ties here—if ever you know of my life here, I think you
will only wonder at the constancy with which I have sustained myself; the degree of profit to which, amid great difficulties, I have put the time, at least in the way of observation. Meanwhile love me all you can; let me feel that amid
the fearful agitations of the world, there are pure hands with
healthful, even pulse stretched out toward me, if I claim their
grasp. . . .

I know not, dear friend, whether I ever shall get home
across that great ocean, but here in Rome I shall no longer
wish to live. O Rome, *my* country! Could I imagine that the
triumph of what I held dear was to heap such desolation on
thy head!

Speaking of the republic, you say, do not I wish that Italy
had a great man? Mazzini is a great man. In mind, a poetic
statesman; in heart, a lover; in action, decisive and full of
resource as Caesar. Dearly I love Mazzini. He came in, just
as I had finished the first letter to you. His soft, radiant look
makes melancholy music in my soul; it consecrates my present life, that like the Magdalen I may at the important hour
shed all the consecrated ointment on his head. There is one,
Mazzini, who understands thee well; who knew thee no less
when an object of popular fear than now of idolatry; and
who, if the pen be not held too feebly, will help posterity to
know thee too.

Mazzini in London had attracted Margaret; here in Rome, as
he stood upon a lofty pedestal as the idol of the people and the
head of the state, she worshiped him. On his success rested the
hopes of Margaret and Ossoli for their ill-fated marriage. If he
won his battle for Italian freedom, Ossoli would be rewarded
for his services with a position that would make him independent of his family, and of the heritage they now held back
because of their disapproval of his politics.

But the cause that was so dear to all of them was fast going down to ruin, as the French kept landing fresh troops to oppose the defenders, who were now weakened by fever as well as casualties. And the relentless cannonade of the city was kept up, weakening the morale of all within it. Early in the morning of June 22 the French succeeded in effecting a breach in the walls. The beginning of the end was now in sight, for day by day they worked themselves forward until their cannon commanded every inch of the city. Garibaldi saw that further resistance would involve only a useless waste of lives, and on June 30 he stated this opinion to the Assembly. That body attempted to obtain favorable conditions of surrender from Oudinot, but he refused even to grant a safe conduct to Garibaldi himself. On the evening of July 2, as the French prepared to take possession of Rome, Margaret was one of the crowd which gathered in the Piazza of St. John Lateran to see the departure of the red-shirted lancers and their leader, for there was still one avenue of escape open. The majority of the other defenders fled with Garibaldi, hoping that they could continue the struggle for liberty elsewhere in Italy. The city, cruelly scarred by the bombardment and with twelve hundred wounded within its walls, was left to the French, who entered still expecting to be welcomed by a large group of Papal supporters. But they were received sullenly by the hostile crowd, and Oudinot felt obliged to fortify the chief squares and put the city under martial law. Margaret refused to appear on the streets where Roman freedom no longer was observed. It gave her a curious wrench to think that this Italian struggle for liberty had come to an inglorious close on the very day that the United States celebrated its declaration of independence. Oudinot shortly issued a proclamation giving all foreigners who had been in the service of the Republic twenty-four hours to leave the city. Margaret thought that it would not have been so bad to have died in one of the cannonades which had rained upon the city as to have had to wait until "every drop of pure blood, every childlike, radiant hope, [is] drained and driven from the heart by the betrayals of nations and individuals, till at last the sickened eye refuses more to open to that light which shines daily on such pits of iniquity." Now, though it broke her heart to abandon the wounded who had been under her care, she was obliged to flee from Rome with Ossoli and seek out her child in Rieti. There was nothing that she could do in Rome, and that city desolated by war was too full of sad memories for her. In her last dispatch to the *Tribune*, written on the day she left Rome, she wrote: "Go where I may, a large part of my heart will ever remain in Italy."

CHAPTER XV

The Last Year

*But it has long seemed that in the year 1850 I should stand on a pla-
teau in the ascent of life, where I should be allowed to pause for a while,
and take more clear and commanding views than ever before. Yet my
life proceeds as regularly as the fates of a Greek tragedy, and I can but
accept the pages as they turn.*—M. F.

THROUGH the influence of Lewis Cass, the American chargé
d'affaires, Margaret and Ossoli managed to secure means of
transport to Rieti, despite the chaos caused by the events of the
last two months. It was a trying trip for them, for neither knew
what to expect at its end, and both had such fears for the safety
of their child that they dared not express them. These qualms
were only too well justified; little Angelo was wasted by illness
and seemed half dead. Margaret questioned the nurse to whom
she had entrusted the child; it seemed that she had had no milk
and so had fed the child on bread and wine. There had been no
money to buy milk; there had been no word from them; what
else was she to do? Margaret was vastly indignant at first, but
after her anger was once dissipated, she could not blame the
peasant girl for something that really was the fault of the war,
to which she and Ossoli had devoted themselves instead of to
their child.

It took a month's tender nursing to bring little Angelo back
to health, and the peace and quiet of those days helped to
restore his parents' strength. Now that the frenzy of devotion

to the cause was over, and that cause dead, Margaret felt life-less and weary:

> I am tired out—tired of thinking and hoping—tired of see-ing men err and bleed. Man will still blunder and weep, as he has done for so many thousand years. Coward and footsore, gladly would I creep into some green recess, where I might see a few not unfriendly faces, and where not more wretches should come than I could relieve. Yes! I am weary, and faith soars and sings no more. Nothing good of me is left, except at the bottom of the heart a melting tenderness—"she loves much."

As soon as the child seemed well enough to travel, the family felt obliged to push on to Perugia, for a detachment of Spanish troops was now stationed in Rieti and the Ossolis feared that disorder might arise. It was also galling to the defeated republi-cans to see the hated invaders making themselves at home in the land whose struggle for liberty they had helped to crush.

And now, since there seemed no further hope for a recon-ciliation with Ossoli's family—for the Papal supporters were extremely bitter toward all those who had lent aid to the revo-lution and the Roman Republic—Margaret determined to end the secrecy about her marriage. She had little love for the Italy that was rising from the ruin of her hopes, and she thought of going to America with her husband and child. She wrote a long letter to her mother:

> This brings me to the main object of my present letter—a piece of intelligence about myself which I had hoped I might be able to communicate in such a way as to give you pleas-ure. That I cannot—after suffering much in silence with that hope—is like the rest of my earthly destiny.
>
> The first moment, it may cause you a pang to know that your eldest child might long ago have been addressed by another name than yours, and has a little son a year old.

But, beloved mother, do not feel this long. I do assure you that it was only great love for you that kept me silent. I have abstained a hundred times, when your sympathy, your counsel, would have been most precious, from a wish not to harass you with anxiety. Even now I would abstain, but it has become necessary on account of the child for us to live publicly and permanently together; and we have no hope in the present state of Italian affairs, that we can do it at any better advantage, for several years, than now.

My husband is a Roman, of a noble but impoverished house. His mother died when he was an infant, his father is dead since we met, leaving some property but encumbered with debts, and in the present state of Rome hardly available, except by living there. He has three older brothers, all provided for in the Papal service—one as Secretary of the Privy Chamber, the other two as members of the Guard Noble. A similar career would have been open to him, but he has embraced liberal principles and with the fall of the Republic has lost all, as well as the favor of his family, who sided with the Pope. Meanwhile, having been an officer in the Republican service, it was best for him to leave Rome. He has taken what little money he had, and we plan to live in Florence for the winter. If he or I can get the means, we shall come together to the United States in the summer; earlier we could not, on account of the child. He is not in any respect such a person as people in general would expect to find with me. He had no instructor except an old priest, who entirely neglected his education; and of that which is contained in books he is absolutely ignorant, and he has no enthusiasm of character. On the other hand, he has excellent practical sense; has been a judicious observer of all that passed before his eyes; has a nice sense of duty, which in its unfailing minute activity may put most enthusiasts to shame; a very sweet temper, and great native refinement. His love for me has been unswerving and most tender. I have never suffered a pain that he could relieve. His devotion when I am ill is only to be compared with yours. His delicacy in trifles, his sweet domestic graces, remind me of Eugene. In him I have found a home, and one that interferes with no tie. Amid many ills and cares we have had much joy together in the sympathy with natural beauty, with our child, with all that is innocent and sweet. . . .

What shall I say of my child? All might seem hyperbole, even to my dearest mother. In him I find satisfaction, for the first time, to the deep wants of my heart. Yet thinking of those other sweet ones fled, I must look upon him as a treasure only lent. He is a fair child, with blue eyes and light hair; very affectionate, graceful, and sportive. He was baptized in the Roman Catholic Church by the name of Angelo Eugene Philip, for his father, grandfather, and my brother. He inherits the title of marquis.

Write the name of my child in your Bible, Angelo Ossoli, born September 5, 1848. God grant he may live to see you, and may prove worthy of your love!

Margaret no longer needed a cause, now that her prayer of many years before for "a bud on my tree of life, so scathed by the lightning and bound by the frost," had been answered. She now found how true was her intuition of that time that "a being born wholly of my being would not let me lie so still and cold in lonely sadness." She had felt that she was "too rough and blurred an image of the Creator to become a bestower of life," but her subjugation of herself to a man in the marriage act, and the bearing and rearing of a child, had made her nature soft and gentle and feminine at last. The psychological change is clearly evident in her writing, particularly in the letters to her friends and family about the silly little doings of her child. She had found happiness in being a woman and in fulfilling a woman's natural duties, and the long struggle between her masculine and feminine traits was ended at last.

Margaret was herself conscious of the change. In a letter to her sister Ellen, written about this same time, she gave a fuller account of her feelings about her husband and child, and of the difference they made in her life:

Had I never connected myself with anyone, my path was clear; now it is all hid; but in that case my development must have been partial. As to marriage, I think the intercourse of heart and mind may be fully enjoyed without entering into this partnership of daily life. Still I do not find it burdensome. The friction that I have seen mar so much the domestic happiness of others does not occur with us, or at least has not occurred. Then there is the pleasure of always being at hand to help one another.

Still the great novelty, the immense gain, to me is my relation with the child. I thought the mother's heart lived in me before, but it did not; I knew nothing about it. Yet before his birth I dreaded it. I thought I should not survive; but if I did, and my child did, was I not cruel to bring another into this terrible world? I could not at that time get any other view. When he was born, that deep melancholy changed at once into rapture; but it did not last long. Then came the prudential motherhood. I grew a coward, a care-taker, not only for the morrow but impiously faithless for twenty or thirty years ahead. It seemed very wicked to have brought the little tender thing into the midst of cares and perplexities we had not feared in the least for ourselves. I imagined everything; he was in danger of every enormity the Croats were then committing upon the infants of Lombardy; the house would be burned over his head; but if he escaped, how were we to get money to buy his bibs and primers? Then his father was to be killed in the fighting and I to die of my cough, etc., etc.

During the siege of Rome I could not see my little boy. What I endured at that time in various ways not many would survive. In the burning sun I went every day to wait in the crowd for letters about him. Often they did not come. I saw blood that had streamed on the wall where Ossoli was. I have a piece of a bomb that burst close to him. I sought solace in tending the suffering men; but when I beheld the beautiful fair young men bleeding to death or mutilated for life, I felt the woe of all the mothers who had nursed each to that full flower, to see them thus cut down. I felt the consolation, too, for those youths died worthily. I was a Mater Dolorosa, and I remembered that she who helped Angelino into the world came from the sign of the Mater Dolorosa. I thought, even if he lives, if he comes into the world at this great troubled time, terrible with perplexed duties, it may be to die thus at twenty years, one of a glorious hecatomb indeed, but still a sacrifice. It seemed then I was willing that he should die.

But Margaret's spirit was refreshed by the quiet summer days she passed with her little family, and soon she regained the strength to face the future with less gloomy thoughts than those she had confided to her sister.

She and Ossoli spent their mornings in the churches of Perugia, studying the masterpieces of the Umbrian painters. In the afternoons they made excursions into the country, or sat and read, content to watch their child growing healthier day by day. Margaret longed to lead a simple, natural life such as this, devoting herself to the child and writing only when the urge was imperative, but their slender resources forced her to renounce what she called "the peculiar beauty of our lives" during this interlude, and to think of making favorable terms with some publisher for her history of the revolution. She wrote to Thomas Carlyle for his aid with the London book-sellers—for the history could only be published in England or America now—and he did what he could for her. He wrote to Emerson about her request and his reply to her—"More power to your elbow!"—and judged the project in these terms: "She has a beautiful enthusiasm; and is perhaps in the right stage of insight for doing that piece of business well." At the end of September the Ossolis went on to Florence, where Margaret planned to finish her book, watching on their way the gathering of the purple Tuscan grapes for the vintage. In the city on the Arno friends awaited their coming: Madame Arconati, who found "nothing offensively strange" in Margaret's revelations about her husband and child, and thought the bond between them was only strengthened, now they could talk as one mother to another; William and Emelyn Story; Greenough, Powers, and the Moziers. There was only one drawback to their life in Florence; the authorities showed too much interest in them, and Ossoli thought he was followed by the Austrian police whenever he went out. They feared for a time that they might be forced to seek asylum elsewhere, but the efforts of Mr. Greenough and the American envoy, prompted by Margaret, rendered the authorities more tolerant of the former revolutionaries.

Margaret was half fearful of the reception that she might get in the English-speaking colony of Florence, now that she suddenly appeared with the "unexpected accessories of husband and child." She was relieved when she was given a warm welcome, no questions were asked of her, and the situation seemed to be quietly accepted. But there was more excitement about the matter under the surface, for Elizabeth Barrett Browning wrote in a letter in December of this year: "The American authoress, Miss Fuller . . . has taken us by surprise at Florence, returning from the Roman field with a husband and a child above a year old. Nobody had even suspected a word of this underplot, and her American friends stood in mute astonishment before this apparition of them here." But doubtless the Storys, who had known the secret since the previous spring, did much to calm the other Americans' doubts and fears on this score. Margaret was less successful in avoiding what she called the "social inquisition of the United States," for the news of her marriage to a "revolutionary marquis" caused a mild storm of gossip when the tidings reached America in the fall of this year, and her friends there reported a certain "meddling curiosity" about the circumstances and a deal of malicious rumors. Margaret was contemptuous of this reaction:

> I had lived in the midst of that New England society in a way that entitled me to esteem, and a favorable interpretation, where there was doubt about my motives or actions. I pity those who are inclined to think ill, when they might as well have inclined the other way. However, let them go; there are many in the world who stand the test, enough to keep us from shivering to death.

This was the last flash of Margaret's pride, now subdued by the feminization of her character. She had written to William Channing that she would come home humbler than he had known her, and that in the future, "while more than ever deeply penetrated with principles, and the need of the martyr spirit to sustain them, I will ever own that there are few worthy, and that I am one of the least."

And she cared less for the opinion of others, now that she had Ossoli constantly at her side with his great devotion to her. She felt that no one but her mother or little children had ever loved her as genuinely as he did. She had been forced to exert her powers to attract affection from others, but "Ossoli loves me from simple affinity; he loves to be with me and to serve and soothe me." She only hoped that in the severe struggle that lay ahead for them she would not neglect either her child or her husband. Their life in Florence was very quiet. Margaret spent her mornings working on her history. Ossoli was content to be alone with her, and since appearance on the streets involved the humiliation of seeing the Austrian troops who occupied the city, he spent most of his time at home, wearing the brown and red coat of his Civic Guard uniform about the house. Their most constant intimate was Horace

Sumner, the young brother of Charles Sumner who had been a friend of Timothy Fuller. This young man had fallen under Margaret's spell at Brook Farm and had recently been sent abroad for his health, or according to his own view, "to see cathedrals and Margaret." He was taken under her wing, and every morning he brought a bunch of flowers for the desk at which she wrote the history. Young Sumner and Ossoli exchanged lessons in English and Italian, and soon became very friendly.

The Ossolis had taken rooms on the Piazza Santa Maria Novella. It was a peaceful place, with a fine view of the Campanile. To those who came to visit Margaret the rooms seemed to breathe forth tranquillity, most welcome to her after the stormy years of the recent past. Of the life of the little family on their first—and last—Christmas together, Margaret painted this picture:

> Christmas Day I was just up, and Nino all naked on his sofa, when came some beautiful large toys that had been sent him: a bird, a horse, a cat, that could be moved to express different things. It almost made me cry to see the fearful rapture with which he regarded them—legs and arms extended, fingers and toes quivering, mouth made up to a little round O, eyes dilated; for a long time he did not even wish to touch them; after he began to, he was different with all three, loving the bird, very wild and shouting with the horse; with the cat, putting her face close to his, staring in her eyes, and then throwing her away. Afterwards I drew him in a lottery, at a child's party given by Mrs. Greenough, a toy of a child asleep on the neck of a tiger; the tiger is stretching up to look at the child. This he likes best of any of his toys. It is sweet to see him when he gets used to them and plays by himself, whispering to them, seeming to contrive stories. You would laugh to know how much remorse I feel that I never gave children more toys in the course of my

life. I regret all the money I ever spent on myself or in little presents for grown people, hardened sinners. I did not know what pure delight could be bestowed. I am sure if Jesus had given, it would not have been little crosses.

There is snow all over Florence. In our most beautiful piazza, Santa Maria Novella, with its fair loggia and bridal church, is a carpet of snow, and the full moon looking down. I had forgotten how angelical all that is; how fit to die by. I have only seen snow in mountain patches for so long. Here it is even the holy shroud of a desired power. God bless all good and bad tonight, and save me from despair.

The note of melancholy at the end of this account had a very real basis. Margaret was beset by financial difficulties. The small share of his family property that Ossoli had managed to secure was almost gone, and soon they would be completely dependent upon Margaret's pen. There seemed to be no future open to them in Italy, and yet the expense of a journey to America was great. Margaret's book was now nearing completion, but she had to give up the idea of publishing it in England when she discovered that no foreigner could hold copyright. She decided that she must go to America, and see what terms could be made with a publisher there. She had written shortly before Christmas to Rebecca Spring of her hopes and fears:

That he (Angelino) may live, that I may find bread for him, that I may not spoil him by over-weening love, that I may grow daily better for his sake—are the ever recurring thoughts, nay prayers, that give their hue to all the currents of my life. Yet in answer to what you say, that it is still better to give the world this living soul than a part of my life in a book—it is true: and yet, and yet, of my book I could know whether it would be of any worth; of my child I must wait to see what his worth will be. I play with him, my ever growing inspiration, but from the solemnity of the thoughts he brings there is refuge only in God. Was I worthy to be the parent of a soul, with its immense capabilities of weal and woe? God be merciful to me, a sinner! comes so naturally to the mother's heart, I think.

When Mrs. Story told Margaret that she seemed so happy now, Margaret protested that the only solid happiness she had ever known was when Angelino went to sleep in her arms. If only she had a little money, so that she could go into strict retirement with her child for a year or two, and live for him alone! But this she could not do: "All life that has been or could be natural to me is invariably denied. God knows why, I suppose."

The problems raised by her proposed return to America were ever with her. She could not think of leaving Ossoli and the child behind; they must all go together. The cheapest possible passage would cost them two hundred and fifty dollars. Margaret racked her brains in thinking how to acquire this sum, which seemed immense to them. Ossoli was of little practical help, for his only trade was that of the soldier and he seemed numbed and dispirited by the collapse of their hopes. Margaret's connection with the *Tribune* had ended, just how it is not clear—perhaps the stories going about at home of her "Fourieristic marriage" had something to do with it. Practically her only source of income now was the trifle gained from her tutoring of young Isabella Mozier, the only child of the American couple who had been so kind to Margaret three years before, when she arrived in Florence alone, ill, and travel-worn. She hated to take the money, but felt obliged to do so on account of her own child.

There were other obstacles besides financial ones. Margaret expected "everything that is painful and difficult" upon her arrival at home; Ossoli had no enthusiasm for a strange land. Both of them dreaded the voyage itself. Ossoli had been warned in his youth to beware of the sea by a fortune-teller. Margaret

had all manner of dark presentiments about the voyage—and
the effect of these was not lessened when word came to Florence
of the loss of the ship on which they had at one time planned
to make the trip. Every time she opened a newspaper the notice
of the loss of some steamer or packet seemed to leap to her
eye. She wrote:

> I am absurdly fearful, and various omens have combined
> to give me a dark feeling. I am become indeed a miserable
> coward for the sake of Angelino. I fear heat and cold and
> even moschetoes, fear terribly the voyage home, fear biting
> poverty. I hope I shall not be forced to be as brave for him
> as I have for myself, and that if I succeed to rear him, he
> will be neither a weak nor a bad man. But I love him too
> much! In case of mishap, however, I shall perish with my
> husband and my child, and we may be transferred to some
> happier state.

And there was the constant vague expectation of the arrival
of some crisis: this relatively calm and peaceful life seemed
soon destined to yield to storms and upsets again. Margaret
thought of her time on earth as drawing to an end: "That
future here on earth seems now to me short. It may be terribly
trying but it will not be so very long now."

But, despite all these forebodings and gloomy reflections,
Margaret found time to become a close friend of Robert and
Elizabeth Browning during this winter in Florence. Elizabeth
Barrett had been a little alarmed and uneasy in her first meetings with Margaret, "she being one of the out and out *Reds*
and scorners of grades of society." But gradually both she and
her husband felt Margaret's magnetic influence, and were
drawn to her despite themselves. Elizabeth noted somewhat
satirically that Margaret talked and Ossoli listened, but Margaret's talk of her meeting with George Sand in Paris was
interesting, and when they became closer acquaintances they
found that they had shared similar experiences in their girl-

hoods. Mr. Barrett and Mr. Fuller were not unlike, and had
influenced their daughters' lives in similar ways, although
Margaret had escaped some of the worst results of paternal
domination because of Timothy's early death. At the end of
this winter, Elizabeth Barrett Browning summed up Margaret
thus: "A very interesting person she is, far better than her
writings—thoughtful, spiritual in her habitual mode of mind;
not only exalted, but *exaltée* in her opinions, and yet calm in
manner." Robert Browning, who according to Margaret "en-
riches every hour I pass with him," characterized the relationship in a few words: "We loved her, and she loved Ba."

Margaret also found time to explain to her American friends
how to address her: "The fact is, it looks to me silly for a radical
like me to be carrying a title, and yet while Ossoli is in his native
land it seems disjoining myself from him not to bear it."

There was something of the queen in Margaret yet, and the
"Marchesa" was not ungrateful to her ears and eyes. They had
a good reason for keeping the title in use, too, for Ossoli's
brothers were trying to disown him for his revolutionary activities, and if he had dropped the title, it might have been taken
as a surrender of his rights and those of his son to the family
property. Ossoli was by no means a howling, wholehearted
revolutionist, he valued tradition and he clung to his Church
despite all Margaret's denunciations of the Papal temporal
policy. All in all, the winter was not a bad one for the little
family of exiles from Rome.

It soon became necessary to set forth, for with the coming
of the spring, the Tuscan police feared another outbreak of
revolutionary activity and made evident their interest in the
Ossolis' departure from Florence.

Margaret hastened her preparations for leaving. She borrowed three hundred dollars on a hundred-day note from a
bank, giving Marcus Spring as security. She wrote to him about
the matter, saying that she would shortly have two hundred
dollars to her credit at the bank and that she hoped to raise the

rest on her book, upon her arrival in America. If anything should happen to her and the manuscript, her family would raise the necessary sum. She took passage in the bark *Elizabeth*, a merchantman which would take two months for the voyage, but the cheapness of the passage offset this disadvantage. The *Elizabeth* lay at Leghorn, and Margaret and Mrs. Mozier paid it a visit of inspection. The ship was nearly new; Captain Hasty and his wife seemed to be pleasant folk and were helpful about the Ossolis' difficulties. A young Italian girl who was going to New York agreed to care for Angelino on the voyage, and Horace Sumner decided to return home with his friends. Margaret was relieved when the matter was finally settled; she had suffered for months from the horrors of indecision. The day before they left Florence for Leghorn, to sail on the waiting vessel, she wrote to her mother:

> I will believe I shall be welcome with my treasures—my husband and child. For me, I long so much to see you! Should anything hinder our meeting on earth, think of your daughter as one who always wished at least to do her duty, and who always cherished you, according as her mind opened to discover excellence.
>
> Give dear love, too, to my brothers; and first to my eldest, faithful friend, Eugene; a sister's love to Ellen; love to my kind and good aunts, and to my dear cousin, E——. God bless them!
>
> I hope we shall be able to pass some time together yet in this world. But if God decrees otherwise, here and hereafter, my dearest mother,
>
> Your loving child,
>
> Margaret

Among all the other worries that oppressed her was the thought that her American friends might not care for Ossoli. She had assured Rebecca Spring that "he is very unlike most Italians, but very unlike most Americans, too." But since Ossoli was without vanity, the regard of others was not important to him. And she wrote William Channing that "I shall embark more composedly in our merchant-ship, praying fervently, indeed, that it may not be my lot to lose my boy at sea, either by unsolaced illness or amid the howling waves; or, if so, that Ossoli, Angelo, and I may go together, and that the anguish may be brief."

The *Elizabeth* sailed from Leghorn on May 17, heavily laden with Powers's statue of John C. Calhoun, some tons of Carrara marble in the rough, and a mixed cargo of other Italian products. The voyage through the Mediterranean was pleasant, and there was beautiful weather on Margaret's fortieth birthday, which fell on the sixth day out of Leghorn. Margaret's fears were allayed, and she enjoyed watching Angelino romp about the deck. He soon became the idol of the captain and the sailors, and was allowed to do what he would. A slight cloud came over the voyage when the captain fell ill; at first he dismissed his sickness as only a touch of fever, but soon he was unable to leave his quarters. And just before the ship anchored off Gibraltar on June 2, Captain Hasty died. The *Elizabeth* spent a week in quarantine here, awaiting favorable winds, but no doctor was allowed on board. At the direction of the British authorities, the captain's body was buried in deep water off the port. On June 9 the *Elizabeth* set sail again, now under the command of the chief mate, Mr. Bangs. Margaret feared that the disease which caused the captain's death was smallpox of the contagious type. On the second day out from Gibraltar, Angelino sickened. He had been much in the captain's cabin during the early stage of the latter's illness, when it was thought to be only some trifling indisposition. There was not much possibility of doubt about the disease now, for the child's closed eyes, swollen head and face, and body covered with eruptions, all bespoke smallpox. Margaret and Ossoli nursed their child day and night, doing what little they could. They despaired for his life, but finally Angelino recovered. Soon he

was as well and happy as before, and made a playfellow of
the goat which had been brought along to provide milk for
him. Margaret was left free to put the finishing touches on her
history of the revolution, and to try to comfort the captain's
widow. Ossoli and young Sumner resumed their lessons in
English and Italian to pass the time.

With favoring winds the *Elizabeth* was off the New Jersey
coast by noon on July 18. Mr. Bangs told his passengers that
he would land them in New York early the next morning, and
suggested that they pack their trunks. The little company
made their preparations for landing and retired early to their
berths for their last night on shipboard. Margaret was greatly
relieved that the voyage had been so uneventful, except for
the outbreak of illness. But the prevailing fresh wind rose to
a gale, and little sleep was possible. In his anxiety to keep clear
of Sandy Hook, Mr. Bangs put the *Elizabeth* on an east north-
east course. Though she was under close-reefed sail, the *Elizabeth* drove farther toward Long Island than the inexperienced
commander anticipated. About four in the morning of July 19,
she struck on a sandbar off Fire Island. The heavy marble in
the hold broke through her bottom and she careened inshore,
while the waves swept over her. The boats were carried away
and the sea poured through a broken skylight in the cabin.
The leeward side of the cabin was soon under water, and the
passengers sheltered themselves against the windward bulk-
head. Angelino cried desperately, but Margaret finally managed
to soothe him to sleep. Celeste, the Italian girl who had helped
to care for the child during the voyage, lost her head and Ossoli
had difficulty in calming her. The officers and crew had re-
treated to the forecastle, after cutting away the main and mizzen
masts. The little group in the cabin, not seeing or hearing them,
assumed they had all been washed overboard or had abandoned
the ship when she first struck. About seven o'clock the cabin
showed signs of breaking up under the pounding waves. Mrs.
Hasty, the captain's widow, caught a glimpse of a figure stand-

ing by the foremast, and shouted and beckoned. The man on the forecastle was scanning the beach, and did not see or hear her at first, in the din of the waves that were still sweeping over the vessel amidships. Finally the second mate, Mr. Davis, saw her, and led some of the men to the rescue. One by one the passengers were brought forward to the forecastle. Angelo made the perilous passage in a canvas bag slung around the neck of a sailor. Now they were less exposed to the beating seas, and the women, wrapped in the sailors' coats, were able to get warm after their chill vigil in the ruined cabin.

There was some hope of reaching the shore, which lay only a few hundred yards off, if the gale should die down. At nine in the morning, there was a lull in the storm and two of the sailors and young Sumner tried to swim ashore, hoping to bring aid to the others. The sailors made it, but Sumner disappeared in the waves, which were too powerful for his slender strength. Another hour or two passed; they seemed like days to the group on the forecastle. Human figures appeared on the beach, but they evidently were more interested in the spoil cast up on the shore as the ship gradually broke up than in attempting a rescue. Finally Mr. Davis proposed a method of reaching the shore without assistance: each passenger should lie on a plank to which rope handles were fastened, and a sailor would swim behind to guide the plank through the waves. He put his plan into execution and brought his captain's widow safely ashore in this fashion. Margaret refused to be parted from Ossoli and their child in such an attempt to win safety. She hoped that Davis would bring a lifeboat to their rescue, in which they could all go together. The others pleaded with her in vain until a boat did appear on the beach. Their hopes rose high, but they soon saw that no attempt was made to launch it. The men on the beach refused to take the lifeboat out until the waves abated. At noon there was another lull in the storm, and Mr. Bangs decided that they must abandon the ship at once, before another tide broke it up entirely. He would take the child himself, and the other sailors would accompany Margaret, Celeste, and Ossoli. But Margaret refused again to be parted from her husband and child. Finally Mr. Bangs impatiently gave the order: "Save yourselves," and he and all but four of the crew jumped overboard, several of them reaching shore safely. A little after three in the afternoon the ship began to break up completely. The four remaining sailors pleaded with the passengers to try the planks which they had made ready after Davis's fashion. The steward took Angelino in his arms and promised Margaret to save him or die. Suddenly a great sea struck the forecastle and the foremast fell, tearing up the deck and hurling the little group into the sea. Two of the sailors managed to swim ashore; the still warm bodies of the steward and Angelino were washed up on the beach twenty minutes later. Margaret and Ossoli were never seen again. Their twelve-hour ordeal, face to face with death, had ended, as Margaret had wished, in their leaving this life together, though her prayer that the anguish might be brief was not fulfilled.

Angelino's body was temporarily buried at Fire Island in a sea chest that had been washed ashore from the wreck of the *Elizabeth*. Later it was placed under the memorial that Margaret's friends raised to her, her husband, and child in Mount Auburn Cemetery in Cambridge. The inscription reads:

IN MEMORY OF
MARGARET FULLER OSSOLI
BORN IN CAMBRIDGE, MASS., MAY 23, 1810

BY BIRTH A CHILD OF NEW ENGLAND
BY ADOPTION A CITIZEN OF ROME
BY GENIUS BELONGING TO THE WORLD

IN YOUTH
AN INSATIATE STUDENT, SEEKING THE HIGHEST CULTURE

IN RIPER YEARS
TEACHER, WRITER, CRITIC OF LITERATURE AND ART
IN MATURER AGE
COMPANION AND HELPER OF MANY
EARNEST REFORMER IN AMERICA AND EUROPE

AND OF HER HUSBAND
GIOVANNI ANGELO, MARQUIS OSSOLI
HE GAVE UP RANK, STATION AND HOME
FOR THE ROMAN REPUBLIC
AND FOR HIS WIFE AND CHILD

AND OF THAT CHILD
ANGELO EUGENE PHILIP OSSOLI
BORN IN RIETI, ITALY, SEPTEMBER 5, 1848
WHOSE DUST REPOSES AT THE FOOT OF THIS STONE

THEY PASSED FROM THIS LIFE TOGETHER
BY SHIPWRECK JULY 19, 1850

UNITED IN LIFE THE MERCIFUL FATHER TOOK THEM TOGETHER
AND IN DEATH THEY WERE NOT DIVIDED

✦CHAPTER XVI✦

Afterglow

MARGARET's friends were overcome with grief when the news of the disaster reached them. The New York papers sent special reporters out to Fire Island to cover the story of the tragedy, and made much of Margaret's memory. Henry Thoreau hastened down to the scene of the wreck, to see if there were any possibility of recovering the bodies of Margaret and her husband, or of salvaging any of the papers she had brought with her. A few trifles were recovered, but the wreckers had scattered or destroyed most of the papers that had reached shore, in their eager search for more attractive loot. The manuscript of the history disappeared as completely as did Margaret and Ossoli; what she had thought her best work perished with her.

Her memory received more honor than had come to her in her lifetime. Emerson, deeply moved by the loss of this dear friend, wrote in his journal:

> On Friday, July 19, Margaret dies on rocks of Fire Island Beach within sight of and within sixty rods of the shore. To the last her country proves inhospitable to her; brave, eloquent, subtle, accomplished, devoted, constant soul!
>
> She had a wonderful power of inspiring confidence and drawing out of people their last secret. *I have lost in her my audience.* . . . There should be a gathering of her friends and some Beethoven should play the dirge.

Thus spoke perhaps her closest friend. But even Longfellow, who had no great love for her, wrote at this time: "What a calamity! A singular woman for New England to produce; original and somewhat self-willed; but full of talent and full of

273

work. A tragic end to a somewhat troubled and romantic life."
Horace Greeley poured out effusive tributes to her memory,
and so did other friends of her journalistic days in New York.
Elizabeth Barrett Browning heard the tidings of the "dreadful
event" in September, and wrote:

> Now she is where there is no more grief and no more sea;
> and none of the restless in this world, none of the ship-
> wrecked in heart, ever seemed to me to want peace more
> than she did. We saw much of her last winter; and over a
> great gulf of differing opinion we both felt drawn strongly
> to her. High and pure aspiration she had—yes, and a tender
> woman's heart—and we honored the truth and courage in
> her, rare in woman or man. The work she was preparing
> upon Italy would have probably been more equal to her
> faculty than anything previously produced by her pen (her
> other writings being curiously inferior to the impressions her
> conversation gave you). . . . Blood colours of Socialistic
> views, which would have drawn the wolves on her, with a
> still more howling enmity, both in England and America.
> Therefore it was better for her to go. Only God and a few
> friends can be expected to distinguish between the pure per-
> sonality of a woman and her professed opinions. She was
> chiefly known in America, I believe, by oral lectures and a
> connection with the newspaper press, neither of them happy
> means of publicity. Was she happy in anything, I wonder?
> She told me that she never was. May God have made her
> happy in her death.

And Robert Browning wrote of "the dreadful loss of dear,
brave, noble M. F., with her husband and child."

Walter Savage Landor, moved by the account of the Ossolis'
deaths which appeared in the *Household Words* for April 24,
1852, raised what he confessed to be his "failing voice"—he
was then seventy-seven—to hymn the tragedy in verse. The
cause of the Italian republicans had been dear to him, and his

THE MEMORIAL, AT CAMBRIDGE

fiery appeals for their cause were the only ones that surpassed Margaret's in enlisting the sympathy of the English-speaking peoples. The poem he wrote, "On the Death of M. D'Ossoli and His Wife Margaret Fuller," was published in *The Examiner* for May 8 and reprinted in the following year, despite its feebleness as verse. It is interesting to note that a third of the lines are devoted to lamenting Ossoli himself. Landor knew his Italy and knew the Ossolis, so the malicious gossip about Ossoli may well be disregarded in the light of this fact. A few lines from the poem will indicate Landor's opinion of Margaret:

> Proud as thou wert of her, America
> Is prouder, showing to her sons how high
> Swells woman's courage in a virtuous breast.

> Rest, glorious soul,
> Renowned for strength of genius, Margaret!
> Rest with the twain too dear! My words are few,
> And shortly none will hear my failing voice.
> But the same language with more full appeal
> Shall hail thee. Many are the sons of song
> Whom thou hast heard upon thy native plains
> Worthy to sing of thee: the hour is come:
> Take we our seats and let the dirge begin.

Thomas Carlyle, who had heard the news from Emerson and sent it on to the Brownings, wrote to ask his American friend whether any competent biographer was to celebrate Maragaret's life. "Poor Margaret, I often remember her; and think how she is asleep now under the surges of the sea." Mazzini was now with the Carlyles again, for Italy offered him no home in these days of reaction, and his references to Margaret's role in the revolution may have prompted Carlyle's thought of her. In that July Emerson told his correspondent that he, William Channing, and Samuel Ward were engaged

in making "a sort of memoir of Margaret Fuller," feeling "a
kind of claim upon our conscience to build her a cairn." He
asked Mazzini to contribute an account of Margaret's Italian
years. The Brownings were also asked to write their reminiscences of their dead friend. But though these accounts were
written and sent to America, they never reached the hands of
the compilers of the *Memoirs,* and no trace of them has ever
been found. It is conceivable that the Italian censors caught
them in the mails and destroyed them. The two-volume memorial to Margaret, finally compiled and written by Emerson,
Channing, James Freeman Clarke, and Frederick Henry Hedge,
was published early in the spring of 1852, after being delayed in
vain for these foreign contributions.

Margaret's old enemy, James Russell Lowell, had been en-
listed by Emerson as an agent abroad to search for the missing
contributions. Upon his return to Cambridge in November
1852, Lowell wrote thus to Emerson of his findings:

The letter of Mr. and Mrs. Browning was addressed to Mr.
Story, and, I suppose, ought to be in the dead letter office at
Washington. (By the way, Mr. Cass also sent a letter which
never came to hand.)

Mazzini said he wrote to *you* and sent the letter by an
Italian, whose name he could not remember and who was in
N. Orleans when last heard of. He said there was not a great
deal in it, and I gathered from his account of it that it related
chiefly to an interview in which Madame Ossoli begged him
to leave Rome when the French entered. I told him that,
however little he might have to say, anything from him
would be of particular interest to the Marchesa's family, and
begged him to write again to you. He promised most faithfully
to do so and to send the letter to my lodgings before I left
London. I wrote my address and put it into his own hands.
Moreover I had already (to make sure) written him a note,
which he told me he had received.

I do not feel that I could have done more (and I would not have done so much) had the affair been my own. I need not say that I felt a particular interest in serving Emerson, and in doing what might in any way console a family so fearfully bereaved.

Spite of all, Mazzini did not write. I feared he would not, for to tell the truth—Guy Fawkes was too busy with his lanthorn and matches to be writing letters.

It would seem that death had ended the feud Lowell long waged with Margaret, for except for the tendency displayed to belittle Margaret's relation with Mazzini—now universally hailed as a great man—the letter is that of a person doing his best to see that the memory of a dead acquaintance was fittingly celebrated. It was one of the many ironies of Margaret's career that it should have been Lowell who sought to discover the papers which might have assured her a more lasting fame.

Emerson sent Carlyle a copy of the *Memoirs,* and it moved the old Scotch sage to a reflection on Margaret's life:

Poor Margaret, that is a strange tragedy, that history of hers; and has many traits of the Heroic in it, though it is as wild as the prophecy of a Sibyl. Such a predetermination to *eat* this big universe as her oyster or her egg, and to be absolute empress of all height and glory in it that her heart could conceive, I have not before seen in any human soul. Her "mountain *me*" indeed:—but her courage too is high and clear, her chivalrous nobleness indeed is great; her veracity, in its deepest sense, *à toute épreuve.*

He gave Emerson an account of the considerable notice taken of the book in England, complaining only that it was too symbolic and not clear and concise enough. And he was at a loss to account for the missing contributions from Mazzini and the Brownings. In writing to Browning at this time, Carlyle referred

again to Margaret: "Poor Margaret meant well, and she might
have read the phenomena infinitely worse, nay it is surprising
she didn't. A gigantic Aspiration: in my life I have seen nothing
stranger in that kind; and very lovable withal." Perhaps he was
thinking, as he wrote, of Emerson's dictum of this time that
"her habitual vision was through colored glasses."

The book caused a considerable stir. Longfellow devoted a
whole afternoon and evening to reading it; he found it so "extremely interesting" that he could not put it down once he
began it. Harriet Martineau was induced by it to make a kinder
estimate of her dead friend, though she had been "completely
spoiled in conversation and manners" and led into self-delusions
by her life "in the most pedantic age of society in her own country, and in its most pedantic city."

> The ensuing period redeemed all, and I regard her Ameri-
> can life as a reflexion, more useful than agreeable, of the
> prevalent social spirit of her time and place; and the Italian
> life as the true revelation of the tender and high-souled
> woman, who had till then been as curiously concealed from
> herself as from others.

Harriet had much to say of the "remarkable regeneration
which transformed her from the dreaming and haughty pedant
into the true woman," and of the beauty and interest of the
closing period "when husband and child concentrated the powers and affections which had so long run to waste in intellectual
and moral eccentricity." The literary journals and reviews
teemed with eulogistic estimates and reminiscences of Margaret,
and ten years after her death the *North American Review*, the
old enemy of that Transcendentalism which had now become
eminently respectable, referred to her as a "noble gift to our
time" and called her life the best of all her works. It even took
pains to refute the most common charge brought against her,
that of arrogance, by quoting Margaret's own words about
Carlyle on this score:

His arrogance does not in the least proceed from an unwillingness to allow freedom to others. . . . It is the habit
of a mind accustomed to follow its own impulse, as a hawk
does its prey. He is indeed arrogant and overbearing, but
in his arrogance there is no trace of littleness or self-love. It
is in his nature, in the untamable energy that has given him
power to crush the dragons.

The other estimates of Margaret in America were in the vast
majority laudatory, though there were a few demurrers and
dissents from the rather sickening sweetness of the universal
hymn of praise. No human being could have been as good and
perfect as her friends painted Margaret after her death, and
their attempt to foist this memory of her upon posterity neces-
sarily brought about a reaction which destroyed their efforts.
But for the first decade or so after her death Margaret was a
glorious memory, a goddess who still walked the earth as a well-
remembered shade. Even abroad, she was considered a queen
without a kingdom and the purest embodiment of the best
qualities and merits of the famous women of the age. Emile
Montégut wrote in the *Revue des Deux Mondes* that those who
found in her neither goddess nor prophetess, and did not share
the enthusiasm of her friends, must yet perforce speak of her
with justice and sympathy. He called her the Circe of the
American literary world, whose one thought was to dominate
and one ambition to reign, whose life was one long fever. He
observed sagely that the "mystic, bizarre, almost occult and
cabalistic" *Memoirs* did not record a life but a character, and
likened Margaret to Lady Hester Stanhope, Madame de Staël,
and Bettina von Arnim. Margaret could rest happily in such
company.

But she was not allowed to lie undisturbed in death. The sly
whispers about the circumstances of her marriage continued,
for her biographers did nothing to lay them at rest with their
idealized account of her life. There were many gaps in the

story of her Italian years, and malicious tongues, surfeited with the praise heaped upon her memory, filled in these gaps with scandalous episodes. And in 1884, a new selection from Nathaniel Hawthorne's French and Italian notebooks was published by his son Julian. Mrs. Hawthorne had published an earlier selection in 1871, but did not include a long passage concerning Margaret's life in Italy, which raised a tremendous furor when it finally appeared thirty-four years after her death. Julian Hawthorne seems to have been a less scrupulous character than his mother Sophia, and not one to shun the sensational, even if it slandered the memory of the dead. The passage which he saw fit to publish was written in Rome while his father was visiting there, some eight or nine years after Margaret's death:

Mr. Mozier knew Margaret well, she having been an intimate of his during part of her residence in Italy. . . . He says that the Ossoli family, though technically noble, is really of no rank whatever. . . . Ossoli himself, to the best of his belief, was ——'s servant, or had something to do with the care of ——'s apartments. He was the handsomest man that Mr. Mozier ever saw, but entirely ignorant, even of his own language; scarcely able to read at all; destitute of all manners —in short, half an idiot, and without any pretensions to be a gentleman. At Margaret's request, Mr. Mozier had taken him into his studio, with a view to ascertain whether he were capable of instruction in sculpture; but after four months' labor Ossoli produced a thing supposed to be a copy of a human foot, but the great toe was on the wrong side. He could not possibly have had the least appreciation of Margaret; and the wonder is, what attraction she found in this boor, this man without the intellectual spark—she that had always shown such cruel and bitter scorn of intellectual deficiency. As from her towards him, I do not understand what feelings there could have been except it were purely sensual;

as from him towards her, I can understand as little, for she had not the charm of womanhood. But she was a person anxious to try all things, and fill up her experience in all directions; she had a strong and coarse nature, which she had done her utmost to refine, with infinite pains; but of course it could be only superficially changed. The solution of the riddle lies in this direction, nor does one's conscience revolt at the idea of thus solving it, for (at least this is my experience) Margaret has not left in the hearts and minds of those who knew her any deep witness of her integrity and purity. She was a great humbug—of course with much talent and moral reality, or else she could have never been so great a humbug. But she had stuck herself full of borrowed qualities, which she chose to provide herself with, but had no root in her. Mr. Mozier added that Margaret had quite lost all power of literary production before she left Rome, though occasionally the charm and power of her conversation would reappear. To his certain knowledge she had no important manuscripts with her when she sailed (she having shown him all she had with a view to his procuring their publication in America), and the *History of the Roman Revolution,* about which there was so much lamentation, in the belief that it had been lost with her, never had existence. Thus there appears to have been a total collapse in poor Margaret, morally and intellectually; and, tragic as her catastrophe was, Providence was, after all, kind in putting her and her clownish husband and their child on board that fated ship. There never was such a tragedy as her whole story—the sadder and sterner, because so much of the ridiculous was mixed up in it, and because she could bear anything easier than to be ridiculous. It was such an awful joke, that she should have resolved—in all sincerity, no doubt—to make herself the greatest, wisest, best woman of the age. And to that end she set to work on her strong, heavy, unpliable, and in many respects defective and evil nature, and adorned it with a mosaic of admirable qualities, such as she chose to possess, putting in here a splendid talent and there moral excellence, and polishing each separate piece, and the whole together, until it seemed to shine afar and dazzle all who saw it. She took credit to herself for having been her own Redeemer, if not her own Creator; and indeed, she was far more a work of art than any of Mozier's statues. But she was not working on an inanimate substance like marble or clay; there was something within her that she could not possibly come at, to recreate or refine it; and, by and by, this rude, old potency bestirred itself, and undid all her labor in the twinkling of an eye. On the whole, I do not know but I like her the better for it; because she proved herself a very woman after all, and fell as the weakest of her sisters might.

This amazingly malign passage, which, even better than *Blithedale* itself, displays Hawthorne's cunning as a novelist in evolving a fiction from a set of facts, made many of Margaret's friends—there were still many of them in 1884—reach for their pens and write violent protests and denials for the press. One of the most interesting, most detailed, and best documented of these rejoinders is that of Margaret's nephew, Frederick T. Fuller, which appeared in *The Literary World* for January 10, 1885. As the son of Richard Fuller, Margaret's younger brother and the head of the family, he had access to her unpublished journals and letters, and from this evidence supplied a convincing picture of the complete falsity of Hawthorne's attack on a dead friend. He showed how entirely different from Hawthorne's account was the opinion held of Margaret by members of the American artistic colonies in Rome and Florence. He pointed out the close relationship which unquestionably had existed between Margaret and the Hawthornes in 1843 and 1844, and remarked: "I cannot think that Hawthorne's memory will be the gainer by the disclosure that he was capable, even in thought, of pronouncing such a judgment upon a former

friend, long since dead, and a woman." He contrasted the superficial likeness and the essential unlikeness existing between the
two portraits of Margaret and her husband—the one presented
by her parents, brothers, and such friends as J. F. Clarke, Sarah
Clarke, Emerson, Hedge, Greeley, Curtis, Mrs. Dall, Mrs.
Story, and others who knew her intimately, which was supported by all her printed works, letters, and journals; and the
other sketched by Hawthorne, which agreed with the early
first impressions of those who never got to know her well—and
suggested that one was a photograph, while the other was a
cartoon, of the real Margaret. He refutes many of the details of
Hawthorne's picture, and there are still others that can clearly
be revealed as false. Margaret was far from being an intimate
of Mozier, an American merchant who had turned sculptor
unsuccessfully in his middle years. He could know little of her
life in Rome at first hand, since he lived in Florence and saw
her for only a few days during her stay at his home in the
autumn of 1847 when she was ill, and no more than twice a
week, at the gatherings of the American colony at the house
he shared with Chapman, during the winter she and Ossoli
passed in Florence after the collapse of the revolution. The
positions that Ossoli's brothers held at the Papal court may
have been distorted into the story of his having been a servant.
The remark about "technical nobility" is incomprehensible.
Margaret admitted her husband's lack of intellectual cultiva-
tion, which would not be at all surprising in a soldier. Ossoli's
half-hearted attempts to while away his boredom and lack of
spirits during this winter of exile from Rome may have drawn
Mozier's fire on his activities as a sculptor. Mozier fancied himself in his artistic capacity, though his contemporaries and posterity did not, and may well have felt scorn for an amateur's
feeble efforts. The speculations about the relationship between
Margaret and Ossoli are Hawthorne's own—for no one knew
what this really was—first because of the secrecy they preserved
and then because they lived in retirement. All those who knew

Margaret well made much of her integrity and purity, and many did so who were only acquaintances. Mozier, a retired business man and a sculptor by avocation, was probably not the most competent judge of Margaret's manuscripts, if he ever even saw them, and surely she had literary friends in high esteem in England and America who were far better placed than he to bring about the publication of the history. There is much evidence for its existence in manuscript form. Margaret's letters to the *Tribune* and her personal correspondence of the last months supply evidence of a great development and ripening of her literary powers, rather than of a collapse of them. And whatever the complete story of her relationship with Ossoli may be—and that can never be discovered—it is not the story of the inglorious fall of a woman who had striven to be great all her life, and labored with some success to elevate her character and her nature to conform to the high ideals she had chosen for herself.

The editors of *The Literary World* came close to the truth in their statement in the issue which contained Frederick Fuller's rejoinder:

> The fact is that both Hawthorne and Margaret Fuller were in some respects abnormal and unhealthy growths of their kind. . . . The genius of each ran into eccentricities, and when eccentricities meet they clash. . . .
>
> However true the delineation may be, she suffers from the making of it rather less than he.
>
> We do not think anyone reading any of the memoirs of Margaret Fuller would derive from them the impression that she was a woman of unmixed loveliness.

But the ill deeds that men do live on after they have gone from this earth. The eulogistic picture that her friends painted of Margaret, touching up the good highlights and shading over the unpleasant features, has largely yielded to the more human, if malign, cartoon that Hawthorne drew of her. It has survived in a hundred aprocryphal tales, and posterity has followed only too well Elizabeth Barrett's counsel: "If I wished anyone to do her justice, I should say, as I have indeed said, 'Never read what she has written.'" The true Margaret, a great woman and a great personality, an intellectual pioneer in spheres new to her sex, whose life was one long struggle to make the fullest use of the rare resources of intellect and emotion given her by God, has been forgotten. This book has been an attempt to bring to life again, with all the strange complexities and difficulties of her character and life, the real Margaret Fuller, who is worthy of being reborn for this age and time.

APPENDIX

BIBLIOGRAPHICAL
NOTE

INDEX

Appendix

Margaret's own summary of her argument, given at the end of *Woman in the Nineteenth Century* "as was done in old-fashioned sermons," offers the fairest idea of her book that can be supplied:

Man is a being of two-fold relations, to nature beneath and intelligences above him. The earth is his school, if not his birthplace; God his object; life and thought his means of interpreting nature and aspiring to God.

Only a fraction of this purpose is accomplished in the life of any one man. Its entire accomplishment is to be hoped for only from the sum of the lives of men, or Man considered as a whole.

As this whole has one soul and one body, any injury or obstruction to a part or to the meanest member affects the whole. Man can never be perfectly happy or virtuous until all men are so.

To address Man wisely, you must not forget that his life is partly animal, subject to the same laws with Nature.

But you cannot address him wisely unless you consider him still more as soul, and appreciate the conditions and destiny of soul.

The growth of Man is two-fold, masculine and feminine.

So far as these two methods can be distinguished, they are so as

Energy and Harmony;

Power and Beauty;

Intellect and Love;

or by some such rude classification; for we have not language primitive and pure enough to express such ideas with precision.

These two sides are supposed to be expressed in Man and Woman, that is, as the more and the less, for the faculties have not been given pure to either, but only in preponderance. There are also exceptions in great number, such as men of far more beauty than power, and the reverse. But as a general rule, it seems to have been the intention to have a preponderance on the one side that is called masculine, and on the other one that is called feminine.

There can be no doubt that if these two developments were in perfect harmony, they would correspond to and fulfill one another like hemispheres, or the tenor and bass in music.

But there is no perfect harmony in human nature; and the two parts answer one another only now and then; or if there be a persistent consonance, it can only be traced at long intervals, instead of discoursing on an obvious melody.

What is the cause of this?

Man, in the order of time, was developed first; as energy comes before harmony; power before beauty.

Woman was therefore under his care as an elder. He might have been her guardian and teacher.

But as human nature goes not straight forward but by excessive action and reaction in an undulated course, he misunderstood and abused his advantages, and became her temporal master instead of her spiritual sire.

On himself came the punishment. He educated Woman more as a servant than as a daughter, and found himself a king without a queen.

The children of this unequal union showed unequal natures and more and more men seemed sons of the handmaid rather than the princess.

At last there were so many Ishmaelites that the rest grew frightened and indignant. They laid the blame on Hagar and drove her forth into the wilderness.

But there were none the fewer Ishmaelites for that.

At last men became a little wiser and saw that the infant Moses was in every case saved by the pure instinct of Woman's breast. For as too much adversity is better for the moral nature than too much prosperity, Woman in this respect dwindled less than Man, though in other respects still a child in leading-strings.

So Man did her more and more justice and grew more and more kind.

But yet—his habits and will corrupted by the past—he did not clearly see that Woman was half himself; that her interests were identical with his; and that by the law of their common being he could never reach his true proportions while she remained in any wise shorn of hers.

And so it has gone on to our day; both ideas developing, but more slowly than they would under a clearer recognition of truth and justice, which would have permitted the sexes their due influence on one another and mutual improvement from more dignified relations.

Wherever there was pure love, the natural influences were for the time restored.

Wherever the poet or the artist gave free course to his genius, he saw the truth and expressed it in worthy forms, for these men especially share and need the feminine principle. The divine birds need to be brooded into life and song by mothers.

Whatever religion (I mean the thirst for truth and good, not the love of sect and dogma) had its course, the original design was apprehended in its simplicity, and the dove presaged sweetly from Dodona's oak.

I have aimed to show that no age was left entirely without a witness of the equality of the sexes in function, duty, and hope.

Also that when there was unwillingness or ignorance which prevented this being acted upon, women had not the less power for their want of light and noble freedom. But it was power which hurt alike them and those against whom they made use of the arms of the servile—cunning, blandishment, and unreasonable emotion.

That now the time has come when a clearer vision and a better action are possible—when Man and Woman may regard one another as brother and sister, the pillars of one porch, the priests of one worship.

I have believed and intimated that this hope would receive an ampler fruition than ever before in our own land.

And it will do so if this land carry out the principles from which sprang our national life.

I believe that at present women are the best helpers of one another.

Let them think; let them act; till they know what they need.

We only ask of men to remove arbitrary barriers. Some would like to do more. But I believe it needs that some Woman show herself in her native dignity to teach them how to aid her, their minds are so encumbered by tradition. . . .

You ask, what use will she make of liberty when she has so long been sustained and restrained?

I answer in the first place this will not be suddenly given. . . .

But were this freedom to come suddenly, I have no fear of the consequences. Individuals might commit excesses, but there is not only in the sex a reverence for decorums and limits inherited and enhanced from generation to generation, which many years of other life could not efface, but a native love, in Woman as Woman, of proportion, of "the simple art of not too much"—a Greek moderation which would create immediately a restraining party, the natural legislators and instructors of the rest, and would gradually establish such rules as are needed to guard without impeding life. But if you ask me what offices they may fill, I reply—any. I do not care what case you put; let them be sea captains if they will. I do not doubt there are women well fitted for such an office, and if so, I should be as glad to see them in it as to welcome the maid of Saragossa, or the maid of Missolonghi, or the Suliote heroine, or Emily Plater. I think women need, especially at this juncture, a much greater range of occupation than they have, to use their latent powers. . . .

Fourier has observed these wants of women, as no one can fail to do who watches the desires of little girls or knows the ennui that haunts grown women except where they make to themselves a serene little world by art of some kind. He, therefore, in proposing a great variety of employments, in manufactures or the care of plants or animals, allows for one third of women as likely to have a taste for masculine pursuits, one third of men for feminine.

Who does not observe the immediate glow and serenity that is diffused over the life of women, before restless or fretful, by engaging in gardening, building, or the lowest department of art? Here is something that is not routine, something that draws forth life toward the infinite.

I have no doubt, however, that a large proportion of women would give themselves to the same employments as now, because there are circumstances that must lead to them. Mothers will delight to make the nest soft and warm. Nature would take care of that; no need to clip the wings of any bird that wants to soar or sing, or finds in itself the strength of pinion for a migratory flight unusual to its kind. The difference would be that *all* need not be constrained to employments for which *some* are unfit. I have urged upon the sex self-subsistence, in its two forms of self-reliance and self-impulse, because I believe them to be the needed means of the present juncture.

I have urged on Woman independence of Man, not because I do not think the sexes mutually needed by one another, but because in Woman this fact has led to an excessive devotion, which has cooled love, degraded marriage, and prevented either sex from being what it should be to itself or the other.

I wish Woman to live *first* for God's sake. Then she will not make an imperfect man her god and thus sink to idolatry. Then she will not take what is not fit for her from a sense of weakness and poverty. Then if she finds what she needs in Man embodied, she will know how to love and be worthy of being loved.

By being more a soul, she will not be less Woman, for nature is perfected through spirit.

Now there is no woman, only an overgrown child. . . .

A profound thinker has said, "No married woman can represent the female world, for she belongs to her husband. The idea of Woman must be represented by a virgin."

But that is the very fault of marriage and of the present relation between the sexes, that the woman *does* belong to the man, instead of forming a whole with him.

An idea not unknown to ancient times has of late been revived, that in the metamorphoses of life the soul assumes the form first of Man and then of Woman, and takes the chances and reaps the benefits of either lot. Why then, say some, lay such emphasis on the rights or needs of Woman? What she wins not as Woman will come to her as Man.

That makes no difference. It is not Woman but the law of right, the law of growth, that speaks in us and demands the perfection of each being in its kind—apple as apple, Woman as Woman. Without adopting your theory, I know that I, a daughter, live through the life of Man; but what concerns me now is that my life be beautiful, powerful, in a word, a complete life in its kind. Had I but one more moment to live, I must wish the same.

Bibliographical Note

ALL OF Margaret Fuller's works are out of print. Since in almost every case her works were poorly edited and were thrown together into book form without regard to anything but the exigencies of the press, a new selected edition of her writings is badly needed. Meanwhile the best approach to her is through the two-volume *Memoirs of Margaret Fuller Ossoli*, by R. W. Emerson, W. H. Channing, and J. F. Clarke; Boston: Phillips, Sampson and Company, 1852. This work, despite the bowdlerizing activities of its three distinguished editors, contains much material available elsewhere only in manuscript, and long quotations from her published writings.

Her works, in the order of their appearance, are:

Eckermann's Conversations with Goethe. (Translation.) Boston: Hilliard, Gray, 1839.

Correspondence of Fräulein Günderode and Bettina von Arnim. (Translation with Minna Wesselhoeft.) Boston: Burnham, 1842.

Summer on the Lakes. Boston: C. C. Little and James, 1844.

Woman in the Nineteenth Century. Boston: 1844, and New York: Tribune Press, 1845.

Papers on Literature and Art. New York: Wiley and Putnam, 1846. (Translation of *Torquato Tasso* appears in later edition of this volume.) Boston: Crosby, Nichols, 1856.

At Home and Abroad, edited by A. B. Fuller. Boston: Crosby, Nichols, 1856.

Life Without and Life Within, edited by A. B. Fuller. Boston: Brown, Taggard and Chase, 1859.

Love Letters of Margaret Fuller, 1845–1846. Introduction by Julia Ward Howe. New York: D. Appleton, 1903.

The dates given are those of first editions. Most of the volumes passed through several, and in some cases were combined in later editions. The earlier ones are preferable, because of errors and omissions which crept in later.

There are two valuable collections of manuscripts. The Fuller Papers in the Harvard College Library have much material bearing on the whole family and some letters to and from Margaret which are unavailable elsewhere. The Fuller Papers in the Boston Public

Library contain the working materials for the Emerson-Channing-Clarke *Memoirs* and Higginson's biography. Unfortunately the value of these papers has been in part destroyed by the unpardonable liberties that the original editors took with them. The collection remains by far the most important source, however, and there is much of interest that was passed over by Margaret's friends and memorialists.

The four volumes of the *Dial,* which was published quarterly from 1840 to 1844, contain many signed and unsigned contributions by Margaret Fuller. The files of the *New York Tribune* for 1845 and 1846 contain many uncollected critical papers by her. The letters from Europe which appeared in the *Tribune* were collected in *At Home and Abroad.*

There are numerous biographies, none of them particularly reliable and none presenting a rounded picture of its subject, though many are good on one phase or another. The most useful, when checked against the manuscript materials, are:

Memoirs of Margaret Fuller Ossoli, by R. W. Emerson, W. H. Channing, and J. F. Clarke. Boston: Phillips, Sampson, 1852.

Margaret Fuller (Marchesa Ossoli), by Julia Ward Howe. Boston: Roberts Brothers, 1883.

Margaret Fuller Ossoli, by Thomas Wentworth Higginson. Boston: Houghton, Mifflin, 1884.

Margaret and Her Friends, by Caroline W. Healey (Dall). Boston: Roberts Brothers, 1895.

Essays on Puritanism ("Margaret Fuller"), by Andrew MacPhail. Boston: Houghton, Mifflin, 1905.

Margaret Fuller, a Psychological Biography, by Katharine Anthony. New York: Harcourt, Brace and Howe, 1920.

Portraits of American Women ("Margaret Fuller Ossoli"), by Gamaliel Bradford. Boston: Houghton, Mifflin, 1919.

Margaret Fuller, by Margaret Bell. With an introduction by Mrs. F. D. Roosevelt. New York: C. Boni, 1930.

GENERAL SOURCES

Alcott, Amos Bronson, *Journals,* edited by Odell Shepard. Boston: Little, Brown, 1938.

Arvin, Newton. *Life of Hawthorne.* Boston: Little, Brown, 1929.

Braun, Frederick Augustus. *Margaret Fuller and Goethe.* New York: Henry Holt, 1910.

Brooks, Van Wyck. *Life of Emerson.* New York: Dutton, 1932.

——. *Flowering of New England.* New York: Dutton, 1936.

Browning, Elizabeth Barrett. *Letters,* edited by F. G. Kenyon. New York: Macmillan, 1898.

Bulletin of N. Y. Public Library, December 1901. Letter of Margaret Fuller to E. A. Duyckinck.

Carlyle, Thomas, and Emerson, R. W. *Correspondence.* Boston: Osgood, 1883.

Carpenter, Richard V. "Margaret Fuller in Northern Illinois," in *Journal of the Illinois State Historical Society.* Springfield: January 1910.

Clarke, James Freeman. *Autobiography.* Cambridge: Houghton, Mifflin, 1892.

Cooke, George Willis. *Historical and Biographical Introduction to Accompany the Dial.* Cleveland: privately published, 1902.

Dickens, Charles. *American Notes.* London: Chapman and Hall, 1863.

Emerson, Ralph Waldo. *Journals.* Boston: Houghton, Mifflin, 1912.

——. *Letters,* edited by Ralph L. Rusk, New York: Columbia University Press, 1939.

Frothingham, O. B. *Transcendentalism in New England.* New York: G. Putnam, 1876.

Fuller, Frederick T. "Hawthorne and Margaret Fuller Ossoli," in *Literary World,* Vol. XVI, No. 1, Jan. 10, 1885.

Fuller, Richard F. *Recollections.* Boston: privately published, 1936.

Goddard, H. C. "New England Transcendentalism," in *Cambridge History of American Literature,* Vol. I.

Greeley, Horace. *Recollections of a Busy Life.* New York: Tribune Association, 1869.

Haraszti, Zoltán. *The Idyll of Brook Farm.* Boston: published by Trustees of Public Library, 1937.

Hawthorne, Julian. *Nathaniel Hawthorne and His Wife.* Boston: Osgood, 1885.

Hawthorne, Nathaniel. *The Blithedale Romance.* Boston: Osgood, 1852.

Hawthorne, Nathaniel. *American Notebooks.* Boston: Osgood, 1868.

———. *French and Italian Notebooks.* Boston: Osgood, 1871.

Hicks, Granville. "Margaret Fuller to Sarah Helen Whitman: an Unpublished Letter," in *American Literature*, Vol. I, No. 4, January 1930.

Holmes, Oliver Wendell. *Elsie Venner.* Boston: Houghton, Mifflin, 1861.

Howe, Julia Ward. *Reminiscences, 1819–1899.* Boston: Houghton, Mifflin, 1900.

Howe, M. A. De Wolfe. *New Letters of James Russell Lowell.* New York: Harper, 1932.

James, Henry. *William Wetmore Story and His Friends.* Boston: Houghton, Mifflin, 1904.

Knortz, Karl. *Brook Farm und Margaret Fuller.* New York: Bartsch, 1886.

Lowell, James Russell. *Poetical Works.* Boston: Houghton, Mifflin, 1887.

McMaster, Helen. "Margaret Fuller as a Literary Critic," *Univ. of Buffalo Studies*, Vol. VII, No. 3, December 1928.

Marten, Willard E., Jr. "A Last Letter of Margaret Fuller Ossoli," in *American Literature*, Vol. V. No. 1, March 1933.

Martineau, Harriet. *Society in America.* New York: Harper, 1837.

———. *Autobiography.* Boston: Osgood, 1877.

Parrington, V. L. *The Romantic Revolution* (Vol. II, *Main Currents in American Thought*). New York: Harcourt, Brace, 1927.

Parton, James. *Life of Horace Greeley.* Boston: Osgood, 1867.

Poe, Edgar Allan. *Collected Works.* New York: W. J. Widdleton, 1867.

Sanborn, Frank B. *Recollections of Seventy Years.* Boston: Badger, 1909.

Shepard, Odell. *Pedlar's Progress: The Life of Bronson Alcott.* Boston: Little, Brown, 1937.

Swift, Lindsay. *Brook Farm.* New York: Macmillan, 1906.

Warfel, Harry R. "Margaret Fuller and Ralph Waldo Emerson," in *Publications of the Modern Language Association of America*, Vol. L, No. 2, June 1935.

Wendell, Barrett. *A Literary History of America.* Scribner, 1900.

Index

Abolitionism, 44–5, 66, 74
Adams, Abigail, 79
Adams, Hannah, 124
Adams, John Quincy, 15, 20
Alcott, Amos Bronson, xi, xii, xv, 32, 34–5, 37–42, 46, 53, 55–6, 58, 60, 63–6, 68–9, 76–8, 85–7, 103–4, 112, 220
Alcott, Anna, 35
Alcott, Louisa May, 35
Alfieri, Vittorio, 21, 37
Allen (farmer at Brook Farm), 105
Allston, Washington (painter), 45, 48–9, 85
Anthony, Katharine, 97, 245
Anthony, Susan, 79
Ariosto, 37
Arnim, Bettina von, 279
Atkinson (mesmerizer), 176, 193
Austen, Jane, 45
Azeglio, Marchese d', 202

Baillie, Joanna, 183
Balzac, 150
Bancroft, George, xi, 21, 66, 107–8, 152, 169
Bancroft, Mrs. George, 75
Bangs (mate of *Elizabeth*), 268–71
Barlow, Mrs. (at Brook Farm), 75, 93, 115
Barrett, Edward, 266
Barrett, Elizabeth, *see* Browning, Elizabeth Barrett
Bartlett (attends Conversations), 65
Bartol, Dr. C. E., 59, 62, 65
Beethoven, 46
Belgiojoso, Princess, 245, 247
Bentham, Jeremy, 43, 184
Béranger, P. J. de, 195
Berni, Francesco, 14
Berri, Duchesse de, 206
Berry, Mary, 183
Berryer, Pierre, 193
Blackwells Island, 157
Blithedale Romance, The (Hawthorne), 106, 114–8, 282
Boston Courier, 35
Boston Quarterly, 62
Bradford, Gamaliel, xv
Bradford, George, 105
Bradshaw's Railway Guide, 174
Briggs (Lowell's literary agent), 147
Brisbane, Albert, 102, 105, 139
Brook Farm, xv, 56, 61, 67, 75, 88, Ch. VII *passim* (102–18), 125, 127, 223, 262
Brooks, Van Wyck, xii, xv, 97

Brown, Brockden, 153–4
Browning, Elizabeth Barrett, xiii, 144, 149, 189, 211, 260, 265–6, 274–6, 277, 285
Browning, Robert, xiii, xv, 144, 149, 186, 189, 211, 265–6, 274–6, 278
Brownson, Orestes, xi, xv, 62, 64, 85, 125–6
Brown's *Philosophy*, 13
Bruce, Georgianna, 106
Bryant, William Cullen, 149, 153
Burgess, Tristram, 42
Burns, Robert, 177, 187
Burritt, Elihu, 174
Burton, Warren, 104
Byron, 14

Cabot, John, 212
Caesar, 7
Cambria (ship), 172–3, 175
Cambridge, 14, 16, 18, 21
Canova, 112
Carlyle, Jane, 186, 189
Carlyle, Thomas, xiii, xv, 30, 35, 40, 57, 59, 78, 87–8, 144, 155, 185–9, 211, 259, 275–9
Cass, Lewis, 254, 276
Celeste (Italian nurse), 267, 269, 271
Cellini, 47
Cervantes, 9, 145
Chalmers, Dr. Thomas, 178
Channing, Ellen (née Fuller), 22, 26, 71, 110–1, 113, 127, 258, 267
Channing, Dr. William Ellery, xi, xii, 34, 36–8, 42, 46, 54–5, 60–1, 63–5, 85, 152
Channing, William Ellery (the younger), xi, 85, 104, 110–1, 127, 153, 165
Channing, William Henry, xi, xiv, 55, 61–2, 64, 102, 104, 139–40, 152, 157, 170, 182–3, 203, 261, 268, 276
Channings, xi, 75, 110
Chapman, 283
Chardon Street Convention of 1840, 55
Charters, Alexander, 121
Cheny, Rose (actress), 192
Child, Lydia Maria, 13–5, 75, 160, 163
Chippewas, M. F. visits, 124
Chopin, 198
Christian Examiner, 57, 65, 82–3
Clarissa Harlowe (play), 192
Clarke, Mrs. Ann Wilby, 76
Clarke, James Freeman, xiv, 16–8, 28, 55, 62, 64, 76, 85, 119, 145, 283
Clarke, Sarah, 75, 119–20, 283

Clarke, William, 120
Coleridge, Samuel Taylor, 30, 34, 42, 55, 57, 78
Columbus, Christopher, 212
Combe, Dr., 178
Conant, Rev. August, 120–1
Condivi, 47
Condorcet, 78
Confucius, 129
"Conversations," 68, 70–9, 82, 88, 91, 106, 109, 119, 125, 216
Conversations with Children on the Gospels (Alcott), 35
Conversations with Goethe (Eckermann, translated by M. F.), 49
Cooper, James Fenimore, 144, 152
Corsini, Prince, 224
Cotton, John, 55
Courier and Enquirer, 203
Cousin, Victor, 55, 57
Coverdale (in *The Blithedale Romance*), 115–7
Crabbe, George, 144
Cranch, Christopher, 85–6, 160, 163, 204
Cranch, Mrs. Christopher, 160
Crawford, Thomas, 48, 204, 211, 243
Crispoldi, Marchesa, 234
Curtis, 283

Dall, Caroline Healey, 76–7, 283
Dana, Charles, 105
Dana, Richard Henry, 42, 48
Dante, 37, 119, 145
Davis (mate of *Elizabeth*), 270–1
Dawson, George, 182
Declaration of Sentiments (Feminist), 135
Delf (friend of Nathan), 180
De Quincey, Thomas, 178
Desatir, 129
De Wette, Wilhelm, 36, 55
Dial, the, xi, 74, Ch. VI *passim*, 102, 109, 112, 122, 129–30, 154, 174
Dickens, Charles, 58
Dickinson, Emily, xi, xv
Domenichino, 204
Duppa, 47
Dwight, John Sullivan, 55, 62, 64–5, 85, 104–5

Eckermann, 49
Edgeworth, Maria, 14
Edmonds, Judge, 156
Edwards, Jonathan, 55, 59
"Elephant" (Fullers' hired man), 27
Eliot, George 188
Elizabeth (ship), 267–71
Elssler, Fanny (ballet dancer), 46
Emerson, Mary Moody, 97–9
Emerson, Ralph Waldo, xi, xii, xiv–vi,
17, 30, 39–40, 46–7, 49, 54–6, 58–60, 64–7, 70, 76–8, 80, 83–5, 87–8, 93–9, 101, 103–12, 144, 149, 152–3, 169, 183, 185–6, 188–90, 205, 207, 215, 221, 226, 229, 231, 250, 259, 275–8, 283
Emerson, Mrs. Ralph Waldo, 75
Emerson, William, 98, 124
Epictetus, 14
Everett, Edward, xi, 63, 151
Examiner, The, 275

Fable for Critics (Lowell), 147–8, 153
Falkland, Lady, 173
Falkland, Lord (Governor of Nova Scotia), 173
Farley, Frank (neighbor at Brook Farm), 105
Farnum, Mrs. E. W., 156
Farrar, Mrs., 18, 25, 27, 30, 44, 75–6, 93
Feminism, xiii, xvi, 43, 70, 72, 74, 79, 108, 122, 124, 131, 135, 142, 183, 205, 217
Fichte, 55, 57
Fielding, Henry, 9
Flaxman, John, 47
Fontana, Lavinia (artist), 205
Fourier, Charles, 55, 102, 105–6, 129, 131, 134, 139, 184, 203
Fox, W. J., 182
Francis, Dr., 59, 62, 64–5
Francis, Lydia Maria, *see* Child, L. M.
Franklin, Lady (wife of British polar explorer), 209
Frothingham, O. B., 59, 66
Fuller, Abraham (uncle of Margaret), 24–5
Fuller, Arthur (brother of Margaret), 7, 22, 26, 53, 122, 127, 283
Fuller, Ellen, *see* Channing, Ellen
Fuller, Eugene (brother of Margaret), 7, 22, 127, 257, 267, 283
Fuller, Frederick T. (son of Richard), 282, 284
Fuller, Lloyd (brother of Margaret), 127, 283
FULLER, MARGARET—
Childhood and Youth: birth, 3; influence of and education by father, 8–10, 21; the "Englishwoman," 10–1; Misses Prescott's school, 11–3; self-culture and Mr. Perkins's school, 13–4; Lydia Maria Child, 14–5; description by Hedge, 15–6; intellectual life in Cambridge, 15–8; described by Clarke, 17; influence of Mrs. Farrar, 18; moves to Groton, 20; teaches her brothers, 21, 26; death of father, 23–5; teaches at Temple School, 34–40; tutoring in German and Italian, 36; Greene Street School in Provi-

dence, 40–9, *see also below under* Emotional Life

Transcendentalism and the Conversations: member of Hedge's Club, 58; introduces Emerson to Goethe, 60; conversational talents, 61, 68, 79; plans courses, 69–70; first Conversations, 70–1; second series, 71–4; influence on Feminism, 74, 78, 79; series for men and women, 75–6; editor of *Dial*, 83–8; relations with Emerson, 30, Ch. VI *passim, see also under* Emerson; relations to Brook Farm, 103–7; relations with Hawthorne at Brook Farm, 106–18; travels West with Clarkes, 119–24; impressions of the West, 123–4

Writings and the *Tribune:* "Mariana," 11; early essay in defense of Brutus, 21; plans life of Goethe, 31; "Record of Impressions of Mr. Allston's Pictures," 45, 85; translates Eckermann's *Conversations with Goethe*, 49; "Short Essay on Critics," and other contributions to the *Dial*, 84–5, 89–90; translation of *Günderode*, 90; of Goethe, 93; "The Western Eden," 121; "Ganymede to His Eagle," 122; *Summer on the Lakes*, 124–6; *Woman in the Nineteenth Century*, 74, 112, 122, 131–5, *see also under titles;* joins *Tribune*, 139; daily journalism, 143–57; America's foremost critic, 144 *ff.; Papers on Literature and Art*, 144, 151–2, *see also under title;* on Longfellow, 145–6; controversy with Lowell, 146–9; on American and English writers, 149–53; on Continental writers, 150; Poe on the Literati, 149, 154–5; trip to Sing Sing, 155–7; on social institutions, 155–9; foreign correspondent, 170 *ff., see also under* New York Tribune *between* 170–264; *History of the Roman Revolution, see under this title;* influence on her of Goethe and Rousseau, 194, *see also under* Goethe; articles on the American in Europe, 218–20; appraisal of her literary career by Elizabeth Browning, 266, 274, 285

Europe and the Revolution: sails for Europe, 172; impressions of English life, 173–5; visits Martineau, 175; meets Wordsworth, 176–7; meets De Quincey, 178; visits the Scottish country, 178 *ff.*; hears English reformers, 182; in London, 183 *ff.*; meets Carlyles, Mazzini, and

Lewes, 185–9; goes to France, 190 *ff.*; sees Rachel, 191–2; attends French court, 193; sees Rousseau MS, 193–4; calls on Lamennais, 194–5; meets Béranger, 195; visits George Sand, 195–8; meets Chopin, 198; visits South of France, 199–200; first tour of Italian cities, 200; explores Rome, 200–4; sits for Hicks, 204; in Bologna, 205; illness in Venice, 206; sees Manzoni in Milan, 207; Switzerland, 208; Milan, 209–10; Florence, 210–12; return to Rome, 215; enlists Ossoli for revolution, 215–6; attitude to Pope Pius, 222–5, 237; relations to Mazzini, 227–9, 243, 250–1; revolution and siege, Ch. XIV *passim;* serves as hospital head, 245–8; flees Rome, 253; friendship with Brownings, 265–6

Emotional Life: sister's death, 5–6; childish nightmares, 7–9; early hysteria, 11–3; early reflections on love, 18–9; religious problems, 28–30; relations with Samuel Gray Ward, 79–80; longings of heart, 80–1, 90–3, 161–2; relations with Nathan, 162–8, 180; meets Ossoli, 201–2; love affair with Ossoli, 215 *ff.*; pregnancy and marriage, 221; child born, 232–3; anxieties of motherhood, 238–40; confides in Mrs. Story, 248–9; flees Rome to child, 253–4; reveals secret at home, 255–9; gossip in America, 261; family life in Florence, 260–6; life on board the *Elizabeth*, 268 *ff.*; death of family, 270–2; appraisals of her character, 273–85

Fuller, Margaret Crane (mother of Margaret), 3–5, 9, 21–4, 26, 32, 53, 127–8, 169, 238–9, 255–6, 283

Fuller, Richard (brother of Margaret), 7, 22, 26–7, 53, 127–8, 232, 242, 282–3

Fuller, Timothy (father of Margaret), 3–7, 9, 11, 15, 17–8, 20–5, 32, 70–1, 90, 97, 207, 262, 266

Fuller, William (brother of Margaret), 7, 22, 127, 283

Fuller, William Williams (uncle of Margaret), 119

Fullers, 8, 267

Furness, William Henry, 64

Fuseli, John Henry, 47

Gannett, Dr. Ezra, 106

"Ganymede to His Eagle" (Fuller), 122

Gardiners, 75

Garibaldi, Giuseppe, 241, 252

Garibaldi's Legion, 244–5

Gibbon, Edward, 30
Gibson, John, 204
Gioberti, Vincenzo, 228
Goethe, 16, 21, 28, 30, 37, 60, 80, 90, 91, 93, 134, 145, 150, 187, 194
Gott (artist), 204
Grandfather's Chair (Hawthorne), 107, 109
"Great Lawsuit, The" (see also under *Woman in the Nineteenth Century*), 74, 122, 129, 131
Greeley, Horace, xiii, 88, 125, 128, 139–144, 150, 152, 155, 157–9, 163, 166–70, 178, 203, 220, 232, 274
Greeley, Mrs. Horace, 140–1, 143, 163, 166–8, 170
Greeley, Pickie, 161, 170–1
Greene Street School (Providence, R. I.), 40–1
Greenough, Richard S., 48, 211, 243, 260
Greenough, Mrs. Richard, 262
Grimké sisters, 78
Guizot, François, 193, 225
Gurney, Joseph John (English Quaker), 42

Halleck, Fitz-Greene, 80, 153
Harvard, 6, 15, 75, 77, 82, 105, 110, 124, 151
Hasty, Captain, 267–8
Hasty, Mrs., 269–70
Hawthorne, Julian, 280
Hawthorne, Nathaniel, xi, xii, xv, 75, 104–15, 117–8, 144, 149, 154, 280–5
Hawthorne, Sophia (née Peabody), 75–6, 107–8, 110–3, 280, 282
Hawthorne, Una, 113
Haydn, 46
Hedge, Frederick Henry, 15, 40, 55, 57–8, 64–5, 76, 83, 93, 102, 104, 283
Hedge's Club, *see* Transcendental Club
Hegel, 55
Heine, Heinrich, 30
Heraud, John, 65
Herder, Johann G. von, 36
Herschel, Sir John, 30
Hicks, Thomas (artist), 204, 230
Higginson, Thomas Wentworth, 62, 87, 114–5
History of Philosophy (Lewes), 187
History of the Roman Revolution (Fuller), xiv, 215, 242, 259–63, 267, 273, 281, 284
Hoar, Elizabeth, 75–6, 195
Holmes, Oliver Wendell, xi
Horace, 7
Household Words (magazine), 274
Howe, Julia Ward, xi, 79, 131
Howitt, Mary, 183
Howitt, William, 183
Hutchinson, Anne, 55

Irving, Washington, 152, 154
"Items of Foreign Gossip" (Fuller), 150

Jackson, Andrew, 20
Jackson, Marianne, 76
Jacksons, 75
Jacobi, Friedrich, 57
Jefferson, Thomas, 21
Johnson, Samuel, 62
Jordan, Mrs. (actress), 173
Josey (Margaret's dog), 165, 168
Journals (Alcott), 63–6, 68, 220
Journals (Emerson), 60
Judd, Sylvester, 153

Kant, 55, 57, 59
Kemble, Fanny, 46, 115
Körner, Karl T., 30

Lafayette, Marquis de, 80
Lamennais, H. F. R., 194–5
Landor, Walter Savage, 129, 144, 274
Leatherstocking Tales (Cooper), 144
Lees, 75
Leger, Dr., 163
Lesseps, Ferdinand de, 247
Lessing, G. E., 37
Leverrier (astronomer), 193
Lewes, George Henry, 186–8
Life of Goethe (Lewes), 187
Literary World, The, 282, 284
Literati, The (Poe), 154, 160–1
Locke, John, 14–5
London Monthly Review, 65
Longfellow, Henry Wadsworth, xi, xvi, 79, 80, 144–7, 153–4, 273, 278
Longfellow, Samuel, 62
Loring's, 75
Louis Napoleon, 241, 245
Louis Philippe, 193, 199, 225
Lowell, James Russell, xi, 84–5, 145–8, 153, 229–30, 276–7
Lynch, Miss, 160
Lyon, Mary, 78
Lyrical Ballads (Wordsworth), 177

Macdonald (artist), 204
Mack, W., 76
Mackintosh, Sir James, 30
MacPhail, Andrew, xiv
Mamiani, Count, 228
Mann, Horace, 17, 75
Manual for Young Ladies (Mrs. Farrar), 18
Manzoni, Alessandro, 202, 207
Margaret and Her Friends (Caroline Healey Dall), 76–7
Margaret Fuller Cottage, 106
Margaret, or the Real Ideal (Judd), 153
"Mariana" (Fuller), 11

Martineau, Harriet, 25, 30, 35, 43–5, 74, 93, 175–6, 278
Martineau, James, 182
Massachusetts Quarterly Review, 87
Matthews, Cornelius, 153
May, 65
Ma~· i Giuseppe, xiii, xv, 185, 189, 198, 208, 227–8, 243, 245, 251, 275–7
McElrath (partner of Greeley), 140
McGregor, Helen, 84
Memoirs of Margaret Fuller Ossoli (Emerson, Channing, and Clarke), xiv, xv, 76, 115, 276–7, 279
Metternich, 224–6
Michelangelo, 47
Mickiewicz, Adam, 227
Milton, 14
Minto, Lord, 224
Möhler's *Symbolism*, 129
Molière, 9, 145
Montégut, Emile, 279
Morrison, 65
Mott, Lucretia, 78
Mount Holyoke College, 78
Mozart, 46, 193
Mozier, 210, 260, 280–4
Mozier, Mrs. Isabella, 210, 260–4, 267

Naples, King of, 224–5
Napoleon, 199
Nathan, James, 162–70, 180–1, 192
Nature (Emerson), 59
Neal, John, 42, 69, 74
Newcomb, Charles, 112
"Newness," 55, 58, 60, 63, 84, 103
New York Tribune, xiii, 88, 125, 130, Ch. IX *passim*, 160, 163, 168–70, 185, 188, 191–2, 194, 201, 203–4, 210, 218, 222, 229, 233, 237, 243, 247–8, 253–4, 264, 284
North American Phalanx (Red Bank, N. J.), 140, 185
North American Review, 42, 65, 80, 82, 83, 88, 278
Nouveau Monde Industriel (Fourier), 129
Novalis, 30, 92

"On the Death of M. D'Ossoli and His Wife Margaret Fuller" (Landor), 275
Opéra Comique, 192
"Orphic Sayings" (Bronson Alcott), 85–6
Ossoli, Angelo (Margaret's son), 232–3, 238–40, 244, 247–9, 253–75
Ossoli, Marchese Giovanni Angelo, 201–2, 215–8, 221, 225, 231–3, 235, 239–40, 242, 247–9, 251, 253–72, 274, 280–1, 283–4

Ossoli family, 215–6, 239, 251, 255–7, 263, 266, 280
Ottawas (M. F. visits), 124
Oudinot, General, 245–8, 252
Overbeck, Johann Friedrich, 204
Ovid, 7
Owenites, 102

Papers on Literature and Art (Fuller), 144, 151–2, 155, 183, 190
Paracelsus (Browning), 149
Parker, Theodore, xi, xii, xiii, 55, 61, 64–5, 78, 85, 87, 104, 182–3
Parker, Mrs. Theodore, 75
Parrington, Vernon L., xii
Peabody, Elizabeth, 35–7, 58–9, 64, 68, 75–6, 88, 105, 107
Peabody, Mary, 75
Peabody, Sophia, *see* Hawthorne, Sophia
Pentameron (Landor), 129
People's Journal, 184–5
Perkins (Mr.) School (attended by Margaret), 13
Petrarch, 37
Pius IX, Pope, 202–3, 210, 222–4, 226–8, 232, 236–8, 240–1, 245–7, 256
Plato, 34
Poe, Edgar Allan, xiii, 88, 144, 149, 154–155, 160
Poems (Longfellow), 145–7
Polk, President James Knox, 140, 155
Powers, Hiram, 48, 211, 243, 260, 268
Pratt, Minor, 104–5
Pratt, Mrs. Minor, 105
Prescott, William H., xi, 152
Prescott, Misses (teachers of Margaret), 11, 15, 45
Putnam, George, 58, 75

Quincy, E., 65
Quincy, Mrs. Josiah, 75

Rachel, 191
Racine, 14
Radcliffe College, 78
Radziwill, Princess, 209, 217
"Raven, The" (Poe), 149
Raymond, H. J., 203
"Record of Impressions of Mr. Allston's Pictures" (Fuller), 45, 85
Rémusat, Comte de, 193
Retzsch, Moritz, 47
Revue des Deux Mondes, 279
Revue Indépendante, La, 190
Richter, Jean Paul, 37
Ripley, George, 49, 55–9, 61, 64–5, 76, 83, 85–6, 88, 102–5, 107–8
Ripley, Marianne, 104–5
Ripley, Sarah, 58, 64–5, 69, 75–6, 98, 104–5, 108
Roland, Madame, 183

Roman Revolution, 240–53
Rossi, Count, 228, 236, 241
Rossi, Properzia di, 205
Rousseau, Jean Jacques, 14, 55, 131, 193–4
Russell, Ida, 75–6
Russell, Mrs. Jonathan, 75–6

Sand, George, xiii, 117, 133, 150, 195–8, 217
Santayana, George, xi
Schelling, Friedrich von, 55
Schiller, 21, 37
Schleiermacher, Friedrich, 55
Scott, Walter, 124, 177, 181, 207
Shakespeare, 9–10, 37, 42, 145, 182, 187
Shaw, Francis, 75–6
Shaw, Sarah, 75–6, 99
Shelley, Percy Bysshe, 30, 144
"Short Essay on Critics" (Fuller), 85
Sing Sing, 155–7
Sirani, Elisabetta (artist), 205
Sismondi's *Literature of the South of Europe*, 13
Smith, Dr. Southwood (philanthropist), 184
Smollett, 9
Social Destiny of Man, The (Brisbane), 102
Society in America (Martineau), 43, 175
Socrates, 35, 91–2
"Sordello" (Browning), 149
Southern Literary Messenger, 88
Southey, Robert, 30
Spain, Queen of, 193
Spring, Eddie, 161, 169–70, 174, 176, 189, 202, 204–6
Spring, Marcus, 139–40, 160, 169–70, 174–5, 179–80, 182, 185, 189, 202, 204–6, 210, 239, 266
Spring, Rebecca, 157, 160, 169–70, 174–5, 185, 189, 202, 204–6, 267
Staël, Madame de, 14, 68, 279
Stanhope, Lady Hester, 279
Stanton, Elizabeth Cady, 79
Stearns, Sarah, 105
Stetson, 65
Stone, Lucy, 79
Story, Emelyn, 216, 221, 235, 246, 248–249, 260, 264, 283
Story, William Wetmore, 76, 147, 216, 229–30, 235, 248, 260, 276
Sturgis, Caroline, 75–6, 108, 128, 155, 204, 209–10, 221
Sturgis, Ellen, 75, 85
Sue, Eugène, 150
Summer on the Lakes (Fuller), 124–5, 130
Sumner, Charles, 174, 262
Sumner, Horace, 261–2, 267, 269–70
Swedenborg, 134

Tambroni, Matilda, 205
Tasso, 37
Tasso (Goethe, translated by M. F.), 93
Temple School (Alcott), 32, 34–6, 42, 53, 60
Tenerani, Pietro, 204
Tennyson, 144, 186–7, 189
Terry (artist), 204
Thoreau, xi, xii, 55–6, 85, 88, 104, 110, 125
Thoreau's mother, 64
Ticknor, George, xi, 63, 151
Tieck, Ludwig, 37
Tirlone, Don (the Punch of Rome), 237
Titan (Richter), 37
Titian, 204
Torlonias, 224
Transcendental Club, 58–9
"Transcendental Heifer," 106, 108
Transcendentalism, xii, xiii, Ch. IV *passim*, 71, 75, 78, 82–3, 85–7, 89, 91–2, 102–7, 126, 144, 153–4, 160, 174, 278
Tribune, see *New York Tribune*
Troy Female Seminary, 78
Tuckermans, 75

Unitarian Church, 30, 57, 63

Vattemare, Alexandre, 194
Very, Jones, 76–7, 85, 144
Vespucci, Amerigo, 212
Vindication of the Rights of Woman (Wollstonecraft), 131
Virgil, 7–9
Visconti, Marchesa Arconati, 208, 231, 242, 260

Wagen, von, 47
Walpole, Horace, 183
Ward, Samuel Gray, 79, 80, 165, 275
Ward, Mrs. Samuel Gray (née Astor), 75–6, 80
Wasson, David, 62
Webster, Daniel, 63
Weiss, John, 62
"Western Eden, The" (Fuller), 121
Western Messenger, 120
Wheeler, Charles Stearns, 76–7, 104
White, Maria, 75
White, William, 76
Whitings, 75
Whittier, John Greenleaf, xi
Willard, Emma, 78
William IV, 173
Williams, Roger, 55
Willis, Nathaniel Parker, 153
Wolff, Albert, 204
Wollstonecraft, Mary, 78, 131, 133

Woman in the Nineteenth Century (Fuller), 74, 112, 122, 131–5, 142, 154, 156, 158, 163, 189–90, 286–91
Wordsworth, William, 30, 42, 176–7
Wright, Fanny, 78

Wright, H. G., 65

Zenobia (in *Blithedale Romance*), 106, 114–8
Zucchi, Minister of War, 236